SURVIVING SEPARATION and DIVORCE

Second Edition

Loriann Hoff Oberlin, M.S.

Adams Media
Avon, Massachusetts

Copyright ©2005 by Loriann Hoff Oberlin, M.S.

All rights reserved. This book, or parts thereof, may not be reproduced in any form without permission from the publisher; exceptions are made for brief excerpts used in published reviews.

Published by
Adams Media, a division of F+W Media, Inc.
57 Littlefield Street, Avon, MA 02322. U.S.A.
www.adamsmedia.com

First edition ©2000 by Loriann Hoff Oberlin.

ISBN 10: 1-59337-276-0
ISBN 13: 978-1-59337-276-7
Printed in the United States of America.

10 9 8 7

Library of Congress Cataloging-in-Publication Data

Oberlin, Loriann Hoff
Surviving separation and divorce / Loriann Hoff Oberlin.—2nd ed.
p.   cm.
ISBN 1-59337-276-0
1. Divorce. 2. Separation (Psychology) I. Title.

HQ814.O34 2005
306.89—dc22

2004026390

This publication is designed to provide accurate and authoritative information with regard to the subject matter covered. It is sold with the understanding that the publisher is not engaged in rendering legal, accounting, or other professional advice. If legal advice or other expert assistance is required, the services of a competent professional person should be sought.

—From a *Declaration of Principles* jointly adopted by a Committee of the American Bar Association and a Committee of Publishers and Associations

In order to protect the privacy of individuals who generously shared life experiences and thoughts for this research, only professional experts are quoted by name and identifying factors. Where more than one expert agreed on particular matters, the term "experts" is used to identify them collectively. All other names and identifying circumstances have been altered to protect their identity. In some instances, composites of two or three persons have been used to obscure them and to clarify the relevant issues. Any similarities between the anecdotes the author presents and any actual person, living or deceased, is entirely coincidental.

This book is intended to provide accurate information for women facing a marital separation, but is sold with the understanding that neither the publisher nor the author is engaged in rendering any psychological, financial, investment, legal, tax, or other advice. If you desire specific advice, consult a trusted and competent professional.

Many of the designations used by manufacturers and sellers to distinguish their products are claimed as trademarks. Where those designations appear in this book and Adams Media was aware of a trademark claim, the designations have been printed with initial capital letters.

This book is available at quantity discounts for bulk purchases.
For information, call 1-800-289-0963.

CONTENTS

Dedication

Michael W. Smith sings a song dedicated to friends, and his words inspire me to dedicate this book to my friends who saw me through difficult times. They believed in me, and I believe in them. Friends are friends forever, and I have some of the very best!

Acknowledgments

Surviving a separation, getting through a divorce, and beginning many new life passages teaches you to call in all the supports, and have I ever! There are simply too many people to list here who have been instrumental over the years as I gained back my confidence, courage, and energy to make a new life for myself and my children. They know who they are—family, friends, ministers, doctors, and other assorted professionals whose wise counsel I counted on, for their encouragement sustained me, and still does.

I would like to thank my two sons, for they never asked for any of this. Just as our lives settled down with new opportunities for happiness on our horizon, it seemed we were all thrust together in coping mode once again, as we headed down the court path. I love my sons more than anything in this world. I'm so very proud of their courage to speak up and know right from wrong, the way they've processed a difficult path and looked forward, and their ability to adapt that continues to amaze me. My sons are great kids, becoming wonderful young men!

My husband Bob deserves my appreciation for supporting us through some of the more recent challenges of litigation and all that goes with it. Bob has added much to my life and to us as a family; I surely felt his presence and warmth tackling the revised edition of this book. Thanks, honey!

My friend Donna Israel-Sapp gave important feedback and encouragement when the idea for this project was first conceived, and the folks at Adams Media, have been enthusiastic supporters as well. Thanks to Danielle Chiotti and Gene Molter, in particular!

Others who contributed their professional expertise include Marc J. Ackerman, Ph.D.; Francesca Adler-Baeder, Ph.D., CFLE; Paul R. Amato; Joye Ashton; Lundy Bancroft; Steven J. Bienstock, Esq.; Joey Binard; Nina W. Brown, Ed.D., L.P.C.; DeeDee A. Burnett; James Carroll, Jr.; William J. Doherty, Ph.D.; William A. Eddy, LCSW, J.D.; Margorie Engel, Ph.D.; Joan B. Kelly, Ph.D.; Randi Kreger; Vicki Lansky; Gail Martin; Roy L. Mason, Esq.; Timothy F. Murphy, Ph.D.; Karen L. Myers, Esq.; Sharon Naylor; Mary O'Brien, M.D.; Sophia P. Paul, Esq.; Steven D. Reinheimer, Esq.; Nola Risse-Connolly; Stanton E. Samenow, Ph.D.; Hedda Sharapan; Michael E. Thase, M.D. and Ara Thomas-Brown, Ph.D.

My professors and the instruction at Johns Hopkins University as I pursue my master's degree have added tremendously to my knowledge. The librarians have also helped me, and they all have my appreciation.

In addition, I'd like to thank the following organizations and personnel for their help in providing information: the Association of Family and Conciliation Courts; the Bethesda Group; the National Council of Juvenile and Family Court Judges; and the National Resource Center on Domestic Violence.

Finally, my sincere appreciation goes out to the many women who freely shared their personal stories, tips, humorous and poignant anecdotes, and general advice for the benefit of my readers. Everyone here has helped to make this a truly meaningful resource with a breadth of views for those who need it most.

Introduction

Back in 1995, upon the release of my first book, our metropolitan paper profiled me in what was a widely read column. I was excited not only for the book's publicity, but because my husband, at that time, never missed reading it. For his eyes and the world's, I'd listed among my greatest accomplishments the work I'd put into our marriage and family. And whom would I most want to have dinner with? Besides listing Fred Rogers and Hillary Clinton, I had listed my husband.

You can imagine how foolish and devastated I felt when two weeks later I learned things that shattered my idea of a happy marriage. If you're like me, you'll never forget the precise moment you realized your marriage was pretty much over, at least in the sense you knew it. Close friends remember the date. I called one at 5 A.M., having failed to cry myself to sleep that night. My doctor remembered the crisis, for I ran to her with my fears, and my minister found me in his office on his first day back from summer vacation. It felt as if my world had hit a meteor, with pieces of my life spinning out of control.

When I first wrote *Surviving Separation and Divorce*, some women wrote to me to say that they, too, felt shocked, numb, puzzled, used, and angry as their dreams were blown away. They connected to the heartache that occurs when you find yourself alone, never truly understanding "why," and wondering "what if" circumstances were different.

A decade has passed since this juncture in my life. After two and a half years, that separation ended in divorce. I took the time I needed to process the changes that had occurred in my life and to focus on helping my children cope as well. Eventually, I ventured onto the dating scene, enjoying the chance to meet new people. Admittedly, it was a little daunting, but one of the first few men I went out with shares my life today. We've been married for several years, but I've never lost touch with those emotions and experiences that first helped shape me into the woman I am today.

In fact, I don't want to lose these memories completely. I remember well my doubts of fitting in. I felt a little helpless at changing realities that I did *not* want in my life. I was afraid of what the future—even the next day—might bring. I remember the sharp pain, unanswered questions, and heavy responsibilities shifted onto my shoulders for my sons who were the tender ages of seven and two. My oldest son had looked forward to a successful start in first grade, and my youngest, born severely premature, had just been diagnosed with gross motor delays that would years later be confirmed as cerebral palsy. They had special needs. I had special needs; I'd lost fifteen pounds and sought help for my anxiety and depression, which had been precipitated by revelations, realizations, and the marital breakdown. Even the house had special needs. That winter we experienced record snowfall, and come spring, I added lawn care to my burgeoning "to do" list. Financial considerations loomed large, since we had made the mutual decision during our marriage that I would cut back my career to care for the children. Personal safety soon surfaced as another concern.

I realized that I couldn't change the situation at hand; I had to change. It took therapy, as well as good, honest friends to reveal my codependency in a troubled, unhealthy relationship. It took some tough phone calls, consultations from lawyers and counselors at the women's center and shelter, and discussions with the police about my rights. I even asked a friend to go to night court with me when I felt sufficiently afraid.

Gradually I started to see positive aspects of the breakup. In just a few weeks of separation, I started to breathe freely again. I saw beauty instead of ugliness, hope instead of despair, and a calm household rather than a rage-filled one. I found strength within myself and companionship with my children and friends—friends who offered objectivity, insight, and encouragement. Mind you, they didn't always tell me what I wanted to hear; they told me what I needed to hear, most importantly. Sometimes, I simply enjoyed the newfound solitude and time to myself. Moments of abysmal loneliness were now reframed as opportunities. I accomplished tasks that had at first seemed too difficult. Patience won out over quick fixes. A can-do attitude guided each day, and I began to dream rather than ruminate.

I ended the first edition of this book with wisdom from a friend. "I'm glad it's over for you, or at least this round is over," he wrote. "You survived. You will survive worse. Now, you will help others to survive as well . . . "

This friend was incredibly prescient on two counts. Years later, facing totally unnecessary and what I truly believe was mean-spirited custody litigation, I drew upon these same survival skills. My friend, knowing how I was trying to channel my righteous anger into something better, bolstered me once more saying, "At least you are using your experience to help others. Some are held back mired in misery and self-doubt; some move forward despite it; and others are propelled forward using their negative experience as a motivation and source of positive energy. You are in that third category, Loriann. Nice work."

Even when you have come a long way in your journey, you may feel forces trying to pull you back to a miserable place. It's a commonality I think many of us have in this circumstance. The first edition of *Surviving Separation and Divorce* has helped thousands of women. For example, in an online review of this book, one woman wrote that she felt as if the book had lifted a huge burden. Let that burden lift from your shoulders as you read this new edition.

Get ready to focus on yourself, your emotional, physical, social, and spiritual well-being. From how to safeguard your health, your property, and your personal safety (and sanity!) to how to maintain your career and finances, your family unit, heck, even your lawn, this is a lifestyle book for you.

In the pages ahead, you'll learn several perspectives from experts in the fields of health care, personal finance, home security, child development, counseling and psychology, and women's advocacy. You'll even hear from pro-marriage advocates on ways you might avoid divorce and reconcile instead. In an expanded legal chapter, I've tried to address many new topics, asking tough questions of attorneys, court personnel, custody evaluators, and professional organizations. I'll also share the experiences of other women who have traveled this painful journey of marital crisis and survived because we can often learn from other women and how they handled difficult situations in their lives. At the end of the book, get ready to relax a little and explore some new horizons that will help you to dream of another place than the one you are at right now—exciting opportunities for yourself, deeper relationships, and the possibility of embracing another man's love as you merge your families for the future.

My realization of my unhealthy marriage came about gradually. When it became overwhelmingly clear to me that circumstances weren't changing, and when I saw the impact upon my children and myself, I altered course. Insanity is colloquially described as doing the same thing over and over, expecting different results. Trust me, I wasn't going to end up divorced *and* impaired!

I look back upon my journey with pride. I held my head up high, cared for my children, had my career on my own terms, and pulled myself together into one confident package. Now remarried and relocated a few hours from my former home, I'm making friends, enjoying the stepfamily my new husband and I created, and setting ambitious professional goals. I am most proud of my children who have weathered much, but emerged from this as happy, empathic, and well-adjusted human beings.

As you read these pages, let new insights take hold and new thoughts emerge, for that's what we all must do to grow from adversity. As I write this, I'm a graduate student in clinical community counseling at Johns Hopkins University. A master's degree was once a "shoulda, coulda, woulda" regret. I had no clue how to make it happen. But where I was then is not where I am today. Your dreams are out there also. So take time—no, make the time—to focus on you and your world without a moment's guilt. You're dealing with a lot right now, and you deserve some time to regroup. I'm proud of you for taking that all-important step here toward recovery and some sort of resolution to your marital crisis. That resolution may be divorce. It may be reconciliation. You'll find your way, just as I did with patience, a little time, and a commitment to forge ahead toward a beautiful future.

—Loriann Hoff Oberlin

Chapter One

Suddenly Separated

The day you realize you're being left, or that you need to leave, is a span of hours filled with mixed emotions that often pierce like shrapnel. If you're leaving, you may feel guilty and question your decision. If you're the one left behind, you might be thrust into a pattern of crazymaking, or you might find you're just coming out of one.

When I say crazymaking, I mean a feeling of being off balance, a little lost (or a lot), with a muddled mind and maybe even broken promises. If you feel that your husband is defining your reality to the point that you're bewildered and you feel increasingly inadequate, then you might be experiencing what experts call crazymaking.

When the true reality sinks in, the prevailing emotion is shock. How could this happen? How could he do this? Shock is followed by fear, anger, and concern for the children. It's an emotional roller coaster. Soon, the very real tasks laid before you require your focus and attention. But right when it's time for action, you'd rather sink into a hole and never come out again.

Realize as you read this book that you're not alone. Plenty of other women have traveled this unpleasant journey, and the good news is, they are living better lives. Hold onto that hope. You have a lot to look forward to, and once you face any unpleasant events, there are wonderful times to come.

When the Bottom Falls Out

When I got the clear message from my first husband not to wait up at night, and that he wanted an apartment of his own, one of my witty friends exclaimed, "What does he want to do, go order pizza with his own toppings for a month?"

Whether it's pizza or some other pleasure, there are lessons every woman can learn. Don't feel weak that you need to regroup and do some remedial work reminiscent of "Emotions 101." You didn't expect this change. Especially at this important juncture, the actions you take and the mistakes you make will most decidedly matter.

If you don't feel up to making decisions on that first or second day after the news hits you, or when you realize you must initiate a separation, allow yourself some quiet time. Taking time to reflect, to pray, to think, or simply to talk through your turmoil is far better than racing into inappropriate action you will regret later. Your strength will come.

In the immediate aftermath of acknowledging that you and your spouse are in fact separating or perhaps divorcing, your mind will race with thoughts, feelings, even pressures—some internal, some very real, and some placed upon you by well-meaning but clueless friends and family. Much of what follows may sound familiar.

How Could He?

The first question you'll often hear when a husband walks out is "How could he?" I hate to be the bearer of bad news, but you may never have an answer to that. Rest assured, you'll hear it again and again. Upon reading the first edition of this book, a reader shared with me that the question "why" seemed to be ever present in her mind, despite supportive family and friends reassuring her that she would be okay.

It's just not that easy to let those questions slide each time they surface. The journalist in me has always sought answers, so it was a real struggle not having any clear explanation in those early days of my separation. I coped by allowing myself time to gain perspective, to see things more clearly.

I reminded myself that I had loved my husband with all my heart and soul, body and mind. I'm sure I could have been a better partner in some respects. Yet my conscience was clear. I held out hope and stood by my mate when other women might have bolted.

Looking back, it seemed that I spent so much time during my marriage trying to keep it together, only to discover it wasn't worth the mental effort. I really had been the partner devoting most of the energy to making things happen in the marriage. Good friends told me later that what I perceived as persistence in keeping the marriage going was coming off to them more like "how much more garbage is she going to take?"

There's no doubt I did the right thing being so persistent. I had two children with special needs. Above all, I did care for this man, despite the pain.

As the weeks passed after our initial separation, I knew my friends were right. I could let go of the "how could he?" because I could live with the outcome. If you have put substantial effort into seeking solutions and standing by your mate, but it has not yielded positive results, try letting go, as well. Shift the focus from "how could he?" to what comes next. What does come after this juncture? A new beginning—for you.

You'll Be Better Off

The morning after my husband walked out, my minister paid a visit. There I was with my box of tissues. I don't even remember if I offered the man a cup of coffee! But something he said—actually several things—made such complete sense that they gave me the peace my heart and my household desperately needed. "I think this separation needs to happen," was one bit of wisdom that I held onto that day.

Several other friends and family members reiterated the same, suggesting I would be much better off. Reluctantly, and slowly, that message sank in.

Many women will tell you that their husbands did them the favor of their lives by leaving them, or by forcing issues so that these women made the ultimate break. Go ahead and sigh at me. If you're not ready to accept that line, I understand. Right now, where you sit, just getting through the next hour might be a monumental task. You may not believe you can make a move without your husband. The longer you've been married, the more firmly planted that belief might be.

Some women—those who have initiated a breakup—also need to realize their new future. Even though they've made an important decision to exit, they will often have mixed emotions. We women are conditioned to be caretakers, and when something in our grasp fails, we feel responsible, as if there's still something else we could do to make it right. Essentially, all women facing a marital separation need to hear that they will be better off. A separation will bring clarity. One way or another, you will have resolution, in the form of reconciliation or freedom.

Sink into Your Support System

The other side of that caretaker phenomenon is that we women are wonderful at taking care of each other. How is it that when we haven't slept, have lost our breakfast, and can't even get the words out right, our female friends know precisely what we need? What's more, they're quickly on the scene.

I remember the constant telephone support. It was my lifeline, in some respects a sanity check, particularly with one friend I must have spoken with almost every day for those first few months.

Having the hindsight of several years now, I can imagine how tedious it must have been to my best friends to continue the reassurance, the reiteration of such lines like "you did the right thing" or "you'll get through this." High on my list of memories is the pan of lasagna that friends brought one evening. This couple had brought dinner to me as a new mom two years before, and we laughed to note that whenever a family member arrived or exited, the simple comfort of Italian cuisine, and my friend's culinary talents, went a long way toward healing!

Hopefully, this type of support is available to you, as well. Friends can be amazingly creative when it comes to comfort, and I'm not just referring to the tangible surprises like lasagna, a box of chocolates, or a tall bottle of bubble bath. I'm talking about calls to check in on you, a shoulder to lean on, arms to hug you when it feels like you'll never again have close contact. These gifts don't cost anything but our friend's time, and they are given freely out of concern and love.

That should say something else to you in your most desperate moments. Friends wouldn't be expending the effort if they didn't feel you were worth it. And if you're like me, you'll often feel you've used up so many methods of support that your IOU list runneth over. Look at it this way, life is never without its struggles for any one of us. In time, you will most surely be able to be there for friends who need a little payback. What you give really does come back to you, and vice versa.

For those women who are facing this marital crisis without family nearby or friends to lend a tangible hand, seek out other available supports. Call the office of your house of worship and schedule a time to talk with someone. If you or your children have experienced abuse of any kind—emotional, physical, financial, sexual—contact your local women's shelter and counseling agency. It's most likely listed in the phone book under county resources or nonprofit organizations. (See appendix for listings.)

Many cities have twenty-four-hour hotline services for anyone going through a crisis. Trained counselors will reach out to you and are often armed with the right words to validate your feelings. They can also provide appropriate information and telephone numbers to contact. Of course, your own physician can be a great support and may often refer you to mental health therapists, social workers, or counselors to help alleviate the burdens you face.

Take One Day at a Time

Who you are today is not who you will be tomorrow, next month, or certainly a year from now. The fears you have will be resolved, in one way or another. The days, with their individual tasks, will come, and they will pass. When this happens, you'll feel growth and accomplishment.

That's largely how separation is, but convincing yourself of this when you desire answers right now is another matter. Of course, every woman's situation is unique. For the woman facing domestic violence, safety decisions are paramount and need to be addressed immediately. Those women left with little or no financial resources need to file for support as soon as possible in order to set a hearing date to settle the matter.

Your circumstances will dictate what deserves immediate attention, and what can wait. As a general rule, your agenda should involve drawing up a safety plan by changing locks or protecting yourself and your property; filing for child and spousal support (which you can do before you even engage an attorney); obtaining medical care if your health has been jeopardized; and caring for the emotional and tangible needs of your children. Much of the material presented in later chapters goes into greater detail in each of these areas.

If you're having trouble coping or even thinking about what comes first, ask a trusted friend or counselor to help you devise daily or weekly goals and a to-do list. An objective party who is not emotionally caught up in the crisis can see things more clearly, more quickly. Just remember not to overwhelm yourself with too many extraneous details that could be handled in the weeks and months to come.

Halt Hasty Decisions

When my separation began, I had known others who had been separated, so I was fairly familiar with Pennsylvania law. I knew, for instance, that there was a two-year waiting period that one party could invoke to halt any hasty decisions.

Honestly, it took me the first few weeks to gather my thoughts and feelings. I needed to listen to my support system instead of my estranged husband. While in anger, it would have been easy to declare "I'm out of this marriage" or "I'm filing for divorce tomorrow." Instead, I'm glad I waited.

Often, quick decisions aren't appropriate decisions. Some distance between the parties might clarify some matters, making reconciliation possible. A hasty judgment to divorce today might make it all but impossible to get back together tomorrow. In addition, if you earn less than your spouse, there might be financial reasons for you to take your time, particularly if there are children involved.

If you haven't separated yet and are reading this book, a word of caution: States vary in their laws regarding separation and divorce. Should your spouse want to move you both to another state, examine the laws closely as they apply to property division, alimony, and child support. It could be that he's seeking a sweeter deal in another place.

Each state varies in the amount of time a couple must live apart before a divorce can move forward. Since my youngest son had just turned two years old when my separation began, I was very concerned about his welfare. Ever since his premature birth, it had been necessary for me to be home with him to prevent illness and facilitate frequent therapy he required. A snap decision to divorce might have disrupted all the care that he needed, and all the supports I had in place. I knew that I had two years in which I could stay in our residence, receive child and spousal support, and have our medical insurance covered. For me, this grace period proved helpful. For other women, circumstances might be different. Just be sure that you don't make important legal decisions too quickly. Sometimes you can't revoke those choices, and you'll suffer unfortunate consequences for your hasty actions.

Waiting also provides a second scenario. You might be tempted to take your spouse back too soon. Reconciliation is certainly a potential outcome, and I don't want to detract from that possibility. However, I do know of many married men who dished a proverbial pile of garbage on their wives and then wondered why these women didn't beg their men to come back. The answer is they'd had enough. They got stronger. They grew. Their husbands didn't.

There is nothing wrong with fighting for your marriage. Just realize that some men will sit back and wait for the ego boost when their wives plead and cajole them back into the marriage. Read this book first, and just maybe you'll discover strength you never dreamed you had.

Avoid Other Actions

When you're most vulnerable, your emotions can pull you in all different directions. Some women use this time to get a better grasp on life, while others can't contain their own anger. These are powerful emotions, and you have a right to them.

But I remember reading an advice column where a troubled teenage girl wrote in about her father who had left the family in an affair and her mother who instantly sought the company of other men in an attempt to retaliate or replace her estranged husband. The girl was clearly ignored by two parents seeking a second adolescence. It sounded very troubling.

Some women retaliate by seeking the company of men too soon. One woman with young children lacked professional patience, getting a full-time job and putting her kids in day care. She ultimately drove herself and her children crazy by the new routine. If you act hastily and get a full-time job too soon, you might jeopardize your chance of alimony. Plus, if you have many men in your life, well, this could be used against you, as well.

Family Fallout

After the reality of a separation sets in, it's often painful to witness the same shock on the faces and in the voices of family members. There are women who hesitate divulging such information, for fear they will be chastised.

In some families when a daughter marries, parents see her husband as a new son. It's quite conceivable, especially in cases of abuse, that she hid from both families the pain she endured in the marriage. In cases like these, some families urge wives to try harder, overlook things, or otherwise downplay the realities she's lived. This is also prevalent in some cultures where a woman is truly scorned for leaving a marriage.

No one wants to believe that a son or son-in-law could be a batterer, a cheat, a drunk, an addict, or even a john. Regardless of your open-mindedness, few welcome the revelation that a son or son-in-law is gay, after he'd committed to a wife and perhaps brought children into this world. Most family members, especially those who haven't been brought along slowly and introduced to your struggles, will be shocked by any of this. When they learn about the separation and the reasons behind it, they may turn to denial: "That can't be" or "I don't believe you." They may even blame you, asking, "What did you do to him?" These accusations could come from either family—most likely from his. Brace yourself for this type of reaction, because whatever is said is likely a defense mechanism masking their inability (at least for now) to cope with new realities. Even if your parents, siblings, or in-laws promised to be there for you, there were probably qualifications on that promise.

Even if you don't appreciate Dr. Phil McGraw's frankness, there is much truth to his notion: You either get it or you don't. Nothing you can do will make people magically face something they're not ready to face, to "get" an issue they aren't capable of grasping. Many times, your in-laws will dump even more complaints or criticisms on you to the extent that you feel like the family scapegoat. What matters most is what *you* think.

I still remember when one member of a family was faced with an unexpected divorce. The husband had left for another woman, and everyone questioned aloud how a man could act with such disregard for his family and the life he'd achieved. These typically tightlipped people made it emphatically clear: Didn't he realize that people would talk? Did this man think he could get away with this behavior? Years later, one of those chastisers did the same, or worse, to his own wife and children. Go figure.

I think if my own boys casually walked away from their families, behaved immorally, or committed a crime, that I wouldn't shift my standards and I'd confront them with their poor behavior. I'd remain true to my beliefs. I know firsthand how troubling it is when others apply a double standard. The same family member who belittled someone else's husband for bolting out the door might have a sudden memory lapse or shift of opinion when it's convenient. One woman shared with me that her estranged husband (and his family) was perfectly nonchalant about his years of substance abuse and infidelity. Denial is far more convenient than the anxiety that truth arouses. Without healthier replacements for a defense mechanism like blame, these folks won't know how to function. Also, some families simply lack a value system that guides any element of their lives or actions. Yes, what matters most is what *you* think, and if you surround yourself with the right support people, you'll triumph. You won't have to worry if others, family members in particular, get it. Actually, for your own sanity's sake, it's probably helpful to assume they'll never understand your side of the story. Accept this and move on.

How to Help Your Separated Friend

Just in case your support system has rallied around, yet you're too confused to consider what you need, here's a handy list to share with those who truly care. Each woman's situation is different, but the following ideas should help most friends and families help those who are suddenly separated:

1. Listen, but don't push your own agenda. Unless you feel your friend is making a grave mistake that will jeopardize her safety, finances, or legal standing, keep quiet and merely lend an ear. Be available for telephone chats at most any hour. Have patience, for you may hear the same ruminations, regrets, or fears until your friend works them through.

2. Offer kind gestures without being asked. If your kids and hers play well together, schedule play dates. Treat them to a movie or park outing when you know their mother has so much on her mind she can't even think of entertaining her children. Drop off a cheer-up gift of bubble bath and tea. Even a home-cooked meal says you care.

3. Provide companionship. Particularly if she's the only adult in the house, your friend will get lonely. Holidays and birthdays are hard that first year. Having a friend takes the oneness out of them. If you fear she's sitting home alone, invite her to a movie or over to chat on your couch.

4. Call daily just to say hi and let her know you're concerned. Don't start ruminating about her estranged spouse or predicament, as you want her to remain upbeat. Also, sending an occasional card to lighten the day sure beats nasty legal letters and bills.

5. Help with objectivity, as best you can. When overwhelmed, none of us is qualified to make too many important decisions all at once. Be a sounding board for practical matters, and always keep your discussions confidential.

6. Accompany your friend to court, a doctor's appointment, a women's shelter, or anywhere else you know she needs to go, but is upset about going.

7. Treat her well. That may sound unnecessary to mention, but especially if a woman is exiting an abusive relationship, she needs the never-ending unconditional positive feedback and empathic understanding that friends, counselors, and others concerned provide.

8. Ease her financial burdens by sharing. Offer clothing your children have outgrown. Provide babysitting so she can save the expense. Share the harvest of your garden when it yields more vegetables than you can consume. If you can afford it, buy a book or magazine you know would encourage her. Little things like these add up, and presented as friendly gestures, they won't affect her pride.

9. Reassure her that this too shall pass. Reiterate that her marriage is only one aspect of her life that continues no matter what. Encourage her to take care of her own needs with good exercise, diet, and health care.

10. Intervene if her condition worsens. Call her doctor or therapist if there is talk of suicide, or alert other friends to check in on her too, once in a while.

The Truth Be Told . . . or Not?

Knowing when to let family ties go is vital when you encounter a separation. Knowing when to speak up and how to respond to questions from friends and family is equally pivotal.

One school of thought is to say nothing, to silence all negative thoughts out of respect for privacy and reputation. I'm more inclined to think that you do need to confide in someone you trust, whether it's a friend or counselor. In the first few hours when my marriage faced a real crisis, I remember a friend advising me, "Just be careful who you tell, because once you say something, you can never take it back." That was wise advice.

For the first few weeks, I confided in only those people who needed to know or who could render assistance. I kept the stiff upper lip and maintained the façade that our marriage was still working. But as time passed, I recognized that there was little point to maintaining the status quo.

If I were an actress, I think I'd be dirt poor. I couldn't hide my emotions and I couldn't pretend there were four of us in a house when there were only three. I also didn't want to wonder who knew what, trying to be open with some, yet closed with others. Thus, in one-on-one dialogue, I shared my feelings with people quite openly.

Honesty about what transpired was the route I chose, partially to end my enabling, partially to preserve my own sanity. It might not be a path you feel comfortable with, given your emotions or your personality. Do what is best for you.

Be Yourself

Similar advice is to be yourself. But even that is difficult to follow if you have endured years of a miserable marriage, emotional battering, and perhaps depression. It's hard to get in touch with your true feelings when you're living a fantasy for everyone else's benefit.

Truly, one of the perks of a trial or even long-term separation is finding out things about yourself, and more important, focusing on your needs. With the wife role sidelined, you can concentrate on your children's needs and on your own interests. It's amazing how much time wives really do devote to their husbands, to making their partner's lives easier or more satisfying instead of their own.

One woman's true sense of humor shined when the husband was no longer in the picture. She could outwardly be the very funny person she'd been years before. Beside her husband, she was chastised into being quiet.

Maybe you've seen other women cautioned to keep themselves in minor roles to bolster their spouse's fragile ego. Maybe these women turned down career opportunities so they wouldn't exceed their husband's income, or perhaps they let friendships slide because he didn't approve. Personally, or even professionally, women sometimes put a lid on who they are in order to please their male partners.

If your partner chooses to be nasty, spiteful, and negative, that's his choice and his alone. You can rise above those patterns, however. You might want to call him a bottom feeder, but you can choose not to. It might irritate you that he can't even send the children home with a card for Mother's Day, but it doesn't mean you have to forget Father's Day.

Take the higher road. While difficult, you'll find it's usually the best course. Be who you are, and allow yourself to grow from the pain and hurt into your true potential, and someone of whom you and your children can be so very proud.

Helping Your Children

Speaking of the children, you might have thought we forgot about them in this discussion of separation and its immediate aftermath. But your children are very much in mind, for they are absorbing what goes on around them.

Don't feel guilty if you've focused on yourself for a while. Maybe upon reading this book, you've become more introspective. That's perfectly fine. Surviving separation reminds me of when the flight attendant cautions you to put the mask on yourself before trying to assist a young child. If you don't feel composed enough or capable enough to parent, a little time to regroup never hurts anyone. Soon your thoughts will turn to the little charges in your care, or the grown children equally troubled by the dissolution of their intact family.

Even when children enjoy time with both parents, they struggle. Anyone who doesn't recognize that it's harder for these children is living in deep denial. Imagine moving from place to place, remembering important belongings, missing the familiarity that comes with a home. It's something we adults take for granted once we establish ourselves in new housing or stay in the dwelling we know as home.

Children aren't exempt from coming to their own conclusions. All kids want desperately to see their parents in a positive light. Coming to terms with someone's misdeeds is difficult for us adults. For the child who hasn't developed a full range of cognitive and emotional skills, it's nothing short of earth shattering.

When parents are openly hostile to one another, which is often the case before some cooling down occurs, the pain at seeing one parent treated poorly by another is immense. For that reason it's important to attempt civility, even goodwill toward an estranged partner. Try at least for the child's sake.

However, you can't make someone treat you well. Rest assured your children will learn important life lessons when goodwill is lacking. If dad fails to show up for his visitation time, he might intend to stick it to you, but he's really hurting his own reputation. Therapist friends I've talked with recall numerous clients who, twenty years later, remember when dad left them sitting with their coat and backpack.

My then preschooler, upon noticing a gift-giving occasion, commented, "I don't think dad likes you." My son knew that in their younger years, I would always send my boys with a card or gift at Christmas, on their dad's birthday, or on Father's Day. I did this because going empty-handed hurts a child, and it speaks volumes about values we're trying to impart. Incidents like this remind me to be who I want to be and not to worry about the choices other parties make.

Seeing how your children struggle is one of the hardest tasks in this process. When your children's father blatantly ignores your child's emotional or physical safety, medical or educational needs, or puts them at risk in some way, it's not just sad, it's sick. Children facing separation and divorce need consistency, more hugs, and affirmations that you will always love them and be there for them. In a child's mind, if one parent can walk out on the family, so can the other. Their security has been shattered. Never forget how important reassurance is to children of all ages, even into their adult years.

What to Tell Children

It's everyone's favorite neighbor, the late Fred Rogers, who often emphasized that grownups are the ones charged with caretaking, and our children shouldn't have to worry who will look after them. In his book *Mister Rogers Talks with Parents,* he encouraged us to explain divorce as a grown-up problem. In addition, Rogers advocated a discussion of which relationships will change in a child's life and which will not. That's because children often worry that they won't get to see or have contact with the other parent.

Chapter Three explores many other coping strategies for helping children through the separation. At the outset, however, there needs to be honest communication, or at least honest in terms of what the child can accept and handle. If left to guess about their family troubles, kids may resort to fantasy answers that are indeed a lot more frightening than reality, and not at all reflective of what will happen to them.

Imparting news of a marital rift is probably a lot like discussing sexuality in stages. Give them enough to satisfy their curiosity, and add a little more when the time is right. When they worry about the future, reassure them: "We'll work it out." They don't need to know anything more than the immediate future for right now. Reaffirm that you will be there for them, and this will help them adjust to almost anything.

When purely adult issues such as adultery are involved, choose your words carefully. For instance, "Daddy likes his new girlfriend better than us" might be what you want to say, but a more tempered "Your dad and I have different ideas about being married" is more general, yet still truthful.

Rest assured that the discussions will be ongoing with a multitude of topics. One therapist advised a mom facing constant harassment to state simply, "Your dad's just tough to deal with sometimes." That pretty much validated everyone's perception. Kids know more than we realize. To ignore harassment or abuse, especially if the kids are present when it occurs, is a mistake. You don't want to teach children that you are someone's doormat. But running the father into the ground in a tirade would surely be a mistake as well. So stick with tempered honesty as best you can, and it should serve you and your children well.

Slowly but Surely

All of this advice might be extremely difficult to follow, particularly when you are ruled by the heart more than by your head. But I can't emphasize enough that what you do and say—in the early stages of a separation and in the days ahead—can and probably will be used against you.

Resist the temptation to give in to your emotions. Anger makes us act impulsively. Use your support system to vent your anger and hurt constructively, or read the next chapter to initiate strategies such as exercise to help you cope.

The golden rule here is to think first, mull it over some more, and then act accordingly. So you get legal letters in the mail, or you hear bits and pieces through the grapevine. This doesn't mean you should pick up the phone, dash off a nasty e-mail message, or incite legal action of your own. You might ultimately decide to respond, but if you think first, sleep on it (or at the very least give yourself a break from dealing with it), and then move forward, your actions will be less likely to haunt you, and more inclined to help you through this journey.

The Road Ahead

Court records, brought to light in an article by Jeffrey Zaslow in *The Wall Street Journal* (January 14, 2003), indicate that divorce filings have been on the rise. Some speculate that it's a reflection of tense times in a post 9/11 world, while others point to the poor economy. In a survey by the American Academy of Matrimonial Lawyers, caseloads either remained steady or increased. Unfortunately, a well cited prediction that 50 percent of first marriages and 60 percent of remarriages end in divorce does seem to hold true in most years.

As you step out, prepare for the worst, and be surprised by the best. Sure, separating could be amicable. One husband insisted on paying spousal support so their children could continue to have a stay-at-home mom. But there aren't too many men like this (and it makes a case for cloning, doesn't it?). Ahead, you'll face unknown challenges, what I call the challenges of change. There will be tough times, and memorable ones. Indeed, if you're like me, there will be deciding moments that shed clear rays of light on old issues, helping you to decide your outcome.

Top Ten Practical Moves to Make When Separation Is Imminent

If you have an inkling that separation is headed your way, peruse this list. Call it looking out for number one, but if you don't—trust me—no one else will. Don't feel guilty about taking these measures if you must. If you are dealing with domestic violence, turn to Chapter Five for additional strategies.

1. Knowledge is power. Know where you and your husband have bank accounts, life insurance policies, mutual funds, certificates of deposit, all other instruments of finance, and important documents such as social security cards, passports, birth and stock certificates, and the details of his pension, 401(k), and other employee benefits. Know the location of and have access to safe deposit boxes. Your county recorder of deeds can help you track down real estate and deeds. If your marriage is just short of the ten-year mark, you may want to wait it out, if you can and if it's safe. You'll have more bargaining power in matters such as alimony, social security, pension benefits, and more. This is because courts tend to view marriages lasting at least ten years or more as longer term. Therefore, you may be eligible for a portion of your husband's pension and social security benefits (when you reach the age to claim these), and you may qualify for alimony. It's all good reason to speak with an attorney before moving out, or asking him to.

2. Become a financial sleuth. Obtain statements and balances for bank accounts, plus copies of wills and trusts. Make duplicate copies of computer files with financial data. The Social Security office can give you a current report of earnings for both of you. Collect as many of your husband's pay stubs as possible. In some professions there are multiple paychecks. For instance, a police officer might receive separate payment for his court appearances.

Or there could be bonuses or commissions accounted for on separate pay stubs. Most of this shows up on a W-2, but this doesn't help if it's July.

3. Safeguard heirlooms and liquid assets. Seek appraisals for artwork, antiques, and other collectibles. Take any sentimental or important objects to a friend's house for safekeeping. Be certain that your name is recorded on the house deed or apartment lease. Do not stash cash in a safe deposit box; for pending litigation, boxes are sometimes sealed. Make sure you revoke any powers of attorney your spouse may have and ask brokerage firms to check for identification before your name is signed to anything.

4. Open a bank account in your name. It only takes one party to raid an account, and you don't want to be left without any money. Certainly do not deposit any more of your own money into a joint account, even if you transfer that into your own name. Establish a new account for future deposits, preferably at another bank. This is where you can keep an emergency fund to live on and pay legal bills, at least until support is established. Don't be surprised if a spouse petitions for joint accounts to be frozen, pending equitable distribution in a divorce. This is another reason to have your own access to funds.

5. Establish credit in your own name. As soon as separation takes place, cancel or report missing jointly held credit cards. Then, go out and set up new accounts in your name only.

6. Pay as many bills as possible. Do this prior to separation so that you are not stuck with the obligations, risk having utilities shut off, or have to fight off a bad credit rap.

7. Take care of household or car repairs. If you've been putting these off, make that upgrade, such as air conditioning, a driveway, or a patio, particularly if you are fairly certain you will maintain and live in the residence at settlement. If you currently have an old vehicle and can afford to upgrade your set of wheels, do so. You'll need transportation, and as long as the expenditure is modest, you won't be faulted for a new (or slightly used) car. Indeed, if there is a manufacturer's warranty, you'll save money in years to come.

8. **Look after your health-care needs.** Visit your doctor for a routine checkup, annual OB/GYN exam, vision testing, or dental cleaning and x-rays. Chances are good your health-care coverage will remain in force for at least several months longer, but you might be responsible for any copays or procedures that aren't covered. So see to these visits now, and order any dental work or new glasses or contacts if they would be covered on your health plans.

9. **Invest in a better work wardrobe.** I'm not suggesting that you buy out Saks Fifth Avenue, only that you purchase some basics to see you through job interviews and career commitments. Focus on a few good suits and the appropriate accessories. But hey, a new bathing suit could do wonders for the self-esteem as well!

10. **Stock the pantry.** This might sound silly, but if funds get tight (and if you're dealing with a belligerent husband, they just might), you won't need to spend as much on groceries if you've stocked the pantry and filled the freezer.

Chapter Two

Looking After You

We were "learning to separate our lives." This was a line I kept hearing over and over when my marriage collapsed to the point of separation. I hated the thought. I grasped at any piece of that marriage that might have been worth saving. Unfortunately, I did this to the detriment of myself.

Over a span of four months, I lost fifteen pounds from stress. You have to realize that I was already thin to begin with. I was too tense to eat well, and as a friend confided, "Loriann, you don't have fifteen pounds to lose." Sure, I fit into something slinky that Christmas without a problem, and I loved finishing those lasagna leftovers my friends had brought me, free of any guilt. But I would rather not have gone through those emotional struggles.

Oddly enough, the line I abhorred quickly became my mantra in the weeks and months ahead. I was learning to separate my life from that of my first husband and marriage. While I remained open to a possible reconciliation for several weeks, I wanted to be strong, at first for my children, but more importantly for my own self-worth. In a matter of months, I realized there would be no reconciliation. This chapter will help you to be strong for yourself regardless of your marriage's ultimate fate. Its focus is you—your well-being and your health.

Shattered Self-Esteem

There are worse things than being separated. Truly, there are. As I looked at my life and career in those days, I saw a scared young woman with battle scars, hardly able to support herself, let alone two children with special physical, emotional, and learning needs. Friends kept telling me that I was strong, that I deserved better than what I was getting in my marriage, and that I had options.

For women who have endured years of verbal abuse, and for those who have been stunned with the shocking news of their husband's secret love affairs, or other illicit behavior, mending the self-esteem is a first step to solid ground. Some women have flat out been told they weren't attractive or desirable. They've listened to a long litany of deficits their partner perceived them to have. Other women are hurt to think that their husband wants to get rid of them so much that he'll be overly generous, as if they can't wait to have it over. Still others have been besieged by their husband's crazy-making behavior, passive-aggression, or years of emotional, sometimes legal, abuse. Worse yet, many women who face marital separation say to themselves, "What did I do to cause this?" or "How stupid I was to waste the best years of my life!"

Wait a minute! No one—I repeat, *no one* is responsible for another person's behavior, choices, or decisions. We are responsible for our own lives. Too often as women, we feel the burden of making relationships work. When they fall apart, we're the first to accept the blame. This notion must end.

The message here is to stop clinging to your marriage and to goals, hopes, and dreams you set as a couple. Especially if one partner wants out of the marriage or refuses to correct patterns that have become major roadblocks, the sad truth is that there's nothing left upon which to build. Your life moves on, yes, even through the challenges of change.

I remember reading that as Oprah Winfrey was addressing a graduating class, she said, "It doesn't matter what you've been through, where you come from, who your parents are or what your social or economic status is. None of that matters." She went on to add that it's how you choose to live, how you choose to love and give to others that really matters.

These remarks speak to me, with a message of hope and the permission to be a little selfish too.

Who you used to be isn't necessarily who you will be in all your years to come. With emotional strength training, you can improve. Your job is to take care of you, because if you fail to, I assure you that others won't do as good a job. And again, it's not their responsibility. It's yours.

If your husband and your marriage seemed to be the center of your life, these efforts of change and rebuilding will be more difficult. Even if you decide to reconcile with your husband, it's probably best to have your own life, your own interests, and your own focus. Men generally want to share their lives with women, not *be* their lives. Remember that, for whether you reconcile or find yourself dating in the years to come, you need to establish your own identity, not his.

The Roller Coaster Ride

Where I grew up, we had some classic roller coasters that could scare you silly or send you on the best thrill of your life. That's the best analogy I can give you in the first weeks and months of separation. One day you'll be blue, feeling another frustrating false start. But the next day you'll wake refreshed, invigorated to tackle tasks, embrace life, and put your world back together. Here's how to have more of the latter and less of the former.

Allow Yourself to Be Angry

So what that you're furious? As long as you don't hurt someone with that anger (namely, your children, yourself, or yes, even your estranged husband), give yourself the right to experience this emotion. You might have every right to be angry. Perhaps you've been lied to, cheated on, or battered about. I sought counsel from a trusted advisor when I felt that I should be forgiving yet couldn't fathom how to do that. He said, "Maybe it's too soon to forgive." The first phase of separation isn't the time to compare yourself to Mother Theresa!

Now please understand. I'm not advocating that you allow your anger to run wild. You need to learn to channel your venom into positive energy that propels you forward and doesn't make you backslide. Journaling is one way of doing this. Venting to a friend or therapist is another. Anger is a sign worth listening to, for if we don't work through these frustrations, we run the risk of miring in misery.

Use your anger as a tool to get in touch with other emotions. In time, you want to discover the appropriate, constructive path for your angry feelings, which may turn to hurt, sadness, and even forgiveness. Ultimately, you will find that holding on to anger eats away at you, and that anger closes doors. Focusing on your own life in a loving way opens those doors to your future. I'll discuss anger in more detail in Chapter Nine, and I've listed several helpful resources for your own bibliotherapy in the appendix.

Let Go of Your Worries

These are probably plentiful right now. I truly know what it was like to be a dependent spouse, thrust into new circumstances and gripped by anxieties from household hassles to financial burdens.

Yet there is an old adage that tells us that most of the things we worry about never come to pass. In many cases, our need to worry stems from our need to be in control—of our own destinies, not of others' lives. When you're suddenly separated, you don't feel in control at all. In fact, you may feel that your estranged husband, his lawyer, or even a court system wields much power over your life. The key then is to focus on the issues we can directly influence, and then gradually let go of all the rest.

Chronic worry saps energy, cripples creativity, and blinds us to real challenges. It can become disabling if we let it. "Worry is a core component of numerous medical disorders, and is central in many solvable, if not medically diagnosable, problems in life," says Edward M. Hallowell, M.D., a psychiatrist and author of the book *Worry: Controlling It and Using It Wisely.* Depending upon your circumstances, you might want to seek medical or psychological intervention to address your anxiety. How do you know when those anxieties are a bit over the edge? Certainly if you feel your heart racing or pounding most of the time, or if you have other physical ailments that you haven't experienced until this stress, that's a sign. If you find yourself taking things too personally, jumping to conclusions and fixating on worst-case scenarios, or if you see things in your life with the pressuring notions of "should," "must," "never," or "always," then anxiety might be getting the better of you as well. Talking through your emotions, combating some of these irrational "shoulds" and "musts" would be a worthwhile step.

Go Ahead and Cry

This might not make sense on the heels of our trying to dump our worries. But indeed a good cry purges mounds of stress. Some women have been taught to swallow their emotions and never let them show. Granted, if your crying scares your children or embarrasses you, then confine it to private moments. But let yourself occasionally have a good cry. If you do find that you are totally engulfed in tearful moments most of the time, use this insight to schedule an appointment and discuss your feelings with a therapist or counselor.

List What You're Thankful For

You've heard the popular expression "count your blessings." Well, by forcing yourself to list what you're thankful for, you do gain a positive perspective again, and what better time to do that than after you've had a good cry? A close friend of mine had been divorced years before me, so she understood exactly what I was going through. We'd often recite to each other the top three things we were thankful for whenever we got a little down. Even if the items on our list were as basic as having a roof over our head, a car that was paid off, or a favorite television program to look forward to, we discovered many positives. If merely listing out loud isn't concrete enough, try writing a journal. Author Sarah Ban Breathnach's book *Simple Abundance Journal of Gratitude* might get you started.

Realize That Friendships Can Mean Friend Shifts

As you've already discovered, having a support system of trusted friends is vital. In some cases, a friend shift will mean that some people side with your estranged husband. In other cases, you'll be surrounded by the loving support you need, but even this can make you uncomfortable if you feel you're receiving more than you're giving.

True, solid friendships are two-way streets. Each party contributes to the trust and bond that endures. Each gives back what he or she receives. But let's face it. You're in crisis mode here, so all the rules get thrown out the window. Don't add this to your worries, because in time you'll be the stronger person in your friend's time of need.

People who have many good friends are physically healthier and live longer than loners. It's also well accepted that those with too few friends suffer from lower self-esteem. But what's a woman to do if friends aren't close by, or have drifted away? True friends are only a long-distance shoulder away, and with e-mail these days, it's so convenient to communicate to our heart's content. If you feel some friends have deserted you, it's time to form new friendships. Put yourself in the company of upbeat, warm-hearted people. Certainly, gathering places like church, school, work, neighborhoods, volunteer organizations, or even the parents of your children's social circle are all starting points to foster adult friendships.

Don't be surprised, though, if some friends can't handle your separation. It may remind them that their own marriages could be headed for hard times. Rather than acknowledge their own fear, they deny your troubles, and your friendship is frayed. Limit your time around old friends who are not positive. If invited to get together with a less-than-cheerful person, merely decline. Right now you need understanding and peace of mind. You don't need hassles with difficult people when you already have enough of those with your husband.

Male Friends

When my marriage fell apart, I first turned to trusted girlfriends to dry my tears and lend an ear. But I soon realized how important it can be for women to have friendships with men.

Granted, a few of the guys I'm friendly with are husbands of my female friends. But not all. Men I met through my career, church, or mutual friends remain confidantes and trusted allies.

Let's face it, raising two boys, dealing with an ex-husband, and dating again, I turned to these buddies for a completely different perspective. Somehow, I think they reap a few benefits from me as well. You'd think most women might be too—dare I say—chatty? Yes, we women do talk more. But when I held back on e-mail to one of my guy friends fearing just that, I got a long-distance call with the disappointed grumble, "My screen is blank!"

Honestly, it's nice to be appreciated by members of the opposite sex, particularly when you've been disillusioned by your marriage

partner. While a girlfriend can agree with my take on things, it's alto-
gether a different validation when a guy says, "He was nuts for
leaving you" or "You look great!" Some male friends even confided
that they've earnestly tried to rebuild my trust in men. I needed that.
It was sweet, if not a pure public service!

So learn to rely upon guy friends, not merely to help you set
up the Christmas tree or fix a leaky faucet. Enjoy their support,
their compliments, and for sure, learn all about the mysteries of
testosterone.

Moral Matters and Problematic Behavior

In a good many separations, one spouse or the other is tackling a
moral dilemma. For instance, you discover your husband's addiction
to alcohol or drugs, gambling, or even sex. On the other hand, you
may have taken a male friendship too far into the realm of infidelity
yourself.

Betrayal often forces problems in the marriage or with the individual out into the open. By betrayal, I don't mean sexual infidelity
exclusively, but this is the most common culprit.

By now, this line isn't new information, but it's important:
Who you were yesterday doesn't define who you will be tomorrow.
If you feel ashamed by a personal failing, there's no need to add to
your burden. The important thing is to take responsibility for what
you've done and move on. If you've been the victim of betrayal, I
understand that the hurt is very real. For most women, honesty is
the bottom line. When that trust is broken, the damage seems
irreparable.

So much discussion has surfaced ever since major Hollywood
celebrities and political figures were caught in moral dilemmas. Of
course, what we call a moral dilemma is a very subjective concept,
but I'm using that term with the popular Western culture standards
that sexual addictions are harmful and that fidelity is desired in

intimate relationships. But just because moral dilemmas are in the headlines doesn't make them any less important to your marriage. You can't talk your way out of a situation you behaved your way into. It's devastating when wives learn of betrayal because of an arrest for soliciting a prostitute, a sexual harassment suit at work, or after contracting a sexually transmitted disease by their unfaithful husbands.

So how do you handle your man's affair or trysts on the seamier side of life? That's fodder for your therapist, for sure, but you do have options. Addictive behavior is usually only the first layer of a deeper problem. One should uncover the underlying cause. For some men who have one affair after another or pick up women on the street, the real issue is not sex. And it's *not* your fault. The roots of compulsive sexual behavior can range from the need for power over another person, deep-seated anger, low self-esteem, a sense of entitlement, and ego gratification to excessive risk-taking, a genuine fear of emotional intimacy, low levels of dopamine in the brain, or even personality disorders.

This long list doesn't absolve anyone; we have choices over our behavior. Many people might suffer problems but choose more moral paths. They recognize the effects of their behavior, and that's enough insight to spur them to seek help.

The person at fault should address the cause and make restitution if there is any hope for reconciliation. No remorse speaks volumes. Don't allow his behavior or guilt to damage your self-esteem. The late Shirley P. Glass, Ph.D., wrote Not *"Just Friends": Rebuilding Trust and Recovering Your Sanity After Infidelity* with Jean Coppock Staeheli. Glass discussed sexual addictions and other extramarital activities. She urged readers to ask themselves whether the infidelity is part of a larger picture of cheating and lying. Is your partner generally trustworthy and dependable in other matters? Is he willing to be accountable for his actions?

Are You Codependent?

Are you enabling poor behavior by denying it? I've already conveyed the popularly held notion of women as the nurturers or fixers in our culture. Most of the time, that's positive, but not when you feel it's your job to take care of another adult of able body or mind. It's not healthy if you take on the responsibility of solving their problems, making life easier for them, and looking the other way while they manipulate to have life *their* way, often at your expense. It's sure not wise to allow your own needs and wishes to take a backseat to someone else's behavior. Codependent partners often truly believe they are helping in some way when they perpetuate destructive patterns. If you're overlooking, smoothing over, and covering up for abuse, alcohol, drugs, gambling, or serial sex, you need to stop.

Couples can survive hard times, and they might even strengthen their marriage, or they may need to end the marriage to end the codependency.

I mentioned in the introduction that a huge chunk of self-awareness came to me when I realized my own codependency. I tried to be the fixer. I tried in so many ways to make my first marriage work and my partner happy that I lost myself doing so. I remember rationalizing with "oh, it must be work stress" or some other, frankly lame, excuse for what were becoming pervasive patterns I could no longer tolerate. In one vivid memory, as I was still keeping up the happy couple façade, I remember a friend wanting to see the layout of our master bathroom. Embarrassed that she might see a gaping hole in the bedroom door, I jogged up the steps, stood shielding it until she passed, joined her looking over the fixtures, then assumed my post until I could follow her down the steps. That hole was the proverbial elephant in the room that no one, particularly me, wanted to talk about that day.

Author Melody Beattie has written several good books on this topic, including *Codependent No More: How to Stop Controlling*

Others & Start Caring for Yourself. The subtitle may appear to be a misnomer for many. Often life is so out of control, such as the case with an addict or an abusive man prone to rage, that yes, many would yearn for some semblance of control under those circumstances. Just remember: You can't change someone else's behavior, only yourself or your reactions to it. If you choose to smooth over, fix, deny, or ignore issues or behavior, it usually festers into a larger problem. Rest assured, you're doing no one any favors, least of all the person you seek to help . . . and yourself. The sooner you realize your role enables poor behavior to come your way, the sooner you can stop the enabling and begin doing a lot of empowering things for yourself.

Reawaken Your Spirit

Reliance upon a higher power and a personal relationship with God helps many women who are facing the crisis of separation. When it seems you can't make sense of your marriage, turning problems over to God might be reassuring. There were many Sundays when I sat in church frustrated and feeling lost. I remember walking away in tears and apologizing for them to my minister. He replied that there was no better place to be than in the company of my church family. And he was right.

As difficult a journey as separation is, you might find that it brings you closer to others, closer to yourself, and closer to God. There are some religions and organizations that frown upon the dissolution of a marriage, and some pastors who urge you to remain together regardless of the circumstances. I personally believe this must be an individual decision. Trust me, I'm pro-marriage. I believe in trying to work out your differences. Vows are important, but sometimes marriages must end. If your pastor, or anyone else, is leading you in a direction that isn't wise given your circumstances, perhaps you need to find another place where you feel more understood. Chapter Five discusses abuse and safety awareness, including how congregations deal with issues of intimate violence and psychological abuse.

Another problem occurs when one spouse wants to annul the marriage and the other is opposed to it. Sheila Rauch Kennedy chronicled her story in *Shattered Faith: A Woman's Struggle to Stop the Catholic Church from Annulling Her Marriage*. If your struggle is similar, perhaps this book will give you strength.

Of course, "How could God let this happen to me?" is a common question when you're feeling rather weak and neglected. You might even have trouble praying. Read with care the sections in this book about managing anger, for you might just be mad at the world, and in this case, mad at the God whom you worship. If you are a person of faith, admit your struggles with God to your friends, and if they are spiritually minded, they'll intercede for you in that department. Just know that plenty of other women before you have found hope in their faith, and you might too.

Books of prayers, daily devotional guides, and the Bible can offer you great strength and help you along the path of spiritual reawakening. Another book unique in its search for answers is *In the Meantime: Finding Yourself and the Love You Want*. Author Iyanla Vanzant uses the analogy of putting a house in order, showing what it takes to learn from the meantime experience—to get out, stay out, and move up to a better place.

Seeking Therapy

Our quest for greater understanding of what's happening to us can often move forward with the help of a trained professional. There are many types of counselors, and if faith-based problem resolution matters most, you might choose to discuss matters with your minister or rabbi. But a psychologist (Ph.D. or Psy.D.), master's-level social worker (MSW), licensed professional counselor (LPC), or licensed clinical professional counselor (LCPC) is perhaps your best bet. Cross off your list any therapist who skirts the credentialing issue.

You might already be familiar with counseling if you and your husband sought marital therapy prior to separating. As a general rule, therapists who worked with you as a couple will prefer that you seek another counselor for individual sessions. However, if enough time has lapsed between the marriage therapy and your own needs at present, then it's largely up to you and the therapist involved. If there are issues involving domestic violence or any form of abuse, women need to seek individual counseling to see things more clearly and remain safe in expressing themselves (see Chapter Five for further insight).

You can find licensed mental health professionals through hospital referral lines, trusted friends, clergy, or your health plan. Many therapists make coming to sessions very convenient, offering evening and Saturday hours. If cost is a concern, inquire with your health plan to make sure that you are using a provider within the network, or if necessary, ask counselors if they use a sliding scale. It's also wise to find out how many sessions your health plan authorizes. If you're limited to fewer than ten visits, then you'll want a therapist who can offer brief, solution-based therapy.

It's very wise to begin counseling in the initial stages of a marital separation. I can't stress this enough. If your husband carries the benefits, you're probably still on the plan. Cost may be a factor once you divorce, and mental health coverage is frequently not rendered with less expensive policies.

Different types of psychotherapy or theoretical approaches suit different people. There's cognitive-behavioral therapy, reality therapy, and brief solution-based counseling to name only a few. Not as many use a pure psychodynamic approach, since the majority of insurers do not cover years of treatment like Sigmund Freud envisioned, though an attuned therapist will use a variety of techniques appropriate for any given client. Group therapy might be effective in treating substance abuse or other addictions, in recovering from domestic violence, and in learning better interpersonal skills. I'll discuss that in more detail in the next section.

Ask the counselor if he or she specializes in working with a particular type of client? If you get the feeling that this counselor, after a few sessions, is promoting a separate agenda, beware. This can be the case with some religious-based counseling. Ideally, you want someone who has had patients going through marital separation or divorce. If you have other concerns, such as domestic violence, eating disorders, or depression, it's best to find a professional who is experienced enough to help you or has adequate clinical supervision.

Women often feel more comfortable discussing personal details with a female, and there is a sound argument for this, says Dr. Ara Thomas-Brown, a licensed professional counselor and life coach with offices in Virginia and Maryland. "While gender need not be a factor in selecting a therapist," she says "if you've got personal issues involving the men in your life then working with a male therapist may be more successful because clinical issues of transference and counter-transference facilitate this process." If you have issues with other women, then the opposite would apply, making a female therapist much more beneficial to you. Transference describes projection of inappropriate feelings onto someone else. For instance, if you are deeply affected by a lack of trust with males in your life (fathers, brothers, husband), you might begin reacting to your male therapist as if he was just like another problematic man in your past. Resolving these issues, once and for all, is wise; thus transference brings this directly into the therapeutic setting. You might get at the problem much quicker. Ultimately, your choice truly hinges upon finding a good match to enable you to do the true work of therapy to get better.

If you begin therapy with a professional and don't feel at ease with that person, then find someone with whom you click. Some patients find therapy quite productive because it gives them a sounding board and trusted advisor they may not otherwise have.

Of course, if you ever feel pressured to follow advice that you aren't comfortable with, this is another sign that you may need to change therapists. A good counselor doesn't tell you what to do as much as he or she guides your thoughts so that you discover the right path yourself.

It's not uncommon that you might be plagued by anxiety or even depression. Individual counseling is often your first course of treatment, but if the symptoms are severe enough, you should seek a medical opinion. If you have suffered a fluctuation in weight, have persistent feelings of emptiness, experience difficulty maintaining your daily routine or sleeping through the night, or feel you might harm yourself or someone else, seek medical care immediately.

Your psychologist can recommend a psychiatrist, a medical doctor who can prescribe appropriate medications to alleviate your symptoms. Of course, you can always discuss what's going on in your life with your primary care physician. While you may feel like the only woman in the world bringing concerns of a troubled marriage to the exam room, I can assure you that doctors are accustomed to helping patients through these rough spots. Thus the referral system works both ways. Your primary care doctor can recommend a good therapist, and if you already have one, that counselor can help you find the appropriate medical practitioner to prescribe and monitor medications while you continue therapy.

Don't feel stigmatized if you do require anti-anxiety medication, antidepressants, or a temporary sleep aid. You're going through a tough time, and if you can get a better night's rest to tackle the next day with more focus, then this is a good thing. Chances are, it's only temporary. If you do need medication, it's wise to engage in talk-therapy as well so that you can really explore troubling issues, and even practice new behaviors to fully overcome current difficulties, rise above them, and learn how to cope on your own next time stressful situations surface. In fact, when you've accomplished this much, met established goals, or have resolved the reasons that brought you to therapy in the first place, then it's probably time to ask your counselor about terminating the therapeutic relationship. If necessary, most professionals will see you again for booster sessions if anything major comes up in three months, or three years.

Choosing Group Support or Counseling

"Group therapy is also useful in addressing issues of separation and divorce," says Dr. Thomas-Brown. "Members receive objective feedback, mutual support and different perspectives. Group members also facilitate the healing process through their interpersonal exchanges."

People often join a support group to obtain counseling or education around a specific topic. In this instance, a divorce support group may provide pertinent information about the legal procedures of divorce as well as the financial, emotional, and parenting ramifications. Group leaders impart information and guide discussions, calling upon their observation skills to draw out more silent members so that they, too, can contribute to the therapeutic process, but it's truly the group members who do the real work. While it may take a few sessions to get to know everyone, successful group experiences are powerful and often very cathartic when the members truly pull together. Of course, they are confidential. What's said in the group remains in the group. Fees vary depending upon your area.

For instance, interpersonal dynamics often drive a wedge between husbands and wives. In the group, you can learn how others perceive you. Perhaps your husband saw you as controlling and domineering, but the group, over a period of time, gives you feedback that no, you're very laid back, open to others, and flexible, or yes, you do come across as wanting your own way all the time.

You'll also find that your role in your family of origin becomes a significant force in your marriage and other relationships. Let's say you were the caretaker of a parent, who while being physically present, may have been in left field much of the time, receiving emotional support rather than delivering it to you. This dynamic may have been fully present in your marriage where you, even unwittingly, smothered your husband, believing that was the role you were *supposed* to play. Trust me, if this pattern existed in your prior relationships, it will play out in the group. Here is your opportunity to change a faulty pattern or behavior through the interpersonal learning you'll receive (and sometimes give) to other group members. You can practice new behaviors through role-play and subtly pick up on good habits and ways of thinking that your group leader (or co-leader) models.

When a group functions at its best, there's much hope, a sense of belonging and togetherness in any given problem, useful information you can apply in everyday life, as well as new social skills and different ways of looking at difficulty. Your conflicts in earlier relationships are recreated, resolved, and corrected. While group therapy doesn't replace individual therapy, it can be an additional resource in helping you heal, and it can help you to continually grow through separation and divorce well after individual therapy has ended. Learning group process and dynamics is also very valuable in handling workplace or personal situations, such as the creation of a stepfamily, where often you'll find initial resistance, anxiety, struggles for control, conflict, and confrontation before acceptance, cohesion, and happiness take hold.

Establishing a Proper Diet and Exercise Regimen

At a time when you are filled with shock and stress or even newfound freedom and gladness, nourishing your body may take a back seat. But it's important to maintain a good diet with the nutrition that will energize your body and mind rather than make you sluggish.

Too Busy to Eat Right

You may shirk the responsibility in part because you lack the time to read labels or prepare proper meals. Grabbing a hamburger at the drive-through window, or heating up a frozen entrée might be the easy route to lunch or dinner. Skipping breakfast might even become the norm, especially if you haven't slept well the night before and are running late. However, you owe it to yourself to practice good eating habits. I guarantee it won't consume much time, but it will yield more energy and an overall feeling of wellness.

When we're in a hurry, we're tempted to purchase more processed foods, grab easy-to-heat snacks or entrées, microwave a packaged bag of popcorn (versus air popping), and open cans of soup. Unfortunately, these types of foods are loaded with saturated fats, hydrogenated shortenings, sodium, and empty calories. By scheduling your time productively, you can add better selections to your grocery cart and combine food preparation with another activity, such as watching the evening news or enjoying a music video. Often it only takes setting aside a block of time to cut up veggies, make no-fat dip, or throw soup ingredients in the slow cooker, and the effort yields leftovers for the week.

Before discussing the food pyramid, know that it's ever evolving with a new one due out in 2005, which will present more distinctions between simple and complex carbohydrates, healthy and unhealthy oils, and starch and leafy, green vegetables. Much of this concern stems from low-carb or no-carb diets, and many people from nutritionists to bread company executives are crying foul.

The current pyramid illustrates that we should introduce six to eleven daily servings of bread, natural-grain cereals, rice, or pasta into our diets along with three to five servings of vegetables and two to four different fruits. The key here is natural, whole grain (not merely multigrain, but look for the word "whole" to describe the grain content). In recent diet debates, most nutritionists have suggested limiting simple carbohydrates (refined grains or white flour products) and opting for the complex carbs (natural grains or whole wheat flour products). During times of stress, our bodies may indeed crave carbs because these act like free Prozac, prompting the production of serotonin. (You get the effect of this feel-good ingredient of such medications that can also be converted naturally from foods into sugar flowing through the bloodstream.)

Toward the top of the pyramid, you'll find two to three servings of red meat, but also fish and poultry (white meat is often leaner), dry beans, eggs, and nuts. You also need dairy requirements of two to three servings of skim milk, nonfat yogurt, low-fat or low-cholesterol cheese, and other dairy products. Fats, oils, and sweets should be used sparingly.

Those fats and oils not only contribute to a thicker waistline but they also raise your LDL levels (the bad cholesterol), which puts you at greater risk for heart disease. When you cook with oil, choose the healthier oils such as canola and olive oil. When you buy packaged food items, beware of trans fats, which will soon be identified under new labeling guidelines. Trans fats are often hidden in many processed and packaged items such as cookies, crackers, baked goods, and many more products.

Too little fiber and roughage in your diet can lead to colon and other cancers as well as heart disease. Fine, you might say. But let me get through this crisis and then I'll worry about good nutrition. Adhering to a certain mind-body connection, I say begin now. Reap the results of good nutrition today and tomorrow, as well as in the years ahead. Two good books to spike your awareness of health and nutritional issues are *Strong Women Eat Well* by Miriam E. Nelson, Ph.D., with Judy Knipe and *The Wisdom of Menopause* by Christiane Northrup, M.D. Yes, even if you don't feel that you necessarily fit into the menopausal audience of readers yet, this last book is good to peruse for the good eating and exercise habits, which you can incorporate early, thereby easing perimenopause when it arrives. In recent years, isoflavones or plant estrogens found in soy foods have provided relief from menopausal symptoms, but have also been linked to the lowered risk of hormone-related cancers of the breast, ovaries, and endometrium.

Curb the Coffee Habit

Here's another vice in times of added stress—caffeine. Oh I know, it's a tough one to cut back on. But caffeine adds no nutrients (the little bit of milk or cream does not count!), and it does dehydrate you more quickly. Instead of coffee, tea, or colas, make a pitcher of lemonade from frozen concentrate. At least the pulp adds a little fiber to your diet. If you must have a hot drink, warm some milk with just a touch of coffee or brew a pot of decaf coffee or herbal tea (green tea is packed with immunity-boosting antioxidants, too). Or make the coffee weaker by purchasing caffeine-reduced blends. These are all much better beverage choices. If you crave your coffee (or other caffeinated beverage), limit your consumption to two cups a day, preferably before noon.

Of course, nothing replaces the value of plain old water, flavored with lemon slices if you want to fancy it up. Water is greatly underestimated and unappreciated according to *Dr. Nancy Snyderman's Guide to Good Health*. This book explains how important good hydration is especially as we grow older. Water helps lubricate body linings, which change with hormonal fluctuations, and it does the same for joints. This literally makes you feel better. Water brings oxygen, nutrients, and hormones to our cells and carries away waste products via the bloodstream and lymphatic system. In addition, remaining well-hydrated means having better digestion and less dry skin. So you can see that even though good nutrition plays an integral role in our lives as we age, it has benefits today. What better time to start feeling better than now, when the rest of life seems out of order.

Necessary Supplements

Even if you eat a balanced diet of at least three good meals and healthy snacks in between, you'll likely benefit from a good multivitamin. Women often require higher levels of certain vitamins and minerals than men, especially iron and calcium. During times of high stress, keeping your resistance up is critical. Therefore, choose a brand of multivitamin that's suited to meet your needs as a woman. In addition to the calcium and iron, you might also want the B vitamins (said to help alleviate premenstrual symptoms and combat stress), as well as vitamins A, C, and E, which are antioxidants and reduce the risk of heart disease and, perhaps, stroke.

An excellent resource for understanding nutrition, as well as women's medical issues in general, is the *American Medical Association's Complete Guide to Women's Health*. In addition, while the release of *Our Bodies, Ourselves* may have seemed radical decades ago, it's a well-respected tome for increasing awareness about women's health, sexuality, aging, and other issues.

Get Moving

People exercise for a variety of reasons. Chief among them is the desire to lose weight, and simply feel better physically and emotionally. Through exercise, our brains release endorphins, feel-good chemicals that give us a sense of well-being. It's hard to believe that working up a good sweat can help reduce depression, anxiety, and mental clutter, but it does.

Before you begin to perspire, however, I'd recommend that you learn as much as possible about fitness and strength training. Seek the approval of your doctor if you're undertaking a diet and fitness program that might tax your stamina or physical condition. After the go-ahead, read articles or books by credentialed professionals on health and fitness. One such book is *Strong Women Stay Slim* by Miriam E. Nelson, Ph.D., with Sarah Wernick, Ph.D. Their book offers health, fitness, and nutrition information, complete with recipes. Also, sign up for an aerobics class through a community college or the YWCA. Some health clubs and gyms even sponsor free orientation sessions or one-time consultations. If you're a true beginner, fitness experts say you might be better off staking out a mirror-free corner of the facility. Looking at your form, at first, may make you more self-conscious and less likely to keep up your routine.

Working out with a friend is a real catalyst for changing your sedentary ways. Just don't compare your progress with hers. And don't be ruled by the bathroom scale; muscle weighs more than fat, so you may not see results in the numbers. Take a tape measure to your waist or hips and use clothing as a gauge of progress.

To stave off excuses that make you miss your exercise routine, have a gym bag ready in your car or near the front door. I do understand that not everyone can afford membership at a fitness facility. In that case, get moving and feel better at the high school track, or around the neighborhood. Keep reading for additional suggestions.

I look back now to those stress-filled months of going through my initial separation and realize that exercise was not an easy alternative for me. My youngest had asthma due to his prematurity so taking him outdoors sometimes was out of the question. I do wish, however, that I had established some sort of consistent exercise routine back then. Cut to years later, my children were a bit older, and there I was listing my house, planning a wedding, house hunting with my fiancé, and then facing unpleasant custody litigation. I really reaped the benefits of a good walking program as well as swimming laps whenever I could. Having turned forty the same year I married a wonderful Italian cook, I found that even happy forms of stress (okay, combined with the pasta!) added a few pounds. So please believe me when I say establish those good eating and exercise patterns; they will pay off in future years.

Choose a Favorite Sport

If you enjoy playing a particular sport, this will increase the likelihood that you'll continue your fitness commitment. Always warm up a few minutes before earnest exercise to prevent injury. Again, community colleges and municipal recreation departments offer seasonal tennis or swimming, self-defense classes, or other sports involving lessons or league play.

Walk Often for a Brisk Three to Five Minutes

Intersperse a minute of super fast walking. Follow this with a brisk walk again for a few minutes, and then another minute of picking up the pace. These sixty-second spurts of energy help you burn more calories. In inclement weather, walk around the local indoor mall. You'll find you aren't alone.

Don't Take the Easy Way Out

Force yourself to take the stairs. Walk a longer distance from your car to the store. Mind the leash when Rover needs a walk. Any activity that gets you out of the sitting or resting position counts.

Work Out Before Eating

This not only reduces your appetite but increases the calories your body burns during digestion. Never exercise on a full stomach.

Use Fitness Videos

Borrow a fitness video from the library or buy your own copy. Just be sure that the tape you invest in has solid guidance from a fitness professional and isn't merely celebrity fluff.

Dance the Night Away

Turn on your favorite tunes and let yourself go for a good twenty to thirty minutes of intense dancing. Who knows, it just might boost your confidence on the nightclub floor!

Seize Opportunities Out of Your Day to Flex Those Muscles

This might mean walking on your treadmill while on the telephone, riding the exercise bike, or doing crunches while watching television. It could mean doing squats while brushing your teeth or waiting for the laundry to cycle. Whatever works for your schedule, works for your body.

Get Professional Guidance for Strength Training

Then relax a day in between sessions to give your muscles a chance to rest. It's during this rest time that muscle building actually occurs.

Alternative Therapies

Plenty of people take a holistic view toward their health and wellness. Several of the suggestions listed here for taking care of yourself and decreasing stress may seem commonplace to some people, indulgences to others.

Talk about taking things for granted. When you're suddenly separated, you do discover the loss of certain things. One of these is the power of touch. I don't mean merely a sexual relationship, but more important, a hug, a hand held, or a snuggle under the covers. Massage therapy offers an outlet for those who have lost the sense of touch. Studies at the University of Miami Medical School's Touch Research Institute have shown that massage reduces anxiety and

lowers the body's production of stress hormones. The health benefits are substantial to diverse groups, including premature infants,
babies, and people with certain medical conditions. So don't feel
embarrassed by your desire to head off to a spa. You're perfectly
normal.

Ask for personal recommendations to find a licensed or certified practitioner. Look in the Yellow Pages under "licensed massage
therapist," not "massage parlor." When you go for your appointment, state your preferences, including whether you prefer to
remain partially clothed in a bathing suit. You should always be
draped with a sheet so that only the specific area being worked on is
exposed. Do speak up if the massage is too uncomfortable. Finally,
check your insurance plan; if a doctor prescribes massage therapy, it
might be covered as treatment.

Of course, a day at a full-fledged spa could encompass all sorts
of pampering, including facials and body wraps. But few of us can
afford these luxuries. Instead, escape into your own bathtub with
bath salts or oils, and let your mind wander. Add some scented candles to the room for aromatherapy. This is relaxation at its best! And
while you wouldn't think that a deck of cards could do the trick for
you, there is an entire fifty-two-card series published by Chronicle
Books that just might perk up your spirits in very alternative ways.
Lynn Gordon has made thumbing through her sets of *52 Relaxing
Rituals* or *52 Ways to Mend a Broken Heart* fun reading. With a little
innovation, your list of looking after yourself just got longer!

Other Health Issues

Other factors that contribute to your lack of overall well-being are
the presence of nicotine, imbibing too much alcohol, and the
absence of a good night's sleep.

There's no question that smoking is bad for you; it leads to
cancer, ages you prematurely, and decreases your endurance. Give

up the habit and you'll not only improve your long-term health but also increase your stamina. When you're dealing with a lot of issues, this is a big incentive.

When life gets stressful, you might be compelled to enjoy a nightcap or glass of wine. True, there are health benefits to drinking red wine, in moderation. But too much alcohol will impair your mental functioning, increase the risk of certain cancers, and make you more prone to osteoporosis. An alcoholic drink may put you to sleep easily in the short term, but later cause you to awaken.

That brings us to the subject of sleep. A good night's rest will make even the most trying day much more bearable. Recent research points to sleep being essential to creative thinking, and when you're dealing with new stressors, you need all of your cognitive abilities, that's for sure. To prevent a lack of sleep, look to environmental factors such as a poor mattress, too much noise near your bedroom, or temperature conditions. Besides, your physician can address anxiety and depression, sleep apnea, breathing disorders (such as asthma), or chronic pain issues.

Of course, stay clear of spicy, heavy, or fatty foods as well as caffeine in the evening hours. Choose warm milk, which contains a natural sleep aid, or brew some chamomile or Linden tea (known as *Tilo* in Spanish); these are known to relax you before bed. Valerian, an herb used in teas or sometimes sold in tablet form (to swallow or dissolve into warm water) is popular in Europe for its sedative effect. Skip these sedating blends if you're pregnant or nursing, however, and discuss them with your doctor if you take other medications

Exercising in the late afternoon often promotes better sleep, as does a warm bath, a body massage, reading, or meditation. Remember, it's not the quantity of hours necessarily but the quality of one's sleep that matters most. If you've tried these approaches and still toss and turn, it's time to consult your doctor.

Your Husband and Your Health

If you've gone through a difficult time with your husband, it's wise to consider how the ordeal has impacted your mental health or physical health. Researchers at Brigham Young University and the University of Utah have found that blood pressure does spike when we're involved in difficult exchanges with people we dislike or with whom we're ambivalent. Throughout this chapter, you'll find you're not alone if you're experiencing anxiety and depression resulting from a stressful marriage.

It's also unfortunate that just when you come to the emotional recognition of a husband's drug habit or extramarital relations, you must endure the added worry that you may have contracted a sexually transmitted disease, or possibly the AIDS virus. But you have to explore this possibility. "The problem is, in this day and age, a little indiscretion can kill you," says Mary E. O'Brien, M.D., author of *In Sickness and in Health.*

While hard to hear, Dr. O'Brien's advice is factual. If a woman even suspects infidelity, she should insist on protected sex only. She should be tested and insist that her husband be tested for sexually transmitted diseases including HIV and hepatitis. "If he is unwilling to comply, it should be clear that (a) he doesn't care about her health and safety; (b) he's selfish and inconsiderate; (c) he's irresponsible and immature; and (d) he has no idea what true love and commitment are all about," O'Brien adds. "That being the case, any self-respecting woman should insist on separation. Marital infidelity is no longer simply a matter of hurt feelings. It can be deadly."

Most of our fear centers around the fatal AIDS virus, but this is only one concern. A researcher from Johns Hopkins University School of Medicine studied the effects of unfaithful partners and found that their wives were five to nine times more likely to get cervical cancer if their husbands had multiple partners and contracted human papillomavirus (H.P.V.). Of course, the more partners a woman has, the same risk increases. Since there are no physical symptoms of the H.P.V. virus, men who carry it are often clueless. In addition, if your husband has had multiple partners and subsequently had unprotected sex with you, your chances of developing a nuisance infection (such as a yeast infection) may also rise.

Thus, if you or your partner has engaged in high-risk behavior (sharing drug needles or syringes or engaging in sexual activities with others or both), ask your physician for a complete round of tests. Don't rely upon your husband's word that he is fine. Go yourself. Go today. It may seem humiliating, but physicians are accustomed to handling situations like this. Your office visit and testing is carried out in confidence. Should you test positive, you'll be referred to a counselor who can help you deal with the results. And in some cases, you may want to follow up with another HIV test six months later just to be sure.

To obtain more information about HIV transmission, practicing safe sex, and being tested, call the National AIDS Information line at 1-800-342-AIDS or the Centers for Disease Control's National STD hotline at 1-800-227-8922.

Dealing with Your Husband

Who said you can't live with them and you can't live without them? Well, part of you might agree with that when life is placid. But during your separation, it usually isn't. Therefore, we need to address how to deal with the men in your life. And truth be told, you *can* live without them.

Attorneys caution that you cannot have it both ways, at least if you want to preserve your legal position. You can't call yourself separated yet continue to have a sexual relationship, even occasional sex, with your spouse. The reason is simple. One of you could claim the marriage is not broken. For instance, if you proceed with a divorce down the road, you'll have to agree upon a date of separation. You may call that date the day he moved out of the residence. But if you've had relations, he may bring up this fact in court and that date might be pushed back. If there is a legal waiting period before a divorce can be granted, and you decide you want it over with soon, then you're stuck. Thus, one brief moment of passion can set back your case. When engaging the heart, just make sure your head has a say.

Communicating

Shortly after my separation began, good friends of mine moved to another state. The wife, known for her sharp wit, was well balanced by her easygoing husband. I'll never forget her advice on how to communicate. "Construct watertight arguments," she'd say. "Don't give any room to wiggle." When her husband concurred, I realized that this was one of those teachable moments.

My friend had learned to stand up to bullies, passive-aggressive types, and other difficult personalities. While she knew how to throw out a sarcastic line or give someone a good tongue lashing, she also appreciated when to relegate such diatribe to friends, not foe. I, too, soon learned to implement such strategies in e-mail and other forms of communication. It wasn't always easy, though.

In fact, e-mail poses such a minefield that you definitely don't want to get mired in a litany of back-and-forth, pointless correspondence. For many couples, especially high-conflict couples, this just keeps the argument or issue brewing and doesn't help toward problem solving. This is where parent coordinators (mental health professionals used by the courts) can help. Parent coordinators will be discussed at length in the legal chapter, but often they can help to establish ground rules of correspondence if there is a truly contentious relationship.

Still, if you have children, you must communicate, and if a difficult dad decides to use the kids to push your buttons, maintaining a no-reaction, purely problem-solving mode is a real challenge.

Stick to the facts. Give only details, without sarcasm, and never assume knowledge or understanding. It might seem exhaustive to restate times, locations, or circumstances, but when communicating in difficult relationships you must. You never want to give your estranged partner the chance to reply with "well, I didn't know" or "that's not what I thought." This is what I meant earlier by constructing watertight statements. For example, say you are e-mailing specific times and locations to pick up the children, and in this case the father is retrieving the kids from your parents' house. You know he knows where your parents live. You know he knows their phone number. You know he knows that 7:00 means in the evening. It doesn't matter. Spell out the address, give an emergency phone number, and put in the "P.M." This covers you, and it gives the opposing party little room to wiggle.

Phrase sentences in terms of "I" statements that express your thoughts and feelings. "You make me so [fill in the blank]" does nothing more than put the other person on the defensive or proves he or she is in control. In fact, it can reinforce negative behavior in manipulative people.

The next communication caveat is a little harder to accomplish. Ignore the person's tone and nasty remarks. Upon learning that parental counseling was available, one woman asked her estranged husband via e-mail if he'd give it a go. What she got back was: "If you think you need psychiatric help for yourself, by all means, feel free." That tone, sarcasm, and innuendo pretty much summed up this guy's cognitive distortions and irritable disposition. The proper response to something like that: none. Gradually, learn to bite your tongue. Friends might get an earful later, but that's what friends are for. If you add venom and sarcasm to your communication with the other side, that's what you'll get back, ten times over. The two of you will be caught in a never-ending cycle of barbs that leads you nowhere constructive. And as a therapist offered, "The more you talk about something, the more mental energy you give it, and ultimately, the more it's still controlling your life." Another added,

"Why are you renting him out so much costly space in your mind?" If you don't want your estranged husband influencing you, then don't be a party to the nasty banter.

Remember, an estranged spouse is usually an angry spouse, not thinking clearly and at times vindictive. And yes, in a marital separation there are two estranged spouses. Him, and you, though it is often difficult to see your own role in prolonging conflict or miscommunication when you're mired in the situation.

You can control how you communicate, and you can indirectly influence his pattern and tone by not going down a nonproductive path. It's no guarantee, particularly for an abusive or game-playing spouse or one with some of his own mental health issues. But it furthers constructive communication, avoids frustration, and assures that whatever you say or write cannot come back to haunt you.

Karen Freed, codirector of the Bethesda Group, and often appointed as parent coordinator to high-conflict cases, gives this simple four-point rule to follow: Start with the issue, write your thoughts about it, focus on what you're asking of the other parent, and end with a specified time by which you'd appreciate a reply. Upon receipt of such, the other parent should answer honestly or at the very least acknowledge receipt, and promise a timely reply as soon as possible. If parties aren't willing or able to communicate like this, lingering strife shows the need for a parent coordinator.

Understanding Passive-Aggression

Army psychiatrist Col. William Menninger first coined the term *passive-aggressive* during World War II. Soldiers following orders and coping with the lack of personal choice resisted, withdrew, and wanted to flee their dictates. Menninger labeled this resistance, for a passive-aggressor thinks of himself as weak to those he perceives as more powerful. Thus, this person easily transforms another into a dictator. It's hidden hostility under the guise of innocence or passivity. I discuss this topic here because anger is almost inevitable during separation and divorce, and it's important to manage it well. Throughout this book, I'll point to examples of poor, passive-aggressive behavior so that you can properly identify it and manage it, especially if you're so consumed by anger that you lash out this way, but also if you're the unfortunate target of someone else's hidden wrath, and may be inadvertently reinforcing poor behaviors. Some are appalled to realize that they have adopted the manipulative behaviors directed toward them in the first place.

"Passive-aggressive behavior is a learned response to handling confrontation," says licensed professional counselor and life coach Dr. Ara Thomas-Brown. "It's not something that usually surfaces in a certain situation, but rather becomes a behavioral pattern that a person may employ when feeling threatened, questioned, confronted, or powerless to assert their desires." She adds that those on the receiving end of negative attitudes, resistance, and stubbornness may end up feeling so frustrated that it increases their stress levels, as well as their own propensity to act on the frustration. For people using passive-aggression as a behavioral default, it makes life much more miserable for themselves because problems go unsolved, and recipients feel pushed away.

Passive-aggressive people are ambivalent. Here, the husband can't decide whether to grow up and take on responsibility or remain the child, thus he may emotionally lose it (explode) if his wife asks something of him. Even if it's just some normal responsibility he's uncertain whether he can do it. Just when he decides to take an active role in something, his passive nature kicks in. One part craves independence; the other is dependent so he often plays the victim or martyr. One woman shared that her estranged husband was supposed to transfer a vehicle they jointly owned into his name alone. They'd agreed to this, but he never followed through. Months passed. When the time came to register the car and have a state inspection, the wife didn't want responsibility for this vehicle.

Communication got her nowhere, so she took the matter to court. When the judge ordered him to sign the paperwork, he blamed his wife for raising his legal fees and causing him to miss work. He failed to recognize his hostility displayed through inertia.

Passive-aggression routinely surfaces in everyday life. In separation and divorce, it arises through defying authority figures (such as judges, trained professionals, expert witnesses, or perceived authority figures, such as one's spouse), and withholding (child support, alimony, medical insurance, or other necessary information). It also surfaces when one spouse sets up the other for his or her own gain. Sometimes, this behavior is little more than an annoyance. Other times, it's a way of life and a pervasive pattern of maladaptive behavior.

Passive-aggression has been described as an immature defense commonly found in adolescents as well as in those with addictions, personality or depressive disorders. For a teenager trying to embrace independence yet without the emotional and financial resources to manage that, responding to a parent's or teacher's authority through passive-aggressive means (e.g., "hold on," "I didn't hear you") is developmentally accurate. Most people develop better coping skills as they mature, but there are often roots in childhood wounds, such as when a genuine authority figure wielded much power or when hiding anger became the norm. Later in life, this individual can't own anger and perceives authority where it honestly doesn't exist, much as Menninger described.

Several researchers place value on a therapist assessing passive-aggression and using it to gauge a client's prognosis. If there is a pervasive pattern of it, as outlined by *DSM-IV-TR* criteria, it's worth a much closer look and should be a goal to overcome in treatment. I think passive-aggressive behavior should be incorporated into anger management workshops and divorce education, and sometimes, recognized as a way that angry people wage war or gain power over others. Legal abuse, for instance, is one way a passive-aggressive spouse can wage war under a veil of innocence (e.g., "oh, I filed for custody because I only want the best for my children"). Since ambivalence, negativity, and dependency issues are inherent in this dynamic, any legal contest keeps two parties bound. I don't think judges give this as much thought as they should when determining motive. I'll discuss legal abuse in greater detail in Chapter Five.

How to Deal with Passive-Aggressive, Manipulative Behavior

While you cannot change another's poor behavior, you don't have to be what psychiatrist Martin Kantor calls a participating victim either. Kantor's book *Passive-Aggression: A Guide for the Therapist, the Patient, and the Victim* comprehensively explores the core causes, including dependency, control, competitive conflicts, cognitive-behavioral errors, and childhood roots. My next book, co-written with Dr. Tim Murphy, deals with hidden anger and passive-aggression, reviewing such professional literature and offering healing strategies.

It takes much cognitive-behavioral work to overcome pervasive passive-aggression so again, realize that while you can change your own behavior, it's quite unlikely you will have much impact if your estranged husband fits this description. However, you can end the enabling. Stop making a passive-aggressive person's decisions and mitigating any consequences, as this teaches him to play the dependent role and fosters codependency.

Constructing watertight phrasing helps combat passive-aggressive behavior. Set artificial deadlines. Don't back down no matter how much the person protests. Confront gently armed with the facts. Decrease their waffling by asking attitudinal questions (a question that begins with "how" is good). The last thing you'll get from such a person is a straight answer or a direct response (remember, they are ambivalent) so get any promises in writing.

Finally, realize that a person prone to passive-aggression distorts much of what is heard (remember, they are manipulative). Passive-aggressive people hear requests as demands. They project and they strive to save face (remember the victim or martyr role). As Kantor points out, "I'm angry with you" becomes "You're angry with me." They drag their feet, refuse to cooperate, and they'll continue to push your buttons, if you let them. My advice: Learn to hide your remote control by not showing any vulnerable spots or buttons to push. Do this and their ability to manipulate usually subsides.

The Temptations of Other Men

Sure, you're thinking. After dealing with difficult men, I want you to think about other guys! Well, not really. But getting back to the old "can't live without them" issue, I think it's important to address the allure of getting involved with other men at this stage in your separation. The best advice I can give you at this juncture is to do yourself a favor and wait to date.

If you're reading this book and you have already exited your marriage for the arms of someone else, you may be tempted to skip this section. Perhaps the two of you will beat the odds and grow old together in bliss. But on the chance that you are rebounding, please read on.

Rebounding is best explained in *Dating for Dummies* by Dr. Joy Browne, where she explains that this is no slam-dunk. Browne advises that one should not date until at least a year after any divorce has been finalized. I know this might seem like a long time when perhaps you might crave validation, affection, mere companionship, or even sex. When anxious, most people have a greater need for closeness. But getting over a man isn't the same as getting over a dog. Replace Fido. Hold off on Harry.

Think about how dating might adversely affect your present case or any attempts at reconciliation with your spouse. "I have no intentions of getting back together," you might say. Fine. But I'd still hold off for several months, if not a year or two into your separation. Depending upon your state's laws, dating or possibly "shacking up" during separation can be construed as fault, strengthening the other side's case. In addition, some states consider total household income in awarding support while other states only include the income of the actual man and woman involved.

Isn't companionship good for your health? Sure it is. Frequent contact with friends, family, a social, religious, or volunteer network makes you less prone to stress-induced health problems.

Meet your social needs by getting together with girlfriends. Join a book club or a volunteer group. I loved the line in Dr. Browne's book, "Hang out with friends, large groups, small countries." It's true. It's easier that way, and you can still meet your needs. Small groups may include guys, but you want to be fair to anyone you date. Wait until you have something to give. This might mean being patient while you tend to yourself, your children, legal matters, your career, and finances, but it will be worth the wait. I'll have more on dating in the last chapter.

Improving Your Self-Esteem

While commonly associated with our self-perception or self-worth, self-esteem is much more complex. Self-esteem researcher Mary H. Guindon, Ph.D. recognizes two types: global and selective self-esteem, meaning the value you place on certain traits and qualities that get factored into your overall judgment of yourself.

For instance, though you might be successful and well-liked, all around, if you get too concerned that your height is a problem, or that you have terrible hair, then these one or two traits may affect your self-concept. Selective self-esteem can be variable. In our example, you can change your hair. On a day that it's styled perfectly, you might feel extremely good about yourself. The opposite could be true if you were rushing out of the house with little time left for grooming.

Adequate self-esteem buffers you from daily trials. If you have low overall self-esteem, you become vulnerable to even the mildest challenges. Certainly, separation and divorce are not mild ones. Indeed, the feedback from significant others in your life impacts your self-esteem. For many women, their parents and their estranged spouse have been significant others. I mentioned earlier how in some cultures, it's frowned upon for a woman to exit her marriage, no matter if abuse or infidelity occurred. Imagine, then, what messages you might still be receiving from significant others. Additionally, our sense of competency plays a part in our self-esteem. A woman facing these scenarios may feel less worthy, less desirable because she may feel less successful in her role as wife or partner, maybe even as daughter. Losses that involve lower self-esteem are more likely to trigger depression, and this is especially true of broken relationships you haven't initiated, or when violence or infidelity played a part.

So how do we boost our self-esteem? That could take an entire book, but it can be helpful to realize that self-esteem is affected by these factors, as well as our thoughts, feelings, values, and behavior. Certainly, doing things to improve our sense of competency—setting up more chances for success, in other words—is one step. Repeating positive affirmations and hanging out with upbeat people are also important. Some of the other self-help measures throughout this book will improve a faltering sense of self-esteem as well.

Getting Out of a Rut

The rut I'm talking about here could mean your self-esteem, or it could just be any bad situation or day you might be having. As you likely know by now, on days where legal matters or some other unplanned task consumes you, this qualifies as a certifiable rut.

Scholars, clinicians, and ordinary folk have embraced positive psychology for years because numerous studies show that optimists live longer, fare better throughout life, and might even have the last laugh over their pessimistic counterparts. When you ruminate on negative thoughts, don't you notice how you feel more run down, both emotionally and physically? So next time you're in a rut:

Check the filter on your thinking. Let each experience enter your mind free of a dusty filter that leads you to see things all black or all white. Truly, shades of gray exist in most every circumstance or person.

Do something different. Buy flowers, sing a song, play a board game with your child, try a new food, plant something in your garden, get your hair cut—you get the idea. Whatever you select lifts your outlook little by little.

Experiment with relaxation. Lie in a hammock with a good book (someone else's saga). Take up yoga or try aromatheraphy. Indulge in a warm bath with candles and classical music. Get a massage.

Lend a hand to someone else. Small acts of kindness or providing help to someone in need makes us feel worthy, important, and just generally more positive.

Act "as if." If you want something, shift your personality in that direction by acting as if you're already there . . . or almost there! Just like the tip above, if you reach out, you receive. If you'd like to be more intelligent, take a class. If you'd like to be more social, join a club.

Chapter Three

Coping with Your Children

After the reality of marital separation hits parents, it turns next to the children. In situations where there has been ongoing discord or public knowledge of a marital misdeed, the news won't be a complete shock to older children. Kids are savvy enough to sense trouble.

But even if your children are clued in to your struggles, they will be affected by the breakup of their family unit. Your emotions will surface as well. It's hard to restrain what you're feeling in front of your children. Issues involving them tend to be triggers for us mothers, especially if estranged husbands aren't really considering the children's interests, but merely their own.

In addition, we are sometimes lulled into a false sense of security regarding custody. While you may opt for an informal custody agreement between you and the children's father, you'll be much better off with a formal custody court order. Otherwise, each party has equal access to the kids, all the time. If there are true problems with your custody exchanges and a threat of violating your agreement and taking the kids, your order is enforceable by the police.

If you have children, this chapter will also give you an understanding into your child's world. It will alert you to common struggles kids face at various ages, for no child is immune to an emotional onslaught. Even college-age kids and adult children, living away from home, experience the impact of a marital separation. Judith Wallerstein has made a life's work of studying the effects of separation and divorce and tells us that college counseling centers are filled with freshmen just learning that their parents split. Later in this chapter, you'll learn important strategies, from helping your children cope to dealing with their difficult dad and mediating child custody issues.

What the Experts Say

Fifty percent of first marriages and 60 percent of remarriages end in divorce. With a million new divorces each year, there are a lot of children living in the wake of their parents' bitterness. One in three children endures a family divorce by age eighteen; there are plenty more struggling with a marital separation before their parents reconcile.

In her book *The Unexpected Legacy of Divorce: A 25 Year Landmark Study*, Judith Wallerstein and her coauthors Julia M. Lewis and Sandra Blakeslee noted that twenty-five years or more following a divorce, many children have significant emotional fallout from their parent's warfare. While one tends to think a separation alleviates the discord, it's only the beginning of a truce, possibly years down the road. Sometimes that truce never occurs.

"Some children are relieved that the arguments may end with the parents' separation, but most children do not react this way," says Timothy F. Murphy, Ph.D., who counseled many children as a psychologist. I collaborated with Dr. Tim Murphy in writing *The Angry Child*. "Children may act more frustrated, impatient, or anger easily," he says. "They may become depressed, withdrawn, or moody. To cope with the stresses, a child may even deny their parents are splitting up."

One barometer Dr. Murphy uses is gauging the child's behavior before the separation. Whatever psychological symptoms exist before parents separate are good predictors of symptoms these children will have later on. These are children struggling to discover where they fit in, especially if it appears that dad has run off to live a new life or that mom suddenly has a steady boyfriend. In their minds, perhaps, wasn't their original family good enough?

But does this mean that children are ruined because two parents have perhaps realized their mistakes and chosen to create new futures? No, it does not. In fact, when her twenty-five-year study was published there were those who believed Wallerstein painted a bleaker picture than necessary. Paul Amato of Pennsylvania State University was one. He wrote about the divergent perspectives in the journal *Family Relations*, citing *For Better or Worse: Divorce Reconsidered* by Mavis Heatherington and John Kelly, to back his position that family scholars see benefits in children of divorce, in addition to the negative outcomes that are more widely publicized.

Parents can make the transition from co-partners to co-parents. They probably can't escape the pain of divorce; nor can their children. However, they can be sensitive to their children's feelings, putting their kids first and learning to forge ahead to a more peaceful future.

Breaking the News

In *Vicki Lansky's Divorce Book for Parents*, the author equates the mention of divorce to your children with shouting "Fire!" in a crowded movie theater. And she should know. Having worked with her ex-husband in a publishing venture, Lansky went through not only a personal but professional divorce.

She makes the point that, to children, parents are a package deal, with no knowledge that the two of you ever had lives before the marriage and will move on to the same in the months to come.

Kids never expect to have two homes, two sets of clothing, toys, and toothbrushes, and two sets of traditions and rules.

So how do you lessen the blow? Can you soften the news so that it doesn't hurt? The answer is, you can't. However, you can choose your words carefully, be as honest as possible about the pain, and mitigate your own strong feelings.

Whatever you do, don't make light of the situation in front of your children. With your adult friends or by yourself, fine. With your children, use caution with honesty. I know the temptation to tell all. One of the hardest comments you might listen to could be "Maybe if you and Daddy didn't argue, he'd still be here." In some cases where there is obvious violence in the home or open courting of another woman, the children will see this behavior for themselves. Your best counter may be to acknowledge the child's pain with a phrase like "I know we argued. I had a right to be angry, and I know that's hard for you to understand. We didn't want to live that way, so we're living apart."

On the other hand, you don't want to enable your estranged husband's poor behavior by covering it up or denying it. Kids are too savvy for that. Where there has been domestic violence, for example, you can honestly say, "Your dad has some real problems with his anger. That's why we need to live apart." Still, rein in the urge to blame. You can be honest without crossing that line.

The most important aspect of conveying this distressing news to your children is the reassurance that the separation or impending divorce is not their fault. The second caveat is to reassure them that their needs will always matter, that they will always be taken care of, and that they are loved by both of you.

It's probably best to speak to all the kids as a group, even if there is a great age differential. Do this at home, not out in public. Use plain language. Kids hardly understand the word *divorce*, let alone *custody, lawyer,* or *court order*. Also, watch how you address money matters. To most children, ten dollars may seem a fortune, so they really don't need to know numbers. The exception might be if they are of college age, where they see the expenditures and have a truer understanding of finances. If there will be some changes in lifestyle, you'll have to discuss these circumstances. Children accustomed to using the health club need to know you won't be renewing the membership. Merely state that you've decided to save money for now.

Finally, it goes without saying that you should never lie, bribe, or promise things you can't deliver. In one case, children were promised a puppy, as if that would replace their mother. Realize that this is a new juncture for you and your children. Their trust in the institution of their family has been broken. Don't fragment that even further by telling them something that is blatantly false.

How Children Feel at Different Ages

Family breakdowns and impending divorces can have major impacts upon every area of children's development, affecting their social, emotional, and learning skills. Some parents manage to soften the pain and successfully bypass problems. But even when parents try their very best, these kids may experience higher rates of depression, sexually acting-out, drug abuse, behavior problems, school difficulties, and delinquency.

So the bottom line is that most kids face some level of psychological difficulty. Children whose separated parents still play out their conflicts are at higher risk. And it's a fact that custodial parents do have their challenges. From the child's perspective, you haven't left them. Your love and acceptance is stable, and therefore there isn't the concern that you'll walk out because of misbehavior or back talk. Unfortunately, you may see your share of both. If you're the noncustodial parent, know that your children may say things and acquiesce in order to try to assure themselves of your support. With children who witnessed abuse, they may not feel free to be genuine, fearing reprisal.

Here is a glimpse of your child's other reactions, dependent upon age.

Toddlers and Preschoolers

Toddlers who sense a change in the air might react with a sense of helplessness, while preschoolers feel a great deal of guilt. They may blame themselves for the breakup: "Daddy left because I didn't clean up my room." If a child, while in a tantrum, previously fantasized about not having parents, she may now feel her temporary wish came true. That's a lot for a little heart to bear.

Furthermore, small children worry about who will take care of them. One of the resounding messages I gained from watching *Mister Rogers' Neighborhood* with my sons, is that no child should ever have to worry about this. Fred Rogers' song "I'm Taking Care of You" pretty much sums that up. In fact, Rogers' company, Family Communications, has compiled a booklet to help parents titled "Talking with Families about Divorce." (See appendix for more information.)

Very young children who seem to have conquered particular milestones such as potty-training may regress during family conflict and upheaval. These children may appear more whiny or may cling to a parent just when it seemed that separation anxiety had been mastered.

Elementary and Middle School Children

School-age children often respond with significant anger or sadness, sometimes culminating in childhood depression. Let's face it: A preoccupied parent is one with a diminished capacity to parent effectively. A parent's own depression makes it difficult to console a child's anxiety. Some children then take on the role of their mom's or dad's caretaker—a clearly inappropriate response.

Crying and sobbing are not uncommon. Fears can run wild. For instance, if your family experienced domestic violence, your children will worry about you, their mother, and your personal safety. For years, my one son worried about our house at night, constantly reminding me to set our security alarm and coming into my room to check on me. It wasn't until we moved out of state that I noticed this fear had abated, and he admitted why that was.

Children between the ages of six and twelve often react with greater rage as they witness the rancor between parents, especially as the separation moves to divorce litigation. Uncertain attempts at reconciliation in plain view of the children might give false hopes, for all children wish their parents would live happily ever after. If those hopes are dashed, it's a double whammy.

Similarly, some children try hard to get their families to reunite. Remember the movie *The Parent Trap*. Children might be extremely helpful in hopes of rescuing their parents' marriage.

Since many children rely upon their family structure to help develop their identities, these youngsters are also frequently confused. They must deal with the threat of a ruptured identity when their parents separate.

Finally, don't be surprised if schoolwork is affected. Sometimes, children bury themselves in their studies just as adults do in their professions. If this occurs, grades may improve. All too often, however, grades suffer because kids can't concentrate or parents are too preoccupied to enforce good homework habits and school attendance.

Adolescents

Adolescents cope with their parents' separation by assuming an air of false maturity. Sometimes overwhelmed parents push these kids' needs aside, feeling that they can manage on their own for a while. But adolescents need love and affection even more because of their changing bodies and confusing thoughts. Thus, to seek approval or affection, it's not uncommon for a young girl to fall for the flirtations of an older boy, giving way to early sexual experiences that she's ill-equipped to handle. It also explains why adolescents fall into the wrong peer groups or experiment with mind-altering drugs or alcohol. Teenagers naturally gravitate to their friends. Add in family stress, and they may want to escape pressures from home even more.

Kids this age also cope with mixed emotions as they see their parents as sexual persons. It's a startling discovery for adolescents to watch their mom and dad show concern about appearance, begin to date, and become physically amorous with other partners. It can evoke vivid sexual fantasies in some children, embarrassment in others, and even cause a few to skip visitation with the sexually active parent. This doesn't mean separated parents aren't entitled to their own lives, but it does indicate the need for sensitivity and discretion.

Preteens might also feel hurried and pressed to quickly assume the independence that their peers typically achieve several years later. This frustrates them. If they must look after a younger brother while you're at work or fix a sister's bike because dad isn't there to do it, they lack the leisure and downtime their friends have. Kids might view every extra chore or favor as a consequence of your separation and divorce. If this happens and your child doesn't feel comfortable discussing the bind he's in, you may see an increase in passive-aggressive behavior as his way of getting back at you or the unfairness of the situation.

Young Adults

As children mature and rational thinking increases, the group best able to cope with separation and divorce is those age seventeen and beyond. This group is on the way out of the family unit, so to speak. They no longer require the protective structure of the family and can better empathize with their parent's individual needs.

However, this doesn't mean that separation and divorce aren't difficult on this group of almost-adult children, especially if there are concerns about how to afford higher education. Again if there is open animosity between the parents, children at any age will take the family breakdown to heart. Their dreams of having happy parents at their wedding or even of having a set of grandparents for their own offspring are now dashed.

If there is any light to be seen regarding a parent's problem behavior, this age is when children will most likely recognize it on their own. For instance, the father who is quite capable of helping with college tuition yet withholds funds to irritate the mother can no longer rationalize his poor behavior to the kids. It just won't work.

College counseling centers are often filled with freshmen whose parents recently split. These kids were merely given a real estate explanation—mom and dad are living apart. Feeling already distanced geographically, they may feel guilty about their parents' separation. Young adults may start to believe that they were the glue that held their family together. Now without a thorough explanation, their family life has changed. If you have a child this age, be on the alert for unusual behavior, depression, or acting out. The worst mistake you can make is to assume that they are now out on their own, no longer needing your emotional and tangible support.

Meeting Children's Needs

Separated parents who are preoccupied with their own emotional struggles, legal battles, and household tasks most likely see an abrupt departure from their own daily routines. Young children, in particular, need the structure of normalcy. Keep the kids' patterns as close to what they are used to, as much as you possibly can.

As hard as it may be to juggle all the demands upon your time, try to carve out moments for individual attention and family activity. From the children's perspective, it seems that the family has fallen apart. So if your household now consists of yourself and your two daughters, show them concretely that the three of you still operate as a unit.

Of course, individual attention is crucial. Nothing replaces one-on-one time with a parent, but this is a challenge when you're playing mom *and* dad. Therefore, look to friends, relatives, and others to help out. Big Brothers/Big Sisters of America has local chapters to pair your child with a mentor. Visit the Web at *www.bbbsa.org* or contact their national office in Philadelphia.

Your child's school or church might also help. One school counselor matched high school and elementary boys in a mentoring-type relationship where they assisted with homework or simply played chess.

When I first was separated, a friend said, "Just give those kids a lot of extra hugs." I did. They needed them. As I stated earlier, touch plays an important role in feeling better. While a massage and spa day is more appropriate for you, your child will benefit by sitting close by, curling up with you to watch television, or reading a book with you, and, of course, by being embraced. Hugs do heal!

If you've tried all of this and continue to sense that your child is troubled, it's probably wise to seek professional help, especially if you see persistent stomachaches, headaches, sleep disturbances, or mood changes, including anger. Your son or daughter could very well be suffering from an anxiety disorder or depression, which if left unattended may get worse. "An early onset depressive disorder colors one's personality development and sense of self," says Michael E. Thase, M.D., a psychiatrist who wrote *Beating the Blues*. "Someone who lacks confidence in his capacity to cope with, or solve problems, will learn to use strategies that rely on others or involve indirect, less active ways of coping." Sometimes this means children will react to their anger passive-aggressively. The goal here is to help your child face new circumstances, stay connected and positive, and move forward.

Ask your pediatrician or school counselor for the names of qualified therapists or child psychologists. Call and interview these professionals. Sometimes having another caring adult listen to their struggles is all a child needs to bounce back. In other cases, your pediatrician may prescribe medication.

Setting Anger Rules

In collaborating with Dr. Tim Murphy in writing *The Angry Child*, I've learned an important rule: It's sometimes okay to be angry, but never okay to be mean. Dr. Murphy points out that anger never exists on its own. There is always a trigger, and your separation is probably behind your children's negative feelings. Your goal isn't to repress or ignore your children's anger but to help them channel and direct it to constructive ends.

Anger is often about unmet need and it may also be a defense to avoid painful feelings, a sense of failure, low self-esteem, or isolation. These are additional triggers. Since a separation is a situation over which children have no control, their anger may surface out of the frustration. Knowing that, use the following guidelines in dealing with an angry child:

1. Help children to acknowledge their anger openly because hiding it comes out later in somatic complaints (aches and pains), anxiety, depression, or passive-aggression. Parents who don't "allow" angry feelings invite these troubles. Being angry doesn't equate being mean.

2. Distinguish between anger that is a temporary state and aggression that is more profoundly an attempt to hurt a person or destroy property. Identifying the triggers helps here. Find out, too, what needs your child might have that aren't being met, or what irrational fears he or she might harbor.

3. Teach acceptable ways of coping with anger, for it's not enough to merely find outbursts unacceptable. Model these by reining in your own anger, and talking it through calmly. Contrary to popular belief, punishment is not a very effective way to communicate your expectations.

4. Reiterate to your children the messages that when angry, they cannot hurt themselves, they cannot hurt anyone or anything, and that anger has the potential for getting them in trouble. Ask them how they can express their anger in better ways. Encourage them to write and talk matters out. Venting with harsh words or thrown objects only teaches aggression. Hiding anger, giving the silent treatment, or getting even through indirect behavior encourages manipulation.

5. Steel yourself to hear such phrases as "I want Daddy" or "I'll go live with my father." Kids know what buttons to press when you, and they, are angry. If you hear those words, ignore them. Most likely, they were spoken out of frustration or the ambivalence your child feels. If he or she exhibits passive-aggressive behavior, gently confront it. Once it's out in the open, there is nothing to hide behind.

6. Catch children doing something positive and tell them how proud you are. Kids facing the loss of a parent, an interrupted routine, and additional worries need to be reminded about what's good in their lives.

7. Provide opportunities for children to exercise. Having a physical outlet like shooting hoops, riding bikes, or even taking walks curbs anger. Besides, it's healthy.

8. Practice affection. Take time for calm conversation. An "I love you" before they leave for school starts the day off right.

9. Diffuse tension through humor. A child who just yelled out in anger might be brought around as you lock eyes and break into a grin. This offers the child the opportunity to save face. Just be certain the humor is understood as such and not perceived as sarcasm or mockery, because hidden anger can escape this way.

10. Help foster a positive self-image. Kids who feel valued and know of their contributions to their family and friends as well as their potential in school and outside activities can better handle anger. They are less likely to feel overwhelmed.

11. Help your child to have a voice. As he or she gets older, navigating the teen years and preparing for adulthood is challenging even under the best of circumstances. If you're involved in custody litigation that directly impacts upon a child's day-to-day existence, schedule, and opportunities, it's important to listen to the child. Sometimes, that means making sure decision-makers (like court personnel) listen to your child as well.

Handling the Tug of War

One mother facing the hassles of separation summed it up by saying, "If you think marriage takes effort, wait until you try divorce." Separating households and building new lives requires far more adjustment than most families face. When one parent or, heaven forbid, both parents refuse to work on adjustments, they are headed for trouble.

"Frequently, the adults are blind to their own anger," says Dr. Murphy. "They use subtle methods of undermining the child's relationship with the other parent." For instance, adults may refer to the other parent by first name rather than the title of "Daddy" or "Mommy." When their child complains about something, even minor, at the other parent's home, they immediately side with the child rather than support the other parent's authority.

Shelve your negative feelings toward your former partner as much as possible around your children. Admittedly, that's difficult. One of the hardest things mothers face is allowing children to have positive thoughts about a person they've seen at his worst.

It's best for everyone's sake if you find ways of communicating with your estranged spouse—whatever works for you, including e-mail, notes, intermediaries, or telephone calls. Don't place a child in the messenger role, and avoid grilling children for a play-by-play of their time with dad.

When parents wage war through their children, it sends a not-so-subtle message of "I am not able to handle this like an adult so I will have you [the child] do it for me." That places an adult burden on a child's shoulders. The kids already have added burdens with their family unraveling. Don't force them to carry more than they can bear.

Mediating Custody and Visitation Disputes

Formal mediation of child custody and visitation is popular, and in some jurisdictions mandatory. First, let's discuss exactly what mediation involves.

A trained mediator has a background in counseling, psychology, social work, or family law. This person doesn't take sides. He or she is there to help a couple define disputes, often because they are so blinded by bitterness or overwhelming emotion that they cannot think clearly. The mediator will help the two arrive at conclusions that they take to individual attorneys to become a court order.

Mediation is not a binding decision. But it does take place in an emotionally safe place. Most quarreling spouses calm down a little in the presence of a third party, at a neutral location. Often, mediation involves attending educational seminars or parental counseling. Each parent pays toward the cost of these sessions.

There are good reasons to use a qualified mediator. For starters, the process emanates from a position of cooperation not antagonism. If you've already received nasty-grams from your estranged husband or his attorney, you know exactly what I mean. Where does this get the two of you, and your children? Nowhere! Therefore, the mere act of going to mediation speaks volumes. As Vicki Lansky puts it, the lawyers then act more as advisors than gladiators.

Mediation also allows parents to make their own decisions regarding their own children. Everyone wants to believe that the courts will act in the best interest of the kids, and they do try. But let's be honest. No one has more breadth of understanding and background on these children than their parents. Furthermore, mediation is less costly than dueling it out through attorneys and the courts. However, while these are all good reasons to move forward with mediation, there are reasons to opt out of it. Where there has been an imbalance of power, such as with physical or verbal abuse, pervasive passive-aggression and manipulation, child abuse, or perhaps an addiction that impairs judgment, mediation may be useless. Often, if you're the victim of domestic violence you can choose a waiver so as not to encounter an abusive spouse. Unfortunately, some courts do not often recognize psychological abuse as being problematic. Psychological abuse is dangerous because it, too, creates an imbalance of power through manipulation.

In addition, some court programs are not spelled out in enough detail. I remember going into a conciliation with my ex-husband. I was trying to get some accommodations made for my children's activities, my career, and our changing lives in general. Originally, my attorney told me that this conciliator would have a mental health background. I found out later that she was indeed a lawyer. Well, Vicky Lansky's gladiator analogy immediately sprung to mind. This woman was just plain nasty. Nasty! She yelled at us the minute we sat down and didn't stop for the entire session. While no doubt this tactic might be helpful to scare some people straight (and into settling their disputes), the whole experience taught me that counseling-based programs had much better potential than someone yelling, demeaning, and even threatening people. Even when I stated that I'd followed our court order, I was threatened that notes might be put in our file if I refused to give in to a ridiculous demand that day, or else to take one of my modifications out of discussion. I took it off the table but still wondered about those notes because the tenor in that room wasn't helpful. Months later, I learned that this conciliator had quite the reputation, and that I wasn't alone in my observations.

Through much debate, I achieved a few goals (like getting Mother's Day weekend), but in my mind, there is no way that shouting fosters cooperation. It only puts people in a defensive posture. You can impact people a lot more positively using empathy than by raising their blood pressure. I'll discuss more positive options in the legal chapter.

Hints for the Holidays

When my first husband and I began living apart, it was late October. Stores already had holiday merchandise on the shelves. In a few weeks, I knew it would be that magical time I'd always looked forward to as my favorite season.

That year in particular, I made a promise to myself, but also to my children. I refused to allow the absence of my husband and their father to affect my enthusiasm for the holidays. I'm not saying it was easy because I'm a fairly sentimental person. But knowing in advance that the season would have its emotional challenges, I was determined to decorate as usual, make our favorite cookie recipes, and get together with cherished friends.

No holiday is ever perfect, whether we're happily married or partnerless. The myth that everyone is supposed to be happy is just that—a myth. So set realistic expectations. Something invariably won't go as planned; if there is harbored anger over the separation, this is almost a guarantee. One woman found that her in-laws used that first holiday season to prove points. While they'd normally heeded their daughter-in-law's views on what was appropriate or inappropriate, they used the opportunity to purchase gifts they knew she was on record as opposing. Passive-aggressive acts like these do no one favors—certainly not the children caught in the middle.

The holidays bring out the worst in people. Add in the strain of separation or divorce, and then factor in any mood or personality problems that exist in the individuals, and you've got a few stressful weeks. In *The Angry Child* and in *Overcoming Passive Aggression*, Dr. Murphy and I featured the different types of families that can even unwittingly create exactly that, an angry child. Sometimes one parent tries to outdo the other in spending or lavish gifts. Here, you've got an already troubled family, and now we're making it indulgent. Mix in perhaps a spiteful motive, like the passive-aggressive example, which I gave above, and now you've got the angry family. Frantic families aren't far behind.

After moving a few hours away, my children and I found ourselves living by an arrangement set forth by the court. When one of us got Thanksgiving Day or the New Year's holiday, the other got Christmas Eve and Christmas Day, and the next year it switched. That worked fine, as did the first year where each parent got two weekends in December. However, a motion my ex and his attorney petitioned for made it a frantic existence—what I not so jokingly referred to as "a holiday season on wheels." My children spent not only Thanksgiving weekend with their father but two other weekends in November, three weekends in December, as well as the week between Christmas and New Year's. That meant three, sometimes four, weekends out of state if there was a makeup. Problems arise with an imbalance like this, especially where there is much preparation, parties, and youth events where children reside with their activities, church, and friends. Holiday time is the stuff of which memories are made, and kids deserve it with both parents and stepfamilies. When devising holiday schedules, avoid being frantic and let fairness rule.

Even in families with adult children, parents need to recognize the strain they put their children under when they demand visits or insist on exclusive time. If your son or daughter is married, and particularly if there are two divorced sets of parents, your child now has four parents or stepfamilies to visit and accommodate. This doesn't even broach extended family like cousins and grandparents. The best gifts for these children of divorce: understanding and flexibility.

As you can see, family issues get stirred up, and there's the potential for a lot of negative emotions. Do your best to keep the holidays pleasant, perhaps low-key, so as to soften the fall to reality. Also, realize that your holiday—whichever one your family puts the emphasis on—isn't merely one day. There's a whole season out there. Celebrate it to the fullest, in daily components if you must. The last thing you want is a child who grows up dreading every holiday season.

Separation Do's and Don'ts

When you have a baby, everyone is full of advice. The same is true when you separate. Here are some strategies to consider as you navigate the weeks and months ahead:

1. Do reassure your children that your breakup had nothing to do with them.

2. Do reaffirm that both parents love them and care for them. Even when you feel the other parent needs a dose of maturity, children need to know that they are loved.

3. Do maintain consistency and discipline. Too often parents relax the rules during a separation because they want to influence the child's loyalty or they're too exhausted to be firm. Consistency and discipline ensure stability.

4. Do allow your children the right to their own emotions. Help them cope with all feelings, even the difficult ones.

5. Don't flaunt new relationships and potential stepchildren in front of them. Some parents do this to replace the family concept they wanted so badly to work out. Others hope word will leak to their estranged spouse. Still others have something to prove, even to themselves. Dating shouldn't replace spending time with your kids. Besides, should your new beau depart, it's an emotional rerun for them.

6. Do gain independence. Children benefit from seeing that both parents can cook, balance a checkbook, and mow the lawn.

7. Do ask children to do age-appropriate tasks to help around the house. Preschoolers can keep their rooms neat, wipe their feet, put dirty clothing in the hamper, and set the table. As they grow older, ask your kids to make their beds, clear the table, wash and dry dishes, rake leaves, and unpack groceries. Teens can prepare simple meals, wash clothes, and clean parts of the house (yes, even the bathroom).

8. Don't threaten to send kids off to their dad. In the event that you slip up, apologize quickly and reassure them that you said things you regret.

9. Do remember to be the parent. If you need a shoulder to lean on, try that of a friend, another adult, a minister, or a therapist. Protect their childhood. Refrain from buying things and indulging your kids.

10. Do realize that though you might dub your former partner a failed husband, he could be a successful father.

Tips for Noncustodial Parents

"Regular visitation is proof to the child that even though the marriage did not last, the love of the parent goes on forever," says Dr. Murphy. "When a parent drops out of a child's life and is inconsistent with visitation, or if a parent undermines the schedule of visits with the other parent, it's the child who suffers."

If you're the parent with visitation rights, understand the impact your actions (or sometimes lack thereof) have on your children. To a child, a promise is a promise. Children wait anxiously for the noncustodial parent to arrive. Understandably, work may prevent you from being on time, traffic may snarl your best efforts, and you do deserve to have a life outside of the parent-child relationship. But your commitment to your children is paramount. Unfortunately, this is an area marred by late-show or no-show parents, often in an effort to infuriate their estranged partner or to prove a point. Trust me—there is nothing worse than the sight of children, ready in coats and backpacks, eagerly looking out the window for a parent to pick them up. I've heard of incidents where the children were left at a restaurant because a parent got frustrated with them or the kids had to sleep at their dad's girlfriend's because it was more fun for him.

One parent purposely arrived early to tick off the former spouse while another came to pick up his three children, leaving the little one behind with mom, merely to create a childcare challenge as she headed off to work. There are parents who leave kids dangling, unable to make plans or schedule fun events, until at the last minute, they save face by calling to "talk about" the child's wishes (not commit, mind you). Sometimes, especially in the case of teenagers, it's too late and the children feel cheated and used by such manipulation. Bottom line: Do what's best for your children. Especially if you have precious little time to spend with them, put their needs first. Being difficult models rude behavior in your child, and encourages acting out through back talk and passive-aggression.

Of course, the other matter involving noncustodial parents is child support. Women are just as likely in this era to earn greater incomes and pay support to estranged husbands who maintain custody. Child support is most always carried through with wage attachment, but if yours is not (because of self-employment or some other circumstance), make the payments on time. Also recognize that children deserve a few extras in this world. That means picking up the tab for the occasional haircut, summer camp, or swimming lessons. And certainly, don't grill your children on how their child support is spent.

Finally, it can't be easy to be separated from your children. There are ways that you can keep in touch, however. E-mail or telephone your kids on a frequent basis. Letters and notes are wonderful, not merely on birthdays or Valentine's Day, but throughout the year. This is especially important for children who are away at school without either parent to lean on. Care packages sent to dorm rooms are instant hits and speak volumes to their recipients!

Keep a calendar listing important dates such as open houses, parent days, and school vacations. If in doubt, contact your child's school counselor or principal (or in the case of older children, the student affairs office) for such a list. You might even send the school a stack of self-addressed, stamped envelopes to mail you copies of tests and other items that you'd like to see. Number these so that you know when their supply is dwindling, but it's another smart way to keep tabs on your child's progress.

By all means, show up when you can. I know of cases where parents live across the country, and yet they make an effort to visit the child, reframing the distance as an opportunity for travel and fun. These parents purposely place themselves at the center of their children's lives versus making demands upon kids to fit into their own adult world. Your presence will be remembered for years to come.

Parenting Despite Difficulties with Dad

I remember someone commenting about the books on my book-shelf, all lined up together. Titles like *The Wounded Male; Angry Men, Passive Men*; and *Dealing with Difficult Men* stood out to this person, who commented, "My, what a sign of the men in your life." Suffice to say, throughout my separation and divorce, I think my bookshelf only expanded its collection. I'm happy to say the book-shelf today is much more eclectic than it used to be!

Indeed, it's tough to be an effective, happy parent if you con-tinually feel that you're hitting roadblocks. It doesn't give you a secure feeling to know your estranged spouse might have had six different addresses in half as many years. It's hard when you see them flaunt expensive lifestyles. It's devastating to watch a father drop out of a child's life when you know how much your son or daughter loves dad. It's galling when you discover that your chil-dren spent the night watching as daddy shacked up with his girl-friend. And it's scary when you realize your children's health or safety has been compromised by irresponsible judgment.

This kind of worry saps energy that you'd rather put toward your children instead of legal battles or back-and-forth squabbles. Indeed, if there is real danger or concern, you must fight for your children's welfare, and even that is terribly draining, as you'll read in the legal chapter.

When you have an adversarial relationship with your chil-dren's father, you're at a distinct disadvantage, for there is no one else off whom to bounce ideas. If you don't trust the other parent to discuss strategies, at least consult another mom or dad you know—a person you trust who knows some background of your child and your situation.

Especially when you are trying to parent with someone you know has some real issues, the struggle is even harder. As one mom at the women's shelter told me, "The same system that's supposed to help me get away from him keeps me intertwined with him." Sometimes the courts believe those difficult dads who say they have their children's best interests at heart, but the judges fail to see just how egocentric the actions are. Nina W. Brown, Ed.D., has written several books about self-absorbed (narcissistic) people. She admits that it's very difficult to separate from or divorce someone you think is very egocentric because this person causes intense emotions and emotional abuse, making it all the more important to protect your children from these influences.

If after all your best efforts to co-parent with a jerk there is still no cooperation, steel yourself to focus on your mission as parent. "Bring up your child with sound moral and social standards," says Dr. Murphy. "Try to give your children as strong a foundation as you can. If there is light to be seen, your children will see it someday." With that light also comes appreciation for all you are and do.

Many adult children who have seen that light still wish that a difficult parent would just grow up, deal with his or her difficulties, and be happy. These kids feel that the difficult parent's poor behavior and repeated patterns were so disdainful that they felt pushed away for a lifetime. It's hard to watch your adult child mourn the loss of the parental relationship that never was.

Earlier I shared that a comeback to questions about a difficult dad could take the form of "Your dad's just tough to deal with sometimes" as a way of validating what everyone experiences. In your effort to bite back what you might really like to say, but shouldn't, you could also offer your child "I'm sorry that your relationship with your dad isn't what you want or need from him." That's another means of validating without adding more.

"As children become aware of and deal with a parent's difficult behaviors, the most important things that the other parent can do are to provide emotional support, a safe place for your children to express their feelings, patience, and understanding," says Dr. Ara Thomas Brown. "It's critical that the supportive parent not reinforce negative perceptions of the acting out parent. The child's awareness that a parent may be causing their unhappiness is a huge emotional load to bear, but they usually continue to love that parent and will even tend to be protective of that parent." Therapy to work through unresolved or negative feelings often helps adult children of divorce, especially when they've come to a certain awareness themselves.

Choosing Childcare

You'll likely need a reprieve for work or a sanity break with adult friends. If you haven't needed it yet, plan for that moment.

The mere mention of finding childcare may be anathema to you, particularly if you have been a stay-at-home mom. You might feel guilty for considering the subject, but don't let your fears consume you. Lots of children thrive in childcare. Perhaps you can't control the fact that you're separated, but you can select a quality arrangement that works for you and your child. Besides, your child may benefit from the active attention of another adult at this time when you're a little overwhelmed.

There are three main types of childcare for working moms. First, there's a private sitter in the home, usually a trusted friend or relative who can watch your child in your own house or in theirs. This could be a college-age au pair who comes to the United States as part of an exchange program. A popular second is a licensed center. Another solution is the family day-care home where a childcare worker cares for several children in a private home.

In his book *Mister Rogers Talks with Parents*, Fred Rogers offered guidelines for selecting childcare. For very small children, consistency of care matters most, as does the caregiver's experience looking after infants and toddlers. Look around to see that there is plenty of safe space to explore, a healthy atmosphere of books and toys, and opportunities for preschoolers to learn.

Most experts agree that the proper ratio should be no more than four infants to one adult, five toddlers to one adult, and ten preschoolers to one adult.

Ask about the level of education that providers have. What are the rates? Do they change as children get older? Are lunches or snacks provided? What activities are there for the children? What discipline methods are used? And, what's the turnover rate for the center's staff?

State and local governments license childcare centers. The National Association for the Education of Young Children (NAEYC) has an accreditation program for centers that exceeds the requirements of the best state regulatory systems. Such accreditation is not mandatory but a sign that the center is working hard to provide the best service. To find an accredited center in your area, call NAEYC at 1-800-424-2460.

For a family day-care provider, ask about registration with the state or local government and get a feel for this person's experiences with children. Is any extra help provided, and if so, who provides it? How many children are cared for total? How many days was the provider ill within the past year? Does he or she smoke? Are there any pets around? Are there any disabilities that would interfere with your child's care? How does the provider's family feel about children, and why did the provider offer childcare in the first place?

Consider the physical surroundings, where the children eat, nap, play, and learn. Look for health precautions (frequent hand washing especially), child proofing, emergency procedures posted, books and educational equipment. Find out what activities go on and if the provider takes the children places (such as the library or the park). Finally, ask the caregiver how he or she would react in certain situations (e.g., if your child is choking, or when disciplining).

For those occasions when your child announces "Mommy, I feel sick," you may need to have a backup plan, especially if you fear that taking time off would jeopardize your job. In Pittsburgh, moms could preregister children with The Get Well Room at Magee-Women's Hospital, a separate area of The Children's Center of Pittsburgh. It provided a warm, loving place for a child to recuperate from mild illnesses such as sore throats, mild bronchitis, diarrhea, pain, and fever from vaccinations. If the center was not filled on the morning that you called, your child could spend the day. Aides help the pediatric staff nurse, and activities were low-key, involving reading, watching videotapes, or sleeping.

Do keep careful records of your childcare expenses, for you might need proof of what your expenses are. Most jurisdictions require that both parents contribute to childcare costs.

Finding Babysitters

You will need to rely upon babysitters from time to time whether you use your own older children, a teenager, or an adult. Parents need to consider a sitter's age and energy level, the qualifications that go into babysitting, and any references provided. Simply put, are rambunctious toddlers going to wear out an older person or put teenagers to tests they aren't ready for? Whomever you choose should be able to handle a variety of situations, including feeding, bathing, and disciplining your children, as well as any emergency measures, such as choking rescue procedures, mouth-to-mouth breathing, and cardiopulmonary resuscitation (CPR).

As children get older, you can use teenage sitters; with very young children, you might feel more comfortable with adults. For overnights, you might prefer relatives. And if you have an older child capable of watching a younger sibling, enroll him or her in a babysitting class available at local hospitals or community colleges. This ensures that they'll know emergency procedures, and it instills confidence.

Perhaps you can find the help you need from mother's-day-out programs or personal referrals. Ask friends, day-care workers, or those in your church for recommendations. You could call upon youth groups, Girl Scout troops, or the YWCA to see if they have a list of qualified sitters.

Finally, if childcare and related expenses arise, your children's dad may feel that "I should be the one to watch the kids if you need a sitter." This is not always the best option, and can prove to be a setup for failure.

For starters, your children might need to be settled in their own home, and that's a place you certainly don't want your estranged husband for many reasons. (See Chapter Five if you have any doubts.) Furthermore, he may leave you in a bind. It happens, particularly when you have a person vindictive enough to play games, jeopardize your employment, or foil your social life. My advice is to build a childcare network that includes trusted caregivers so that you don't need to rely upon the children's father.

Support for Single Parents

I know that raising your children alone is not what you had anticipated. When my separation began, my oldest son was struggling in first grade and my youngest was diagnosed with asthma in addition to the developmental delays most preemies encounter. I had my hands full. It couldn't have occurred at a worse time.

There have been moments when I'm saddened that my children didn't have the traditional family. However, there are other moments when I realize what an incredible bond I'm forging with my boys, and now, what a bond we have as a stepfamily with those attachments in their lives. Yes, as the custodial parent I'm busier and taken for granted at times. Moms might also get the brunt of bad moods or anxiety, even when it stems from other people's actions. Many moms can relate to this, yet we find coping strategies.

In Chapter Two, I discussed finding your own therapist to help you sort out matters. I'll add here that joining Parents Without Partners, perhaps the best-known support group for single parents, lends camaraderie. With chapters throughout the United States and Canada, you can reach them at 1-800-637-7974.

Advocating for Your Child

Getting through a separation and divorce can make you feel like a lobbyist, only the powerful interests behind your cause (namely, your children) don't pay you! This advocacy typically comes at a cost to you, in time, effort, and legal fees. For example, I knew a mom who had to take extended leave in order to care for a cancer-stricken child. Another mom had her employment jeopardized because of the school's frequent phone calls about her son's emotional adjustments at school and home.

Hopefully, community members, family, and friends rally around. There are folks out there to help if you only ask. I know how frustrating it can be to divulge to others your difficult circumstances. My one son's doctors urged as much activity as possible to strengthen him and prevent problems as he grew into adulthood. Karate soon became the buzzword because it forced all-body movement, so I enrolled him in a karate school headquartered a few miles from my former home and his dad's house. This came about five months before I got engaged and needed to relocate. When I discovered that the same karate school had a satellite school in Maryland, I really felt that a higher power was looking out for us. I continued to pay the tuition and drove my son roughly twice the distance in Maryland in order to keep up the continuity and treatment plan. What hassles I had in getting support for that plan when my son was away! When he lost ground due to inactivity three summers straight, it became another legal hassle, not to mention how it necessitated further medical treatment that was anything but comfortable for my son, lost academic time for him, and lost work time for me.

Never give up advocating for your child. I'm not talking about enabling poor behavior when they're older, but even then there are growing needs that you may need to address. For instance, two teenage twins (a boy and a girl) were angry at their dad for his selfish demands and harsh temper. They wanted to live a normal teenage life. If they ever spoke directly to him about their concerns, they faced reprisal, yet yearning for a voice, who do you think heard the children's complaints? You got it—mom did. (As I said earlier, if frustration can't be openly expressed, it will most assuredly surface somewhere.)

Things got plenty intolerable—to the point that mom tried to seek help from the courts. However, there were no procedures in place for these kids to speak directly to hearing officers, without lawyers present, and the fear that their honesty would leak to their father. "Nothing is simple," she shared with an exasperated sigh. When you feel caught in the middle, it's hard to keep advocating, but often you must.

Making Each Day a Little Easier

If you do nothing more for your child, reconcile yourself to bring pleasure into every day. This is especially true during those initial periods of separation or when divorce litigation is wearing on everyone. Help your child to appreciate what she has, not focusing on what's lost. Mastering what might seem a small skill makes a child feel particularly large in stature. Show your child how to be a giving, kind person. That payoff will last forever.

When tempers flare or harsh words fill the space between you, apologize. Show them that you're human and admit that you blew it if you were at fault or overreacted. In fact, it's very easy to confuse roles when angry or in a low mood cycle. If you find yourself reacting to your child because the behavior reminds you of your ex, you're dealing with transference (see Chapter Two), and you'll need to consciously remind yourself: "This is Johnny . . . not John."

Write notes to your child to celebrate special accomplishments, or sometimes just to slip into the lunch box as a midday "hello . . . I'm proud of you" note. Spend one-on-one time whenever possible.

Single parenting can be a challenge, but what you might resort to out of desperation can have surprising rewards. After I was remarried, I thought my boys were so well adapted that they might look back on the years of just them and me as, well . . . less than fun perhaps. That was until my ten-year-old son commented, "Mom, remember the good old days when we'd pile into your bed and watch Disney movies at night. That was fun!" Hearing that, I stood there smiling because as a single mom with two young boys, I did wonder how to entertain them on a budget, especially on cold winter nights. We'd curl up with books, crayons and coloring books, and they'd sometimes play a board game in my room while I worked occasionally on my laptop. Obviously, what I saw as a single-parent backup plan made wonderful memories instead! So never underestimate what the simple acts involving your children can accomplish. The results may amaze you.

Chapter Four

Navigating the Legal Landscape

While the purpose of this book is not to give legal advice or assistance in obtaining the best divorce settlement, it's necessary to navigate the legal system. There are various issues you'll need to address even if you strongly believe that you and your husband may eventually reconcile. An attorney can help you at each juncture.

How do you find trusted counsel and save money doing so? Is it a good idea for you and your husband to share one attorney? Would it be best to employ a mediator? What if you need to relocate? What if you're dealing with a very difficult spouse or ex-husband, and you honestly see very maladaptive patterns that might be better addressed by mental health professionals yet you can't get this mental health issue before the courts? These are all potential concerns, as is legal abuse and harassment, which I'll cover in more detail in the next chapter.

In addition, you'll most likely revise your will and change beneficiaries on retirement and other accounts. I'll also discuss taxes because many legal decisions have tax ramifications. You may even be able to represent yourself on minor matters, such as filing a contempt of court motion, because you've exhausted or wish to conserve your funds. You might also wonder what to do if your attorney has not managed your case well. If you plan to remarry, consider a prenuptial agreement, discussed in the last chapter.

After reading these pages, you'll hopefully feel more comfortable navigating the legal landscape. In addition, you'll learn to separate the divorce path into the three areas of property division, alimony and support, and child custody.

Having gained quite a few expert insights and learned of some innovative programs and approaches, I'll raise some serious questions in this chapter to create further awareness. There are no easy answers to issues that plague our family courts. Many describe this path as an exhausting, demoralizing process. Thus, why not try something new, something different?

Should You Call an Attorney?

It's conceivable that you've never before had to hire an attorney, except to write a will. Frankly, it can be upsetting. The day my hands reached for the phone to merely get a referral for a family law attorney, I broke down in tears. I couldn't believe my marriage had come to this.

Like any profession you encounter, there are good attorneys and poor ones. Your job is to weed out the individuals with whom you don't feel comfortable, those not successful with this type of litigation, and those you simply cannot afford to retain.

Getting over the emotional paralysis of making that first phone call is easier if you look at your initial move as merely a consultation. And indeed that's all you're looking for, in most cases, is a free consultation to briefly outline your case. In *Money-Smart Divorce*, Esther Berger writes, "Your first visit to a lawyer will not set in motion anything permanent or irreversible." In fact, she advises that if you ever feel pressured to undertake action you aren't comfortable with, trust your instincts. Voice your concerns. Refuse to sign any agreements before you've had a chance to think. Or, get up and walk out.

Chances are good, however, that you will leave your initial meeting knowing at some level what to do next. It could mean that you need other opinions. It could also mean that you feel very satisfied with this attorney's advice, having chosen the lawyer who will work on your case until its conclusion. Don't be afraid to take notes or ask the lawyer to clarify legal language in everyday English. You're probably under stress, and that alone impacts your ability to comprehend and listen accurately.

But the problem might not be you at all. Avoid any attorney who talks down to you, or anyone that you believe is not being completely forthright. So too, avoid those who feel entitled to run up your bill at their choosing (and you may not learn this until much later). Some attorneys have egos that will be difficult to endure over the long haul. Some make it difficult to penetrate that male inner circle, thereby placing female attorneys and sometimes female clients at a distinct disadvantage. Others, who have never been parents themselves, may be inept at asking questions to children and leveraging the children's say in matters. These realities exist, and I present them so that you can make wise choices in selecting legal counsel.

Don't be surprised if your spouse pleads with you *not* to see an attorney. As I've said before, knowledge is power. For whatever reason (and usually selfish ones), your husband may very well be threatened by your moving ahead in the legal process. Get the legal knowledge and ignore his opinions, for the moment. The same advice applies if he encourages you to use the same attorney to represent both of you. One attorney can't look out for both sides.

Very often, the party who seeks legal input first has an edge in the months to come. An initial consultation with someone reassures you. Perhaps your spouse has threatened to sell the house. An attorney can tell you that if the asset is held jointly, your estranged spouse is merely blowing smoke.

Your attorney can also warn you about anything that could jeopardize your standing in a subsequent divorce and give you additional pointers prior to separating. The take-away value of such advice is often substantial, ranging from major details like bank account transfers or relatively minor ones like possessions. For instance, if you really think your future happiness depends upon the brass lamp you got as a wedding gift, best to take it with you in the separation. The same goes for anything of sentimental value, or anything that could be fought over later. And, of course, the children's care should be given great thought. Without a formal custody order, which an attorney can help you with, each parent has equal access to the children. If one shows up to claim them at school or anywhere else, there is little you can do about it without such a document that outlines shared custody times or visitation.

Finally, securing an attorney is a step toward the inevitable outcome. As Esther Berger writes, "Divorce is a difficult journey, but for many women it's the road to a much better place."

Selecting an Attorney

Friends or family members who have been pleased by legal services they've received are the best source of referrals. After an initial consultation with one attorney, something inside of me didn't feel right, even though I'd been given great pointers. A family member urged me to seek a second opinion. I'm glad I did because I ended up with her attorney. Unfortunately, this attorney—probably the best I'd had—left practice for a position within the family court. So I've had my share of experiences with a variety of legal and interpersonal styles.

Lacking personal referrals, call your county bar association or look at the National Register of Lawyers. The American Academy of Matrimonial Lawyers in Chicago (312-263-6477) may also refer you to an attorney in your area. Of course, you could also consult the Yellow Pages. It's wiser to use an attorney who regularly practices family law.

Some of the questions you'll want to ask any attorney you interview include:

1. What percentage of cases are settled out of court? Do you consider your legal style that of a litigator, negotiator, arbitrator, or mediator?
2. How will state laws affect what I'm looking for in custody, support, alimony, and property division?
3. Is there a charge for the initial consultation? If so, how much? What is your hourly rate? Are invoices broken down into detail?
4. When is a retainer required? What's the amount, and is this money fully refundable in the event that it's unused or if I do not proceed with any litigation?
5. Are there other costs the legal firm bills for, including photocopies, messenger services, etc.?
6. Can some research on my case be conducted by paralegal support, which is often less expensive than attorney rates?
7. Could my husband be required to pay a portion of my retainer or counsel fees at settlement?
8. How long might my case take? Is it considered complex? Are you willing to take some risks, in that case?
9. How able is the attorney in accepting your opinion and intimating knowledge or history of your case?

In addition, it's wise to ask during your initial interview for some background about the firm and this lawyer's particular experience. For instance, if your case involves domestic violence issues, you'll want someone who truly understands the dynamics of an abusive marriage. William A. Eddy is a family law attorney and worked as a clinical social worker before that. If you suspect that your spouse (or ex-spouse) is difficult because of psychological problems, Eddy advises that you ask those in the mental health field for lawyer referrals.

During that initial meeting, you'll need to give a brief summary of what transpired in your marriage that led you to need an attorney. Be as concise as possible. Avoid the "he said, she said" approach.

Do not lean on your family law attorney for emotional support. Sure, some handholding might be necessary. But each professional in this world is there to provide a service. A therapist is much better suited to addressing your emotions than an attorney, whose primary role is to look out for your legal interests. Still, choosing an attorney does involve the personality factor. The two of you should relate well, or you may be better suited to another attorney's style. If you discover questionable character traits or business practices when you're well into your case, you may feel stuck—so I can't emphasize those questions enough.

Saving Money on Lawyers and Taxes

Usually the cliché refers to death and taxes as being unavoidable, but when you're separated, it may seem like you're dying under a mound of legal expenses instead. It doesn't have to be this way.

For starters, choose an attorney whom you know is fiscally conservative. Ego and entitlement often go hand in hand; this may be tough to take. Find out about billing practices from friends or relatives who have used the same counsel. I've had attorneys slash items off my bills because they knew my income was not substantial. They understood that I was fighting for my children's concerns in many instances, plus facing unnecessary litigation at various junctures. In other words, some lawyers have a heart. Some have a bedside manner that wouldn't comfort a fly, and I hate to say this, but there are also attorneys who will steer your case down a longer path in order to pad the bill. Plus there are those who will be adversarial at every opportunity for much the same reason. Sending another nasty letter or taking a matter to court adds to their coffers. This posture doesn't help your sanity, your bank account, or the ongoing relationship you must maintain with your children's father. All attorneys are not like this, and in some parts of the country the idea of therapeutic jurisprudence is taking hold. This approach allows for less strife and more healing.

In other words, you can control the actions of your attorney by doing proper research in selecting one, and by having some frank money discussions. Realize from the start that most phone calls or meetings with your attorney will cost you, since most attorneys bill in minimum minute increments. That means if you have a five-minute call, you could be charged for ten or fifteen minutes of your attorney's time. Think through your arguments and write down questions before discussing them with your lawyer. Or if you prefer, put your thoughts on paper, review them, and fax them to your attorney. Several attorneys have thanked me for laying things out in detail while another's ego seemed unable to handle much client input.

If you have questions about items on your bill or if there have clearly been mistakes made in your case, you have the right to speak up and ask for a billing modification, especially if your work was to be billed at a paralegal rate. Watch out for the attorney who bills you for the time that it takes him to hand-deliver material to the court since he's generally marching to court every day to represent other clients—that's double, sometimes triple—billing.

Whenever you personally gather data, make calls to banks or investment firms, or deal with your estranged spouse to work out minor matters, you do save the cost of an attorney. In my opinion, most litigation costs are unnecessary; you'll read later why and how other approaches might matter more.

With taxes, you'll want to pay close attention to the way court orders are written and designated with regard to alimony and child support payments (see Chapter Six). Typically, the custodial parent receives the tax deduction for minor children. Only when an IRS Form 8332 (Release of Claim to Exemption for Child of Divorced or Separated Parents) is signed can the noncustodial parent claim any children as exemptions. Determine your tax standing and refund potential before you sign any release forms. Even low-income custodial parents can obtain a refund if they qualify for the earned income credit and file as head of household.

Analyzing your tax position is easily accomplished using tax preparation products that make your returns less expensive than using a private accountant. Just remember, if you do choose to release the exemption to the other parent, make sure it's only for one tax year, and specify that year on the form. Other sound tax moves to consider include taking advantage of the $4,000 IRA deduction (beginning in 2005) if you receive alimony equal to or above that amount. If you receive less than $4,000 in alimony, contribute up to that amount. For those who are 50 years or older, the deduction is increased to $4,500 annually in a traditional IRA. Your future retirement will benefit.

If you are living in the marital residence and maintaining it through support payments, take the mortgage interest deduction if it makes a difference on your taxes. Of course, the standard deduction may at any time be a better move, but the point here is to prevent you from forfeiting this sizeable deduction to an estranged spouse who might hassle to improve his bottom line.

How you file also deserves some discussion. Some couples file joint returns when they are separated; others wouldn't dream of it. The problem is that the IRS has been known to crack down rather severely on both spouses, even if one spouse was unaware that the other partner made a mistake, cheated, or simply refused to pay

Uncle Sam. Tax reform laws passed in the late 1990s gave some tax relief to the "innocent spouse." But the wronged party still must establish innocence and show that the other spouse was at fault or accrued the tax responsibility. Who wants this additional hassle?

Therefore, think twice before signing a joint return. If you do, make sure the figures are accurate by viewing supporting material (such as W-2s, 1099s, etc.). If there is any doubt as to the return's accuracy, do your own and check "married, filing separately" or "head of household," whichever applies. When figuring your deductions, plan wisely. Realize that a tax credit is always preferable to a tax deduction because of the effect on your adjusted gross income.

For those women who do file joint returns during their separation, make sure that the refund check gets sent to your accountant or tax preparation office, or better yet, comes to the marital residence in which you are living.

Finally, if all this talk of lawyer fees and potential tax liability gets you down, just try to mentally reframe the issue. I often thought my personal ad might some day read "Gives good tax return." With several cute exemptions, yourself, and maybe some mortgage interest, you're sure to attract the desire of every bean counter in your community!

Exploring Other Legal Options

You've seen the ads for do-it-yourself divorces, legal clinics, perhaps mediation or arbitration. Are these divorce settlement methods beneficial to your cause? It depends.

First, know that you get what you pay for. People are often lured by the ads they see in the paper that claim the attorney can achieve a divorce for them for less than $200. I met a woman who told me her divorce in the late 1990s cost her only $250. I was happy for her, of course, but talk about having a jealous moment! To keep the fees low, these attorneys go off and file for your divorce in another county, where filing fees are significantly less. Sounds good—until you realize that in order to litigate any issue, you may have to drive five hours each way. To transfer the case to your jurisdiction, it costs even more money.

If you are young, have been married for a relatively short period of time and have few if any assets and no children, you might want to proceed with a do-it-yourself divorce. Your local court can probably give you the necessary paperwork to file, and if you feel you can easily untangle the marital ties that bind you, you would save money. However, this is not the best route for anyone with children, substantial assets, or arguments over alimony (or, really, arguments over anything).

Legal clinics can offer you trained paralegals who have a better knowledge of family law than you might. Again, if you're young, have been married briefly, have few assets and no children, this could prove beneficial.

Some jurisdictions use alternative dispute resolution where a contested case is sent to a seasoned law practitioner who acts as a mediator, often when a trial looms in the future.

"Approximately 80% of cases I see are settled this way," says Steven J. Bienstock, an attorney and mediator practicing in Rockville, Maryland. "This obviously reduces the burden on the courts and averts the bloodbath that occurs through trial." If you go to trial, Bienstock warns, no one walks away happy. "Even if you win, you come out losing because you hear things that will infuriate you. You're not mending, you're tearing," he says.

Mediation only succeeds when the two of you bring accurate information to the table. If you feel bullied, coerced, or lied to, mediation might be senseless, especially in abusive relationships where there is clear power over one party in a psychological sense. "More than half of what I do deals with the psychology of the situation rather than pure legality," Bienstock says. "Some clients are so angry they can't hear me. People are so mired in a problem that they need to step back, looking at the big picture." When child custody is the disputed issue, some jurisdictions employ a parenting coordinator or appoint a guardian ad litem, which I'll discuss later in this chapter.

Arbitration is another route for avoiding a costly and prolonged legal battle. Here, the arbitrator presides over a mini-trial of sorts, where the individuals and their attorneys present information. This legal option is sometimes used when the court system is severely backlogged with cases. With arbitration, you can decide in advance whether the arbitrator's decision will be binding or advisory only. And like mediation, you can use arbitration for only some or all aspects of your divorce. If you can stipulate or agree to certain issues, it saves time, money, and frustration. Sometimes, the court will approve going to a special master to resolve a particular issue, such as equitable distribution or perhaps a custody dispute. Your attorney should help you decide if going to a master is your best choice because often these decisions are binding.

Do know that in mediation, arbitration, and special master options there is no attorney-client privilege. Thus anything you divulge could come out in court. Still, I can't emphasize enough how wise it is to attempt settlement.

"I remind clients that the judge, while knowledgeable in the law and possessing a fair amount of wisdom and common sense, doesn't know them, doesn't know their children, and likely has different life experiences than the parties involved," says Steven D. Reinheimer, an attorney in Oakland County, Michigan. "I also remind them that the judge is going to make a decision based upon a limited amount of information that he or she can glean from the testimony provided."

Whether you choose one of these legal avenues, truly consider the level of communication and honesty between you and your estranged husband. If either party operates in a passive-aggressive mode, your chances for success are slim. Those couples with realistic requests, no power or control struggles, and the ability to compromise will be much better off. Also know that people who go to court rarely get everything they want. How you proceed is an important decision, to be considered carefully with legal counsel.

Top Ten Legal Mistakes

While many clients have complaints about their lawyers, it's only fair to point out that plenty of attorneys have their lists of factors that cast clients into one of two categories: from heaven or hell. According to attorney Karen Myers of North Versailles, Pennsylvania, calling over and over to check the status of a matter is silly because it's your attorney's responsibility to send any information or documents to you. Not dealing with your anger is another pivotal problem because it blinds you to problem solving, and as Steve Bienstock added, there are no winners on a warpath.

Know the true facts regarding common law marriages in your state. In Pennsylvania, for instance, common law marriage is not automatic just because a couple lives together for seven years. You must prove that you had an informal ceremony or used the same last name. How you filed your taxes matters as well. This book's appendix provides numerous legal resources, and often the publishers' Web sites have resources regarding your state's laws.

Review the blunders we women make as legal clients. You'll be glad you did, and so will your attorney. Here are the top ten legal mistakes I've compiled:

1. Believing your spouse will be fair and cooperative. Expect the worst, but allow yourself to be surprised.
2. Having totally unrealistic expectations or demands regarding your case.
3. Not asking appropriate questions, or signing documents without understanding them.

4. Withholding information from your attorney and dumping the entire case in her lap. You should not be a passive participant here.
5. Not double-checking facts and figures that were given to you by the other side or even by your attorney. This includes any invoices from your law firm.
6. Allowing emotions rather than logical thinking to rule your legal decisions. Knee-jerk responses are usually inappropriate. Give yourself time to calm down and think first.
7. Expecting the legal system to be fair and for court personnel to see things from your perspective. They only see a fraction of the arguments at hand, and often what's presented is colored by opinion, thereby, not the "whole truth."
8. Allowing too much time to pass before enforcing a court order or agreed-upon support.
9. Forgetting the tax ramifications of legal decisions. That's why having a separate financial advisor or, at the very least, seeing issues from another perspective helps immensely.
10. Being a hindrance—not a help—to your case. For instance, it's not wise to annoy your attorney by not paying her or pestering her ad infinitum, unless there is true financial hardship or if you suspect billing errors that need to be addressed once the litigation concludes.

Residency Matters

The state in which you or your husband files for divorce is important because each state's laws vary. Some states have no-fault divorce, whereas in others you might file for a more old-fashioned fault divorce based upon grounds (such as adultery, abuse, mental cruelty, addiction, or insanity).

These days no-fault divorce seems to be more popular because parties readily acknowledge incompatibility or an irretrievable breakdown of the marriage. It lessens the need to spy upon or catch a spouse at a particular misdeed. However, there are those who claim that no-fault divorce hurts women who have stood by their marriage and relinquished their careers for their family's nurturance. In some states, fault can only play a factor in certain divorce outcomes (such as awarding alimony). There are those who feel fault should be considered in property division (sometimes called equitable distribution).

The State of Louisiana made news in 1997 as its legislature passed a law enabling couples to opt for a traditional marriage contract or a new covenant contract, aimed at lessening the divorce rate. Couples choosing the covenant contract have to stay married unless they can prove misconduct such as adultery, abuse, abandonment, or conviction. Before they can divorce, the couple has to be separated for two years unless there is such proof.

Many states do invoke a waiting period of several months to several years as a cooling down period, giving a husband and wife the chance to think seriously about the decision.

A legal annulment of your marriage is always an option if you meet your state's criteria. This court action voids your marriage as if it did not take place. (This is separate from a religious annulment.) Annulments aren't as common today since the social stigma of divorce barely exists. Check your state's laws, but an annulment may apply if your spouse lied to you or misled you in some way (perhaps you want a family but your husband cannot have children, or even worse, he's already married), your spouse isn't of legal age, you were forced to marry, or you were under the influence of drugs or alcohol when tying the knot. While an annulment might legally void your marriage, it will not change your responsibilities to any children resulting from your relationship. In other states, legal separation is granted. More on that in a moment.

A default divorce can sometimes be granted if you cannot find your estranged husband. In most states, you file for divorce, publish legal notice, and if your spouse fails to respond, you can be granted a divorce by default after a particular length of time.

Though you've undoubtedly heard of the quick celebrity divorces, most states maintain a residency requirement. Look with suspicion to any husband who wants to move abruptly when the marriage is plummeting. He could be trying to move to a state that would grant a divorce more to his liking. The same caveat applies for custody and visitation issues though most courts are on the lookout for "court shoppers" and adhere to the Uniform Child Custody Jurisdiction Act (UCCJA) and the Uniform Child Custody Jurisdiction and Enforcement Act (UCCJEA) following it.

In addition, the county matters a great deal. Two adjacent counties may have different laws. Technically, you can file for a divorce in the county either party resides in, or the county of the marital residence. But if one allows you to bifurcate the divorce more easily (grant the divorce first, the property division later), this is a substantial consideration. Bifurcating means you will cease medical insurance coverage and other benefits from your husband, so weigh this in your decision-making.

Legal Versus Informal Separations

Some states have legal separation. If this is the case, you may want to file a petition for separation with your family court. After you've worked out the terms, the agreement is also filed with the court. It's wise to consult an attorney to ascertain your state's laws. There have been instances where the wife walks out in a fit of rage only to discover later that she's jeopardized her claim to the marital residence, many of the possessions, perhaps even primary custody of the children.

A formal separation agreement addresses any issues you'd like spelled out including who will stay in the house, how you will share your joint assets, who will have custody and care for the children (or visitation times), alimony and child support, and other expenses, such as health care. It's wise to include mention of debt and credit, for if one spouse mismanages the money or racks up joint debt, your credit history will be damaged (Chapter Six goes into greater detail about finances). Someone will have to pay off any joint debt that you already owe. Stipulate that your spouse will not include your name on any new credit cards, debts, or bank accounts—that he must not sign your name to *anything* without your written consent.

If your state allows for a legal separation and you and your husband are no longer communicating effectively consider entering into a formal agreement. Without such a document, you can't ask the court to enforce it should the relationship turn sour. And if you reconcile, great. Providing your agreement doesn't need to be withdrawn from court, simply file it away or tear it up.

Custody Concerns

Stanton E. Samenow, Ph.D., is a clinical psychologist, researcher, and at times, expert witness in extremely adversarial child custody disputes. He shares his insights in his book *In the Best Interest of the Child*. If a problem-solving parent is married to another problem solver, she is able to settle the dispute with her spouse or with the help of an attorney. If the problem solver is married to a controller whose agenda is unyielding, problems begin. In the next chapter, I will discuss legal abuse and harassment because these are closely intertwined issues. For now, I point you to Samenow's book so that you know what's in store if your case heads to court.

"A custody evaluation by a clinical psychologist can run thousands of dollars," writes Samenow. Add to that all the other court-related costs outlined in this chapter, plus lost earnings if you must take time off from work for the interviews and observations, plus psychological testing and home visits. I once traveled for a re-evaluation that my ex-husband had attained in court then called off, only *after* I'd driven more than 225 miles. Not only was I disgusted, but the evaluator seemed annoyed, and my children were upset by the inconvenience. The court ordered reimbursement for the session cost, but not for other expenses, lost wages, or lost summer time since my kids had just returned to Maryland, leaving us with little more than a week before school started to sandwich in recreation with friends, back-to-school shopping, and vacation.

Factor in that the evaluation process itself is draining, especially if you question the credentials of the evaluator. Each jurisdiction sets its own standards. One woman actually heard the evaluator say that he'd gotten out of corporate work and coaching to do these evaluations because it was "recession proof." One evaluator told the parent to stop answering questions midway through the psychological exam thus ruining the reliability and validity of the exam.

This cavalier attitude appalls but doesn't surprise Marc J. Ackerman, Ph.D., author of *Clinician's Guide to Child Custody Evaluations*. "A lot of people go into this work for the money because managed care has taken over insurance payments for mental health practitioners," Dr. Ackerman says. Many clinicians are making 25 to 75 cents on the dollar as a result, unless they're fortunate enough to have private payment. He points to California, one state whereby evaluators must have forty hours of training in areas such as domestic violence, developmental psychology, sexual abuse, and law.

While advocates are working hard to mandate recognition of domestic violence, psychological or substance abuse, and parental alienation, there are many evaluators who simply do not grasp certain issues, have no background in family therapy, and their written reports may be colored by misperceptions or other errors.

For example, I had to address a problem when I realized that I'd been misquoted from both my written questionnaire and interview comments. The evaluator wrote that I had stated that I had a particular diagnosis that was never—ever—mine, even after I'd presented a very clear written outline, as requested, to him and the court-ordered program, and could prove the error was not mine. Also, I'd been asked to photocopy and send material that was never mentioned in the final report, and I'd never been given the chance to respond to certain accusations either. Despite the recommendation that I should maintain custody, I felt very used by the sloppy reporting procedures and the process, especially since I had politely asked in writing for a corrected addendum. The county court system didn't have a procedure in place to correct such data, making it nearly impossible, and because of court rules once the custody case was dropped against me, my attorney could not call this evaluator as a witness. Therefore, I was stuck with whatever (inaccurate) picture this painted of me.

"You have to determine how important the incorrect material is," said Ackerman when I shared my poor experiences with him. "If it's a misquote of a child having chicken pox at age eight instead of six, that's fairly insignificant. If it's a wrong diagnosis or attributed to the wrong party, that's an egregious error and you'd start questioning the evaluator's competence." Indeed you might face adverse consequences with inaccurate information unless you document your attempts to correct it. Even then, a state complaint may take two years or more, stepping through different procedures.

Another potential problem with custody evaluators is the sheer cost. Ackerman told me of a 400-page report detailing a case that lasted two years and cost $75,000 for the evaluation alone. "That's an annuity, not a case," Ackerman declared.

Everyone agrees that the evaluation process is packed with pressure. "If your partner is a bad actor, you don't have to prove it. He'll prove it," says Ackerman. "And if you try to prove it, and they're not, it's going to be on you—not on your estranged spouse (or ex-spouse)." Experts admit that few bad actors can keep it together long enough so that others (especially evaluators and court personnel) won't get the true picture. One might wonder, though, if the evaluator and court personnel lack insight or proper training to be on the alert for these types of people.

Court-appointed psychologists or evaluators are entirely separate from guardians ad litem, a legal term for an attorney who represents the child's best interests, including the child's health, education, welfare, medical needs, and more. This attorney is often court-appointed and paid for by both parents, based upon their incomes. "In the child's best interest" is a pivotal phrase for it does not always reflect the child's wishes. For instance, a five-year-old child may wish to remain with the parent who affords her more candy or the teenager might be tempted to go with the parent providing a set of wheels, but neither scenario may be in the child's best interest. A guardian ad litem should understand this.

Preparing Your Case

If you want a crash course in litigation, *The Everything® Divorce Book* by Mary L. Davidson guides you through legal terminology and the litigation process. Again, this assumes that you don't settle out of court.

Davidson discusses pretrial motions, the process of discovery, interrogatories, pretrial conferences, and hearings with a judge. Becoming familiar with the legal procedures on your own will help you save time and money.

Depending upon the complexity of your case, if you go to trial, be forewarned of the expense. You'll have to pay not only for your attorney's counsel but also for filing fees, court reporters, expert witnesses, subpoenas, exhibits, transcripts, guardians ad litem or parenting coordinators, and miscellaneous fees.

Remember that it is important to have the documents and paper trails on hand that you need to prove your claim on various assets, or even prove that these assets exist. Nothing will help you obtain a favorable settlement like good sleuth work, organization, and being prepared.

Having Your Day in Court

Try to settle your case outside of court, even reaching such agreement on the proverbial courthouse steps. It happens all the time.

However, there may be issues where you must appear before a hearing officer or judge. Here are some guidelines.

For starters, be prepared and appear on time. Dress neatly and conservatively. You don't want to wear flashy clothing or expensive jewelry, nor do you want to appear poverty-stricken. Show respect by not chewing gum, smoking, swearing, acting overly angry or even flippant. If you must display an emotion, crying is better than most choices. Even the slightest thing can annoy some judges, according to attorneys who routinely appear for motions, hearings, and trials. Unfortunately, if you're not used to the environment— and most of us aren't—family court is a terribly confusing place to find yourself. At the beginning of a proceeding, don't be afraid to ask questions, but if you do ask, be aware that you might offend someone (such as the hearing officer who urged you to speak up in the first place). Pretend that you're guilty until proven innocent, was one tip a court-weary soul shared with me. Make sure that you understand any questions posed to you. If they are unclear, ask politely if the question could be repeated. In addition, learn to rein in your responses. In court, less is more. Answer only what you must as concisely as possible. This is difficult especially when you know the truth and yearn to get it out in the open. Sometimes, attorneys will summarize your testimony to save time as the court docket is always an overloaded one. This can be helpful but frustrating since you know the details best. Unless your attorney is well versed in certain minutiae, you might be cast in an unfavorable light by the other side.

Be courteous. "Yes, Your Honor" or "thank you, Attorney Smith" goes a long way in creating favorable impressions. If you want to communicate with your lawyer prior to a recess, scrawl a note on a piece of paper. Let your attorney present the case, and slip notes of important points his or her way if you're seated next to one another. Otherwise, hold your thoughts.

Sure, you'll be uneasy and perhaps upset during court appearances, particularly if you are charged with doing or saying things that never occurred. Take a friend to wait outside for moral support and be with you on the way into and from court that day. Or keep a small photo of your children in your pocket during cross-examination.

Of course, if your case is decided in court, you may not be pleased with the outcome. You can appeal a judge's decision, but appeals on divorces aren't always easy to win. The biggest issue you may want to consider is the cost to your pocketbook and your sanity. Keeping up the fight is draining to all parties involved, and it does filter down to the children. In some cases, the amount of money you'll spend to fight the decision will impede other goals (such as hanging on to your house or completing your education).

Furthermore, an appeal may not be heard for many months, and then you face yet another trial. Living in this kind of legal limbo prevents you from obtaining the emotional divorce that you need to get on with your life. The appeal process may force you to switch attorneys if your present lawyer doesn't feel confident that he or she can win the case. You also have no guarantee that a new judge will rule any more to your liking than the first. A faster and less expensive way to appeal particular aspects of your case could be through modification, legalese for a change (such as with custody or support issues petitioned separately). This can become a lengthy process, too, depending upon the court system involved.

Representing Yourself on Minor Issues

When does it make sense to ask your attorney to withdraw and represent yourself on minor issues? Well, there is no easy answer. During a separation most couples encounter a variety of issues that warrant an attorney's intervention, advice, and services. So I am not going to tell you to ask your attorney to formally withdraw from your case prematurely.

But if you're like me, there comes a point when you are weary of lawyers and their fees. Indeed, some estranged or ex-husbands see the legal system as a toy or weapon they can use to vent their anger. They might know, for instance, that every time their lawyer writes a nasty-gram to your attorney, you might choose to ignore the contents, but indeed you'll be billed for the time taken to read and forward the letter to you. If one party is in a more secure financial position and vindictive enough, this becomes another form of abuse, which I'll address in the next chapter.

During your separation, I'd hang on to your attorney but choose your battles wisely. Every letter you receive doesn't require a response. Indeed if you dash off a reply, you're fueling the flames of anger, which might be exactly what your estranged husband had in mind. Why give him the satisfaction? (It might just tick him off more if you ignore the issue, and you'll certainly be less in debt to your legal firm.) However, there will come a day when your case reaches a settlement, and at that juncture or shortly thereafter, you may want your attorney to withdraw.

Sure, there might still be squabbles. But an ordinary mortal can present a motion in court. If you aren't an assertive and communicative type, this might not be the best strategy for you. Knowing my own nature, I gave it a try when I needed to enforce an issue to reach closure in my divorce settlement. I figured that if I could write 110,000-word books, I could darn well draft a simple motion by following the format of so many I had in my files.

When you represent yourself in court it is considered pro se representation. People do this in small claims court all the time. In the case of family law, it might make sense to go to court pro se over an issue of minor expenses due you or for a form that needs to be signed. For instance, if your ex-husband owes you approximately

$300 in unreimbursed medical expenses, you could conceivably spend more in attorney's fees than the ultimate amount of the reimbursement. Some pro se motions courts offer free legal assistance depending upon income, while others have a desk staffed by legal aides to assist you on the right path with proper paperwork.

Considering that you might choose a pro se court action at some juncture, do hang on to prior motions, drafted court orders, briefs, and other legal documents when you begin weeding out your files. Keep these merely to follow the format in the event that you might have to write a motion or brief yourself. If there is one judge assigned to your case, you'll want to bring the matter before his or her attention. To find out the court schedule of when particular judges will hear motions that month, look at a copy of your county legal journal in the library. You might know a kind-hearted attorney friend who could give you the information and dates you need. Another option is to call the judge's secretary, stating that you have a pro se motion to present and would like to know when Judge Smith is hearing motions. Some court personnel are kinder than others, but if you're courteous, hopefully you'll get the information you seek.

If you have a few items to discuss, the judge may slate your case for a judicial conference where the parties (and attorneys if there are any) meet with the judge a little more informally, reviewing unresolved issues and receiving the judge's take on the matters involved. This one meeting might be enough to get one or both of you to settle the dispute.

Gather your paperwork in an organized manner. If you write a motion, photocopy particular evidence and label these as exhibits. It's always best to be more prepared than less. You will have to conduct yourself with the utmost professionalism, remaining as dispassionate about matters as possible. However, many lawyers have shared that judges typically grant you a little more latitude when representing yourself because they know you're trying hard and you're not used to the environment.

Upon representing myself a second time to defend a brief and try to obtain some modifications to a court order, the entire experience taught me one more key reason, beyond fiscal conservancy, why you should think about representing yourself at times. If you're not there, especially if the judge has not seen nor heard from you in months or years, it's much easier for the other side to lob barbs, innuendo, or just plain misstatements and lies against you. In other words, they'll sling mud, and without you there to flick it off, it may stick. It's much harder for the judge to have a negative impression of you or the facts when you are there live and in person, with sound arguments, facts, and nonverbal demeanor that conveys who you really are and what you're trying to accomplish.

What If You Must Move?

There may come a day when you determine that you want or need to move closer to your family of origin in order to carve out a better support system, or you may need to relocate for your work. In my case, I had met my husband-to-be in Pittsburgh, but upon a corporate merger, he lost his position and later found one located a few hours away.

I never treated the decision to relocate myself, and my children, lightly. I had lived in one area for forty years. This was home. This hurt a little. On the other hand, my life was changed forever when my marriage collapsed and divorce papers arrived. I had done my best as a single mother for six challenging years. Change was likely around my corner, one way or another with a rising house assessment. Not to mention, I had found a man with whom I wanted to spend the rest of my life—a man who accepted my children with open arms, and continually told me how proud he was of the choices that I made for them.

"Relocation is a realistic possibility, especially with people who have transient jobs or people who have lost their jobs," says Sophia

P. Paul, a family law attorney in Pittsburgh. "In some families relocation has been a routine part of their family life. You run into problems, therefore, when someone deciding your case may have been born and raised in the same locale, not understanding the need or desire to live or work somewhere else."

Making a Move Happen

When my second husband found his new position, we made the best of the distance for eighteen months, but we wanted to marry and be a family. Practical by nature, I knew the new arrangement *could* work. In fact, I pictured what cooperation could look like. Knowing how much my boys already enjoyed the new area, wouldn't it be nice if they could maintain ties with their birth town, in addition to this new adventure? Since life, as we all know it, is a series of adjustments, wouldn't it be great if all the adults in their lives could support this change, especially since they were embracing the prospect themselves with unbridled enthusiasm?

Unfortunately, my daydreams turned more into nightmares. Once engaged, I met with an attorney, and I meticulously pondered a new custody plan for my relocation. I wanted to be fair and foresee all sorts of needs and possibilities, but my plan didn't work. My ex-husband had rejected this proposal without discussion or comment, and we found ourselves on a protracted journey through the family court system because my ex-husband had filed a custody suit. I earned the right to relocate after a lengthy court hearing at which I gave detailed descriptions of my children's needs, their medical care, educational background, social and religious development, and more importantly how I as their mother was instrumental in these areas. In addition, my husband (then fiancé) took the stand to explain his career, his job loss, and new position.

In addition to recognizing such knowledge and care, many times courts decide a relocation based upon whether your standard of living will increase by the move (and subsequently that of the children), your motives, and if you've got a workable proposal to continue visitation with the other parent, and whether you presented sufficient notice to the other parent. Children might also be asked to share their preferences.

In researching this a little more, I've heard from several estranged spouses (or divorced couples). In one Internet dating case, east coast mom met west coast man, only she was married to her children's father at the time. Convinced it was the love of her life, after two months online, she left for San Diego, with her two children, and her wounded husband's agreement that she could take their children. Very shortly after they settled, new man walked out, and mom shacked up with someone else. Dad couldn't fathom the money and the negativity that a court battle would bring to his children and his own life, so he kept in touch, planned visits, and flew them home for five weeks out of the summer. I was amazed because if ever there was a case against relocation of the children, with the distance and the casual lifestyle decisions, this seemed it. But I share it to show the range of people's choices and responses. Each case must be weighed on its own merits and the criteria outlined—criteria that are used by most courts in the land. Court personnel are increasingly searching the intent of the parties involved in either petitioning for or blocking relocation. Women I've spoken with report an increase in acting out behaviors as well as litigation upon their steady dating, engagement, remarriage, or relocation attempts. Looking beneath the surface, some litigious ex-spouses who are trying to block a move are actually more threatened by the presence of other adults in their child's lives than they are threatened by the distance that a move creates.

Disappointing Decisions

If you're looking for emotional justice, you will not find it in family court. Long ago, I adopted Fred Rogers' advice to "look for the helpers" when explaining difficult matters to children. When we traveled down the court path, I framed the process this way for my boys. As they grew older and saw how things worked they, too, felt incredibly discouraged. For instance, after getting used to speaking with our judge, they really wanted to share their opinions with him again at a subsequent hearing. "We liked it better just the three of us," was the collective sentiment. They wanted a voice since they would have to live with the outcome of the decisions. Like me, they also felt stuck.

When reviewing a court transcript of their testimony, I was appalled at how hearing officers can actually add remarks to the end of a child's testimony, leading a child in a particular direction or stunting whatever that child might really have wanted to say.

It's not easy when you put so much effort into advocating for what you believe is best for your children, only to have others see things another way or not grasp the true problem. It leaves you feeling stalled and taken advantage of.

Even trying to schedule a medical appointment became contentious for me. As many parents know, appointments with specialists must be booked at times six months in advance. Physicians may have scheduling considerations such as surgical days and time booked at satellite locations. My son's doctor was brought on board to establish a pediatric clinic; I had no ability to control the schedule of a major medical center. I also found it frustrating when my attorney conveyed that court personnel assumed that a condition was progressive when it was not. Rather than find out or ask, decisions are sometimes based upon assumptions. My son's doctor and I joked at how she must add copious detail because our reports end up in special places, like court. But, this is not a laughing matter at all. It's embarrassing when you must ask very busy people to spend even more time on your case, with reports, sometimes even testimony, when they could be treating other children.

Alas, it's also possible to reframe some disappointments into possibilities. The proposed plan that we followed throughout our first year of relocation never directly allocated time over the next summer, assuming our case might be settled. Though we'd discussed four weeks, it wasn't written down. Even though he saw the children frequently, my ex-husband petitioned for the bulk of the summer, and per court order my sons spent most of their summers away. While it was hard hearing their complaints, I could do nothing but accept this, and they had to do likewise.

As adults, we made do. My new husband and I enjoyed time to ourselves. We took a long overdue Caribbean honeymoon. I attended a conference for an editor, and there, was bitten by the graduate school bug. I soon realized that I could reframe these months as a chance to further a dream, one that finding childcare arrangements had previously deterred. Now I had time not only to myself, but the laundry and grocery bills were significantly less without the boys in the house. I missed my children, but like The Serenity Prayer reminds, control what you can, let go of the rest.

Commit every possible scenario to paper, and of course, be reasonable. If regular visitation throughout the school year is provided, then parents should each share in the children's summer break. Even if one parent lives a substantial distance away, children still need some summer enjoyment where they reside, and all families deserve the chance to go away for a week's vacation.

Help for High-Conflict Cases

Earlier, I wrote about how parenting coordinators are becoming prevalent in high-conflict child custody cases. Joan B. Kelly, Ph.D., cowrote "Children's Adjustment Following Divorce" with Robert Emery for an issue of *Family Relations*, stating: "Although high-conflict post-divorce is generally assumed to be a shared interaction between two angry, culpable parents, our clinical, mediation, and arbitration experience in high-conflict post-divorce cases indicates that it is not uncommon to find one enraged or defiant parent and a second parent who no longer harbors anger, has emotionally disengaged, and attempts to avoid or mute conflict that involves the child."

Parenting coordinators, having a background in mental health and specific training in separation and divorce, are court appointed to contain a conflict post-divorce, after there has been agreement reached by consent or court order. This approach is used in some states, such as in Florida, Kentucky, Maryland, New Jersey, Oklahoma, and California, where it has a long history of use.

"High-conflict cases occur with conflicting perceptions of many things, decisions stuck at opposite poles, alienation, or the suspicion of it, distrust, or the continuous use of the legal system to resolve problems," says Karen P. Freed, a licensed social worker and codirector of the Bethesda Group. According to her experience, it's generally a characterological problem that rests at the root of continuing conflict. "This causes a person to perceive things in a distorted way, and they base their behavior on those distortions." Characterological is often a more polite term for what clinicians recognize as a personality disorder made up of pervasive, maladaptive behavior.

Philip M. Stahl, Ph.D., author of *Complex Issues in Child Custody Evaluations*, writes, "For many high-conflict families, it seems that the parents' characterological personality dynamics get manifested in a relationship disorder with the other parent. They may be able to manage some of their chronic traits, including their narcissism, over-reaction, rigidity, and anger, in some of their other relationships." Thus, it's possible that long-standing patterns don't become evident with extended family, coworkers, even a person's children. These maladaptive patterns can surface more prominently in interactions with former spouses.

What court personnel and attorneys typically see is a lot of "he said, she said," data that goes nowhere fast. What's needed is a problem-solving approach, and parent coordinators provide this, even if they have to monitor e-mail between parties to teach a skill set that might not otherwise exist. This might mean teaching parents to word questions differently, and working with parents to adjust unrealistic expectations they might seek.

In the most extreme cases, where a parent takes a rigid position and refuses to work with the other parent, the court may appoint a parent coordinator as the sole decision-maker or one with ultimate authority. States, like California, sometimes appoint mediators and special masters under the family code with authority to make recommendations about all areas of conflict, including pickup times and dates, vacations and holidays, transportation, education and after-school activities, as well as health care management.

High-conflict cases can be prevented, and it's always advantageous for both parents to work together to be part of the solutions for their children rather than be part of the problems. Unfortunately, it takes two willing people to do this with congruence in what they profess and how they act.

"We're asking people to do something outside the marriage that they weren't able to do inside the marriage," says Dr. Ackerman. "Had they been able to [problem solve] inside the marriage, they may not have needed a divorce in the first place." According to Ackerman, there have been times that he's suggested the need to minimize contact between parent and child, due to a parent's personality disorder, poor judgment on the part of that parent, and his or her poor problem-solving skills.

Using parent coordinators or special masters might be necessary. Once again, it adds to the costs of a divorce (both emotional and financial), and it usually is not nearly as effective as when reasonable co-parenting occurs. Be sure to look to the appendix for important resources, including books and Web sites that might be helpful to you.

Have You Been Misrepresented?

It's not a pleasant topic for you, and certainly not for any legal counsel, but there are cases when a litigant does not feel she's been properly represented. Perhaps your attorney left out important matter from an important document or settlement. Perhaps you weren't protected during difficult testimony. Perhaps your attorney has turned out to have some difficult character or business traits that interfere with cooperative progress on your case.

You can always relieve your attorney of his or her duties, but if you do so in the final stages of an approaching trial or other matter, you may not be granted additional time for a new attorney to play catchup. It might also make you look like a difficult person, even if that's a totally false description. Annapolis attorney Roy L. Mason takes on legal malpractice cases. He suggests that women first compare notes of an attorney's performance with other women who have been involved in domestic disputes. Also, be certain from the outset that your attorney has experience in domestic relations by checking with your local bar association. If you're concerned with the progress of your case, get a second opinion.

"If your lawyer is not communicating with you, not sending correspondence, never returning phone calls, or gives you very little notice of hearings, these are signs of disorganization," says Mason. Observe your lawyer. Is he or she on time or early for proceedings? Is he or she prepared with the necessary documents that the judge requires? Have you been prepared? Was your attorney accurate in what he or she told you? Does your lawyer push forth your case or backburner it? Observe also what the judge says to your counsel and how the judge responds to any presentations.

"All domestic attorneys have a style of how they handle emergency situations," says Mason. In addition, you should be introduced to others in the office who might help your case in your attorney's absence. While human error happens in billing, it's your role to carefully review your invoices and question if any time was overbilled. This can include billing you at an attorney rate instead of secretarial and paralegal rates. "If the lawyer makes a mistake that causes prolonged litigation, then you shouldn't be charged for it," says Mason. "If counsel has done something that caused you to get less money, then you're talking malpractice."

Washingtonian magazine featured an article titled "Running from the Law," in which the author spoke of the pressure attorneys face to work and bill unbelievable hours. It's called "timesheet padding," a dirty little secret that indeed goes on in some law firms, with associates having been known to ask if they could bill for shower time, if they were thinking about their cases while lathering up. The answer was an astounding, "yes." For someone trying to hold onto assets, and not add to any further rancor, this behavior would disillusion, if not sicken, most readers.

Your first remedy is to talk with your attorney, presenting facts of what testimony or evidence was left out, and then ask for the attorney to credit this, or correct the matter at no charge. Ask "What can we do about this?" as firmly, but politely as you can. If the amount of money is large enough (typically amounting to $100,000 at minimum, even when added up over time), then you can conceivably get another lawyer interested, but as Mason points out then you must prove a case within a case, that not only did original counsel make a mistake, but that you would have won on that issue and how much. Your former husband, who may likely be a good witness for you, is unlikely to cooperate. Thus, you're in a jam.

"Suing your lawyer on a custody loss doesn't really apply because the court always has revisory power regarding children as long as they are minors," says Mason. "By taking custody back to court, what you could recover is money you had to pay your new lawyer to correct the first attorney's mistake." If your attorney is ignoring your polite requests, a little extra pressure might work as a last resort. Suggest that you'll alert the local bar association of any practices that you felt damaged your case. Most attorneys will not want potential clients to know of problems and would rather settle them quietly.

Jurisdiction

Changing the jurisdiction of your case can be easy or difficult. "Certainly if both parents are in different locations, a motion to the court where the child primarily resides should be successful," says Rockville Attorney Steve Bienstock. It may be more difficult if one parent still resides where the order was issued and protests. If both parents move away from the area where your original litigation took place, cases are typically transferred to where the children reside. Especially if experts to their education or care would need to provide testimony, you may be able to change jurisdiction also providing the children have lived in the new locale full-time for a minimum of six months. Be sure to petition promptly because a court may modify a custody or visitation order from another state only if it has the authority to do so and if the court in the issuing state has declined to do so. Also, be sure to move your entire case, as custody and support are essentially separate matters.

Child custody cases conceivably involve a range of jurisdictional statutes, including the UCCJA, UCCJEA, the Parental Kidnapping Prevention Act (PKPA), the Violence Against Women Act of 2000 (VAWA 2000), and the Indian Child Welfare Act (ICWA), among others.

When there is domestic violence, most states exercise emergency jurisdiction if it's a state that has enacted UCCJEA, giving more protection to victims than UCCJA, which it replaced. This can allow you to flee with your children without a custody order, but you ought to know beforehand the legal standard in your initial and refuge state.

I got my own case moved because of UCCJA. For several months, my children indicated that their dad was moving out of state, but I couldn't get any official confirmation of this, and when my former counsel made inquiries, I was told what he was told: No move anytime soon. About two months later, now representing myself, my ex's attorney served me a motion stating his client was moving and wanted our case to go through the court system again, never even proposing a consent order, just court intervention. If the judge granted this motion, I would have been put down a miserable path for my own relocation, as well as his. I thought not. Using UCCJA, I urged the judge to dismiss this motion, and move the case to where the children resided, in Maryland. Thankfully, he did. I was especially grateful since our judge had heard this motion after opposing counsel had given me the wrong time to appear in court, then contacted me *after* I'd driven 225 miles to get there. Staff members that day were very kind, but learn from this example to always get your facts straight, as well as your dates and times.

Does Gender Play a Role in Litigation?

For many years courts have pretty much given credence to the "nurturing years" doctrine whereby mothers were usually granted custody of their children, at least during those tender infant and toddler years. Many fathers' rights groups have protested this, so depending upon this notion is no longer a safe bet.

The question arises, though, if there are other instances in which the courts favor one gender over another, or make stereotypical decisions. For instance, Lundy Bancroft, who practices in Massachusetts training various state and judicial agencies about domestic abuse, feels that women are at times discriminated against, even in custody evaluations. "When a woman shares her difficult journey and may admit to battling depression (common among domestic abuse survivors), she's held accountable, and it might even be used against her as proof she has some problem, not that she's being honest and working on a problem," he says. "A man though can share a similar complaint or even diagnosis and he's applauded for his honesty. It might be looked at differently."

When in my own case, the Pennsylvania court gave complete decision-making authority to my ex-husband over our weekend schedule for visitation, several friends of mine were outraged, for they knew it was extremely difficult for me to commit to professional obligations, book a teaching date out of town, or even plan to attend a conference, more than a few weeks in advance. Often, these events had to be prebooked months ahead since they were publicized. One was this blunt: "If you were a self-employed man, I doubt they'd allow his ex-wife to control his schedule this way." I had to agree and everything I've learned about the court system where my case was first jurisdicted has clearly cast doubts on equality and open-mindedness toward women. I say this because nearly two years after this court order was issued, I proved the point of how constricting it truly was. It got changed, but I asked for certain changes immediately, paying an attorney to follow procedure, only to be brushed off. In Pennsylvania, you're given a written order, where I'm told in other states, the judge may advise the parties verbally to at least hear some preliminary questions. Now there's a solution!

For me, it took nineteen months, two frantic and frustrated children later, and at minimum $6,000 to $8,000 per side to effect a needed change. It all could have been avoided by just really trying to understand the double bind this order put us in in the first place.

As I've shared in this book, court personnel aren't always at their best. One man on a judge's tipstaff sent me on a fishing expedition for a date he refused to give me, and even that county's helpdesk couldn't find it readily on the Web site where he sent me. Being short with me, in that instance, got me out of his way, even though court personnel are essentially public servants, funded by taxpayer dollars.

In drafting this edition, I spoke with others who shared a similar view that some courts are the "old boy's network."

Many court systems are provincial rather than forward thinking or even equitably minded, one female attorney told me after she'd left practice. She'd surely seen it and heard it from colleagues.

Surprised at the tenor of it all? I've seen occasional kindness in family court, but not as much as should be there. One could argue: Shouldn't court personnel model appropriate behavior? You get what you give sometimes. Start with rough demeanor, and see a self-perpetuating cycle.

This is why I raise inequality as a concern among our family courts, and our family court laws. I don't think it's ever wise to allow such total authority of one gender over another or of one former spouse over another, in any circumstance, but particularly if there has been a high-conflict or abusive relationship. From a clinical perspective, it feeds the circular nature of an unhealthy dance in which two people are engaged. All this truly feeds are the lawyers' bank accounts. I hope it's not this way for you. I hope I never travel such a path again, and so far, I've found the tenor of family court in my new state to be worlds apart from my experiences in Pennsylvania. There is hope!

If we women don't speak up, sharing such eye-opening experiences, the picture won't change. As I've learned in preparation for counseling work, we teach people how to treat us. It looks like we have a lot of educating left to do.

Chapter Five

Abuse and Safety Awareness

A marital separation can be a volatile time. Data from stress questionnaires indicates that marital separation ranks up there under death of a spouse as being a highly stressful event. These pressures sometimes cause people to act impulsively in a marital separation, without thought to consequences, and with retribution in mind.

For all of these reasons, this chapter is devoted to ensuring your personal safety, and the protection of your children and your property. It will also deal with preserving your sanity if there is emotional abuse, stalking, and harassment, including the misuse of the legal system against you.

I'm not trying to alarm you with instructions to secure your house like Fort Knox or to take precautions you might term extreme. However, in cases where there has been domestic violence, a woman is most vulnerable to attack (emotional or physical) when she tries to break away and establish a new life. Whether exerted with physical aggression, emotional cruelty, or legal force, that hold upon the wife feels like, and is, an attack.

Even if you feel you have not experienced abuse, still read this chapter. You'll become familiar with patterns of abusive behavior and know exactly how to protect yourself if you feel sufficiently threatened. Besides, now that you are living alone, these are safety measures that any woman can benefit from learning.

Before I begin though, let me fully admit that women can be the abusive party in many instances. Since this book is written to support women facing separation or divorce, this chapter then takes the tone of men being perpetrators. Much research now provides us with the awareness that women can batter men, emotionally, physically, or in regard to their finances, and they can certainly act as the problematic spouse in contentious, ongoing litigation. In fact, Randi Kreger, who writes many works on borderline and other personality disorders, offered the genderless descriptor of "persuasive blamer," as one who, for mental health reasons, fabricates abuse claims. If you read this chapter, and you realize that some of the descriptions fit your behavior or thought patterns, you have the same responsibility as any man who has to seek help.

What Is Domestic Violence?

So often we view domestic violence solely as physical assault. For many years in my marriage, things didn't seem right. No, I never ended up in an emergency room—not with bruises—though I do remember one ER visit and some doctor's appointments stemming from the mounting stress brought because of my marriage. I felt threatened, terrified by certain actions, and abused by words and behaviors. It wasn't until I sought individual therapy and counseling at a women's shelter that I came to terms with the fact that I, too, was a victim.

Domestic abuse knows no boundaries. It occurs without regard to race, religion, income, profession, neighborhood, or social status. As I previously stated, it knows no absolute gender either. In addition, domestic violence encompasses the following:

Physical abuse is hitting, pushing, shoving, kicking, slapping, burning, and choking. It involves objects or weapons intended to cause injury, and it includes physical force that might prevent you from leaving home or fleeing an attack.

Mental abuse includes telling you what you can and can't do, calling you names, using foul language and words that hurt, threatening you, or belittling you in verbal assaults. This type of abuse also includes withholding postures, the persistent use of passive-aggression, and manipulation.

Sexual abuse is identified as rape, forcing you to perform particular sexual activities against your will, or touching you in a manner that you deem inappropriate or unpleasant.

Property and economic abuse entails stealing or destroying personal belongings, even if those belongings were marital property. Examples include kicking doors, breaking windows, and smashing your favorite antique vase. It includes hurting pets, withholding money, or refusing to meet needs for shelter, food, and clothing.

Legal abuse serves as a weapon, especially when a rage-filled spouse has no other means to inflict harm because the victim has successfully left or is attempting to extricate herself. This entails the misuse of the legal system to keep a battle brewing throughout a marriage, divorce, or thereafter. It's often an attempt to win power over a woman, sometimes the children, too, and yet with child custody issues, legal abuse can be hidden or couched as being a loving, concerned parent. It's about power, however, not true regard or love. Legal abuse might also take the form of blocking a woman's choices as she tries to move forward with her life.

Having read these descriptions, many of us might remember a time in our own behavior when perhaps we called someone a name in an argument or threw the newspaper down at the end of a rough day. It's the persistent pattern of poor behavior that makes it abuse. In many cases, emotional abuse is the precursor for physical violence and property destruction. When a man kicks in a door or hurls a glass vase, the woman thinks she's next.

One minute your husband is calm, the next he's raging. In cases like these, a wife becomes the lightning rod for all the emotional storms in her husband's life. He might be able to change this pattern of behavior, but he might not. Domestic violence or other forms of abuse is never the victim's fault. The responsibility for behaving well (nonviolently) is an individual one. Bottom line: There is no excuse for abuse.

I compiled this list of abusive behaviors—after much research and consultation with experts. Looking over that list, there isn't a doubt in my mind that I sought the right kind of counseling for my two sons and me. After my divorce, there was a period of calm followed by another storm. But the good news is that I'm a survivor, and you can be one also. No one—I repeat, *no one*—deserves to be abused.

Control Issues and Crazymaking

The mistreatment of a woman by a man with whom she lives or has had a romantic relationship is an attempt to gain and maintain control over her. Such power is exerted through physical force, terroristic behavior, economic deprivation or legal abuse, and sexual abuse. In a subtler sense, control manifests itself through withholding, countering, blocking, diverting, and blaming. Sure we all may block or blame occasionally, but an abuser uses whatever methods he can to relentlessly perpetuate a cycle of oppression and control.

Donald G. Dutton, Ph.D., a professor of psychology at the University of British Columbia, has written books on domestic abuse and has served as an expert witness in prominent legal cases, including the O.J. Simpson trial. He writes that when we try to control something, there is usually anxiety or anger. Unfortunately, there is still not enough awareness, particularly in our family courts, that this anger manifests itself physically, but also covertly, such as through legal maneuvering, mental abuse, property destruction, and economic impact. Suffice to say men who employ such methods to intimidate and abuse are dealing with larger problems, covert aggression among them. An abuser becomes skillful at projecting negative traits onto his partner, such as finding a fault in her that indeed he perceives in himself. This can be an unconscious behavior or what clinicians call projective identification. The abuser doesn't fully disavow what is projected and remains aware of his impulses yet misattributes them. He regards his behavior as justifiable reactions to the victim involved.

Have you ever wondered if your partner is actually two people: the public persona who gets along with others and the private man who only rages in the intimate relationship?

I came to the conclusion in my own life that it didn't quite matter what I did. Something—anything—would spark resentment or anger. I couldn't win. I remember planning a vacation to an island that we'd both dreamed of visiting. I took both our hobbies into account. We'd saved for this trip, and I had checked with my husband before making reservations. Closer to departure, I got the impression that he perceived me as "controlling" for making these plans.

This type of crazymaking, as author Patricia Evans calls it, is a way of life for some. If your partner seems irritated or angers easily, denies being angry when he clearly is so, doesn't work with you to resolve important issues, rarely (maybe never) shares thoughts or plans with you, or dismisses your concerns as unimportant or senseless, then crazymaking is a word to add to your vocabulary.

"Whether control is exercised verbally or physically, the dynamics are the same," Evans writes in *The Verbally Abusive*

Relationship. It all revolves around oppression and control. A raised fist, a push, or an unspoken threat like punching the wall leaves a woman in fear of her partner for a long time to come. "Of course, when this occurs," Evans writes, "the relationship is definitely one of oppression."

Is It Mental Illness or Just Abuse?

Beverly Engel, author of *The Emotionally Abusive Relationship*, says that sometimes emotional or verbal abuse stems from a personality disorder. Personality disorders are characterized by longstanding patterns of maladaptive thinking and emotional responses, poor interpersonal functioning, lack of impulse control, and inflexibility leading to impairment or significant distress in social, work, or interpersonal relations. These disorders often go undiagnosed through most of that person's adult lifetime because difficult people generally do not seek out therapy themselves. Rather, they are thrust into therapy (usually as unwilling participants) by concerned significant others or by court order. Lacking their own awareness or motivation to change behavior that, frankly, may have met their needs, they don't heal but continue to hurt others, often creating self-perpetuating problems.

There are several types of personality traits and defense mechanisms (like passive-aggression, projection, and denial, among others), which raise a clinician's suspicions that perhaps there is a deeper, more pervasive problem. In her book, Engel devotes a chapter to these disorders, casting the brightest light on borderline personality disorder (BPD) and narcissistic personality disorder (NPD) because these are said to have emotional abuse or neglect at their core.

Both men and women can suffer from BPD and NPD, but since men typically hold in their emotions more and are not as encouraged to express feelings openly, they build up strong walls to defend against getting wounded or hurt by others. This is very much the case with a narcissistic man. He may display a sense of false bravado and self-sufficiency, but inside, he's extremely needy, often viewing a woman as an object intended to serve his every need.

William Eddy, Esq. wrote *Splitting: Protecting Yourself While Divorcing a Borderline or a Narcissist* based upon his years in law and social work. High-conflict divorces, he believes, often involve a partner with borderline personality disorder who is the high functioning type appearing normal to strangers but emotionally abusive to someone in private.

If this is a concern for you, extra care should be taken in litigating your divorce. Unfortunately, courts have the ability to place women right back in the dynamics of a poor relationship (even post-divorce) after these women drew tremendous inner strength in order to live better lives. When the court places power over one individual in order to placate an often manipulative spouse (or former spouse), it's wrong. Simply and extremely wrong . . . but it happens.

Personality disorders cannot be medicated, though mood disorders often coexist and these can be treated by various medications. Therapy is very much called for, but here again, if you are the victim of someone else's disorder, there may be little you can do but extricate yourself from the relationship if that person fails to seek treatment. If you have children with this person, it's much tougher to extricate yourself.

Many experts agree that certainly not all abusive men fit with the criteria for a mental health disorder or diagnosis. Even if they do, it does not exempt them from owning and ending their abusive patterns. Some men might even have particular traits as opposed to a full-fledged personality disorder, and some might even score well on certain psychological tests such as the MMPI-2, according to some experts I interviewed. An abused woman, however, may show scale elevations on the MMPI-2. She might answer honestly that she does believe someone is out to get her or is following her. She may admit to having trouble sleeping or may feel that there is someone who is at the root of her problems. Frankly, there just may be, but you can see how this might cause a raised eyebrow, unless there is real training to recognize and reach out to abuse victims. For now, review the signs of abuse in this chapter and really think about your husband's behavior. It might even be wise to run the list by a trusted friend who has seen you and your partner interact. Sometimes a third party can be more objective, recognizing things we remain blind to.

Dealing with Verbal Intimidation

When a woman faces the dissolution of her marriage, it's more the rule than the exception that she will endure a tirade of remarks to convince her to reconcile or to intimidate her during the litigation process. Often these remarks come from her estranged husband. Be prepared to hear such comments or feel the actions below:

1. I'm going to drag this case out forever. You'll get nothing.
2. I'm going to file for custody and take the children from you.
3. I've got a pitbull lawyer who will eat you alive.
4. Your attorney is a crook out for every last dime.
5. I was going to give you a fair settlement. But you went and got yourself an attorney (moved out, got a restraining order, etc.), so now forget it.
6. I'll tell our children how terrible you are, and they'll never love you.
7. If you don't settle this case my way, I'll drag your boyfriend (family, friends) into this case and make all of you miserable.
8. If you try to move forward (remarry, relocate, go to school), I'll stand in your way.

When faced with such a nasty litany, remember that when people aim to control with harsh words, they are indeed the ones with the fear and anger. Your best defense is to ignore the remarks. Sure, they hurt. Sure, you should look out for your legal interests and protect yourself in every way. But words are words. Just because they are uttered does not mean these words will impact your life.

As a woman and a wife, you have every right to demand respect from your partner, even when you are separated. If there is any possibility of reconciling, you should not have to endure the silent treatment, stored grudges, or unfinished arguments handled in anything less than civil discussion. You should expect heartfelt apologies when called for (but do read about contrition below). Even if divorce is imminent, never tolerate abuse—whether it involves physical, emotional, or verbal battering.

"A good man will generally treat a woman the way she demands to be treated," says Mary E. O'Brien, M.D. "If a man will hit you once, he'll eventually hit you again, no matter how passionately he pleads forgiveness." I think the same can be said of verbal intimidation. If he feels that he can accomplish something with senseless remarks or nasty letters from his attorney, he has no incentive to stop. Some programs such as Steven Stosny's Compassion Power attempts to rescue marriages from the grasp of domestic violence. Stosny has written that one such approach for offenders rests in restoring responsible fatherhood, for the more a dad values his children, the less likely he is to strike out at their mom. That may be and Stosny's work is to be applauded, but there are quite a few manipulative abusers—men who will talk one way and behave another.

"For a lot of abusive men, children are personal possessions or extensions of themselves, even if their actual involvement in the children's care has been very limited," says Lundy Bancroft, author of *Why Does He Do That: Inside the Minds of Angry and Controlling Men.* "A connected issue is that sometimes he's okay with the divorce until she has a new partner, then he has to establish that he's the owner, even if the new man in mom's life poses no threat or shows no hint of jeopardizing his relationship to his children."

Signs of Abusive Behavior

No woman pictures herself with an abusive partner. All too often, she was swept off her feet by a man whose complex behavior unveiled itself as time went on. Use the following list to tell if your husband has abusive characteristics. Having one or two traits does not make him abusive though he may be. Certainly if you spot several, discuss your thoughts with a counselor.

1. Do you see signs of controlling behavior? Abuse is about the struggle for power. A man who interrogates you about where you were or sets limits over whom you can interact with and when you have time to yourself is high on control issues. Post-divorce you might see frequent demands, passive-aggressive behavior, and underhanded maneuvering, including legal abuse where winning matters most.

2. Were you pressured for a quick commitment? Abusers prey on weak women, those ending another relationship or otherwise vulnerable. Did you have little time to get to know your partner? Beware if a man who just ended a relationship comes courting you.

3. Does he exhibit signs of jealous rage? If you're made to feel bad about talking with another man, accused of flirting, or called nasty names that imply that you're unfaithful, there's jealousy. And if your husband follows you, monitors your phone calls, or has fits of anger, there is a serious problem. Love is not isolation.

4. Is he the blaming kind? Abusive men are savvy at turning the blame around to partners, manipulating feelings to make it seem that they are the victims, that they have been harmed. It's crazymaking. You'll rarely find an abuser who accepts responsibility. Abusers shirk it. Remember, there is no excuse for abuse.

5. Have you been verbally abused? Cruel and hurtful remarks are never called for. And it's a sad fact that a great deal of domestic violence begins with verbal and emotional battering. This includes name-calling, insults, undeserved and harsh criticism, and distortions of your own words and actions. If successful with words, some abusers become empowered. The abuse doesn't end there.

6. Does your man use physical force? Whether it's destroying property, blocking your exit, raising fists, pushing, threatening to harm, demanding sexual compliance, or actually assaulting you, it's not right. Force is frequently a means to manipulate and control.

7. Do you see a pattern of contrition? Do you see a pattern of acting out, then a remorseful stage in which you're promised it will never happen again? Well, it usually does happen again, only with more severity. Promises rarely work, and flowers won't fix it. Explosive mood swings deserve medical and mental health care, before your well-being suffers further. Many abusive men are also quite good at playing the victim when it can elicit sympathy.

8. Has anyone reported episodes of previous battering? If someone in this man's past (a former girlfriend, an ex-wife, or a child) has reported being battered, listen with both ears. He isn't going to own up to his responsibility. He'll only justify and rationalize his behavior.

9. Do you see a pattern of incongruence? If you are hearing one thing yet seeing another, this incongruence is a very important piece of insight. If he claims to care about the children yet puts them in harm's way or hurts them, this is incongruent behavior. If he tells you how much he loves you, yet continues to explode at you, it's just as incongruent.

10. Have you noticed a pattern of punitive behavior? This could include excessive litigation, his filing for custody or taking visitation issues to court on a routine basis. According to Lundy Bancroft, the abusive man is very punishment oriented, demanding a high price if he feels defied in any way.

11. Is there chronic infidelity or use of pornography? Bancroft writes that chronic infidelity is more than being unfaithful to one's vows, but a symptom of a deeper problem. Such men see women as playthings, refusing to take their partner seriously. Pornography often portrays women as available and submissive. It depersonalizes women.

12. Are there mental health concerns? Not that this is an excuse for poor behavior. It is not. I repeat: No one has the right to abuse you, regardless of a diagnosed or undiagnosed mental health condition. Knowledge of any psychological concerns is a powerful tool toward remediation, and certainly equips you (or others, such as court personnel) to make better decisions.

Legal Protection from Abuse

If you're a victim of domestic violence, you can choose to end the struggle and begin a better life. Police forces across the country are becoming more aware of domestic abuse, for it is a crime. They can arrest your husband or ask him to leave. Many police departments have informational sheets on how to file for a restraining order (a protection from abuse or protection of the peace order).

If you find yourself sufficiently threatened, do file for a protective order. There is no guarantee that your estranged husband won't violate it, but if he does, the law is definitely on your side. Such an order will keep him away from your home, job, or school and forbid him from assaulting, threatening, harassing, or stalking you. It may also provide protection for your children.

Protective orders can spell out exactly what an abusive man can and cannot do, and indeed what he is required to do (such as pay interim support, enter a counseling program, refrain from drugs or alcohol, or have supervised visitation with his children). Temporary or emergency orders are granted for approximately seventy-two hours, and remain in effect until you can appear before a judge for an extended order. Truly, you can get this kind of emergency protection at any time of the day or night. District magistrates often hear cases, or you may petition in night court. You do *not* need an attorney for this initial step though taking a friend for emotional support is a good idea. If granted, you'll be given duplicate copies of the court order. Take these to the police, who will need to serve your estranged husband with the order. They keep a copy, and you keep a copy for your records.

Once you have a temporary order, the services of an attorney may be helpful to you. Judges often see domestic abuse cases, but they also see a misuse of protective orders. Many attorneys representing the other party will argue against the judge granting an extended order because then it becomes a criminal charge, but if the facts and evidence are on your side, you should not let this deter you from any needed protection.

If you cannot afford counsel, there is often free legal aid rendered to battered women regardless of income. Most counties provide this help. Knowing your rights is another reason to consult a shelter. To find one near you, call the National Domestic Violence Hotline at 1-800-799-SAFE (7233). And to learn more about legal protection you can read *What to Do When Love Turns Violent* by Marian Betancourt.

Legal Abuse and Harassment

Have you ever wondered if your estranged spouse or ex-husband is using the legal system as a means to intimidate you, destroy you financially, or create undue stress and havoc in your life?

One area of family law that is not well defined is the dual issue of legal abuse, whereby one party (usually the more financially sound) wages constant litigation as a weapon of sorts, and also the issue of harassment. These two issues can be one and the same. Upon speaking with a few district attorneys, I was dismayed to learn that even when you are living apart and divorced from a spouse, complaints you might have (including excessive phone calls or a barrage of e-mails) may be looked upon as a domestic issue, even if you're both remarried to different spouses, and may live in two different states. Often, the harassing party can claim that he or she is "only trying to reach my child." However, check your state's laws. Maryland authorities have begun to take a tougher stance on Internet harassment, and as more awareness is brought to these issues, you may find remedies easier to attain. *The Times-Picayune* in New Orleans, Louisiana, reported that a state judge ordered two years probation and a six-month suspended sentence on cyberstalking charges, stemming from a single e-mail a man wrote to his wife during their contentious divorce. Thus, we can infer from what might appear to be idle words much more serious threats to inflict injury or harm through electronic communication—all because of statutes and misdemeanor offenses added to state criminal codes around the turn of this century. According to cyberstalking statistics released in 2004 by Working to Halt Online Abuse (WHOA), online harassment escalated from 39.4 percent in 2001 to 62 percent in 2003—a substantial increase. The majority of such victims were Caucasian females between the ages of eighteen and thirty. Most were single, and nearly 60 percent knew the offender previously.

Some states have laws whereby offenders of telephone harassment must cease all contact except on specific days and times and pay court fees and costs associated with changing a phone number. However, the burden is on the victim to prove the allegations and show costs. A less costly approach would be to employ caller ID and block certain e-mail addresses from your account.

The question of what exactly is legal abuse is subjective. Lawyers are notorious for sending "nasty-grams," that is, letters with no other intent than to intimidate and run up a legal bill, one that benefits them and unfortunately harms another. One woman received a letter claiming her ex-husband tried to reach his daughter.

Here is mom's side, the story behind the letter. Told by her stepdad that the little girl was in the bathtub, dad agreed to call back later. Upon picking up what she anticipated to be the call back, mom answered, "Hello," waiting for a reply. She repeated this three times and with continued silence on the other end, she assumed it was a wrong number and hung up. You can see the end of this story coming, right? Sure enough, three days later a letter appeared in her mailbox to the effect of "your client prevented my client from reaching his daughter." Dad never identified himself.

So what's that whole scenario about? What it's *not* about is dad wanting any kind of communication with his child—anything but. When there is no real purpose, or when an attorney knows his or her client won't achieve some positive means, there ought to be some remedy for this type of abuse also. But tell that to state legislatures and judicial committees made up almost entirely of—you guessed it—lawyers!

Remedies to Legal Harassment and Legal Abuse

Concerned citizens need to demand better protection for their rights to live peaceful, harassment-free lives. We also need to seriously consider the opinion many experts voice in this book—that much litigation could be better addressed by mental health professionals than by the courts and lawyers, with perhaps an increased chance of eradicating problematic behavior through counseling, rather than enabling poor behavior (which empowers them) or slapping a punishment upon abusers (which further enrages them).

"The social pressure on men to change is so very low because he's only hearing it from the woman—a woman he doesn't take seriously, and that's the nature of the problem," says Bancroft. "So how is she going to convince him? When we start seeing a lot more pressure from family and criminal courts, media outlets, abuser's friends and relatives, then we'll see higher rates of change in abusive men."

William Eddy, an attorney, social worker, and author, shared that in his experience, many women (and men) are victims of legal abuse or legal harassment. "Once a spouse realizes that attorneys and judges will accept their statements at face value, they use the system to try to control and at times humiliate the other spouse," says Eddy. "This is often not a conscious process . . . It may be an unconscious cognitive distortion, which the person actually believes when it is said. Or it may be a bold-faced lie."

Certainly looking at patterns helps to prove intent because as we know in the mental health field, behavior reveals itself over time. Some jurisdictions place domestic relations cases with one judge to follow through various conflicts. This is wise, but only if judges are willing to look at the record and hold abusers accountable with, as Bancroft put it, "real, meaningful, lasting consequences."

William Eddy added that court personnel are not yet trained as they should be to deal with personality disordered litigants with their distorted thinking, perceiving themselves as chronic victims, and that these people easily mislead the courts, even their own lawyers. "They need to be gently challenged: Is that really true? What is your part in all of this?" says Eddy. "If legal professionals would ask these questions from the start of a case, most with this type of problem would not make false allegations or become preoccupied with blaming the other party." Repeat court visits, in his mind, stem from the unquestioning belief of those in the court system, as well as the no-consequences approach. Eddy describes this as a disservice to the person suffering the personality disorder, as well as a significant tragedy for those they blame.

As a graduate student in clinical counseling, I feel compelled to ask the tough question: Why can't we mandate more counseling, as outlined in the previous chapter? Some of these continually cantankerous individuals need treatment. Also, when one spouse is willing to work out differences, but the other one digs in for a legal fight, what's that about? Folks, it's *not* about problem solving. Sometimes, it's about winning. Rest assured, happy people—those fulfilled by life—do not try to cause misery in other people's lives. They just don't.

If you have any doubt about the unfair goals of an argument, you need look no further than the book *The Angry Child*. Plenty of litigious adults act like angry children. My coauthor and I discussed that the only good reason to argue is to solve a problem. Among the unsavory goals people use for arguing: to win, destroy, vent, or just for the sport of it. The experts whom I interviewed have seen too much of this behavior.

Another means of ending legal abuse is for judges to enforce penalties for perjury in family court (rarely done according to several sources I contacted) and to impose counsel fees upon parties who brought frivolous actions to court. It's not enough to dismiss a stupid motion. Plenty of experts would contend that awarding counsel fees to a legally abused party is not only prudent but also compassionate. In some proposed bills, the Pennsylvania Senate Judiciary Committee attempted to add a provision for judges to award legal counsel fees, but as of this writing, the legislation was stuck in committee. As I found tracking this bill, nothing happens quickly. Nothing happens very slowly either. It's as if these legislators are waiting for William Penn to return with a little guidance; meanwhile, I've spoken with several women in Pennsylvania and other states who feel they've been financially raped by a poor system of supposed justice.

Awarding counsel fees in this way compensates the lawyers for court appearances, and it may serve as a deterrent to the growing problem of legal abuse. Given the telephone setup I outlined before, sanctions should also be placed upon attorneys who profit from nuisance and harassing correspondence. The "do no harm" edict that guides medical professionals ought to be applied to lawyers as well.

Battered Woman Syndrome

"Why didn't you just leave?" is always the first question people wonder. If you're the woman, perhaps you wondered why on earth you've stayed in a poor relationship.

But a woman who has been abused is running on empty with little self-esteem, and has a shattered concept of her place in the world, few resources including money, and perhaps a deficit of job skills. Frequently, battering escalates at times when a woman is most vulnerable, including during pregnancy.

The battered woman forgives her abusive spouse, she hopes that he will change, and she continues to love him, until she's so confused that the next cycle occurs. The battering escalates. It explodes. There's the honeymoon period again. Over and over again.

Lenore Walker presented her groundbreaking research in 1979 in *The Battered Woman* in terms of the tension-building phase leading to the explosion (the battering incident) and ending with contrition (professing love, sending flowers, promising the abuse will never happen again).

The good news is that recovery is your right. A battered woman's best chance of escaping abuse is to get herself appropriate counseling as quickly as possible.

Counseling and Recovery

For me, education was key in breaking away from a poor relationship. Fortunately, I'm an avid reader. Once I began reading about domestic violence and the patterns of abuse, I didn't feel as overwhelmed. In their book *When Men Batter Women*, the late Neil Jacobson, Ph.D., and John Gottman, Ph.D., make a good case *against* seeking marriage counseling to remedy abuse. First, they suggest, marital therapy puts the couple together more frequently where they are encouraged to deal with conflict. And if the couple is treated together, it's implied that each party is responsible for the problems. This is sure handy for your husband if he's abusive since it supports his point of view.

So what kind of counseling should you seek? Your own. Cognitive therapy will help you adjust thinking patterns that became unhealthy and may have led you to put up with poor treatment.

Outside of psychotherapy, you'll find that advocates and counselors at your local women's shelter are very helpful. It's a big step to call a shelter for help, let alone walk through the doors for an appointment. But I've been there. I'm so glad I sought that kind of support because I realized I wasn't alone.

There is a wonderful life of peace and happiness out there for you. In time, the wounds of mistreatment and violence will heal. The sooner you seek help, the quicker you will recover.

Others Advocating for Abuse Survivors

One effect now recognized is the impact that abuse makes on the survivor's spirituality. "The whole area of looking at religion's role in abuse and the effect abuse has on the survivor's ability to trust God is fairly new," says Gail Martin, Director of the Refuge Project, based in Charlotte, North Carolina. The Refuge Project is a research effort exploring how the faith community can welcome and accept adult survivors of abuse. "These studies really coincide with the first generation of women to become theologians, established ministers and rabbis, and divinity school teachers."

Extensive interviews with counselors, clergy, advocates, and survivors reveal a pattern of difficulty trusting God to be good, says Martin, because abusers often use religious language to back up their claims of power and control. Even well-meaning houses of worship are often misinformed about the nature of abuse.

"Abuse victims are often victimized twice," says Martin. "Once by their abuser, and again by a personal belief system and faith community that unintentionally create a climate ripe for abuse." This includes an environment that emphasizes personal worthlessness, requires blind obedience, perpetuates inequality between the sexes, and places little stock in psychology or outside intervention. "I hear horror stories all the time from counselors about women who went to a minister for counseling and were told to 'go home and pray' or 'be more submissive' or sometimes, even exposed to harm by having the minister break trust and contact the abuser," Martin adds.

Fortunately, a growing number of programs are helping churches, synagogues, and other houses of worship understand the cycle of abuse, recognize the signs, and provide safe and appropriate intervention. The Refuge Project develops presentations and materials to help congregations understand how abuse forever alters the way survivors perceive Scripture. It also encourages clergy to talk about all forms of abuse from the pulpit, noting how validating that can be for survivors.

In addition, many domestic violence advocates are urging that lawyers in training receive much more education on abuse issues, and they are also expressing concerns about state marriage initiatives potentially using federal welfare funds for marriage promotion. Advocates do not wish to see women pressured into attending marriage preparation classes that eventually result in relationships with abusive spouses. The compelling argument is "educate but don't mandate."

How Abuse Affects Children

Children who witness violence early in life come to see the world as a dangerous, unpredictable, and unloving place. Some researchers have found that many children exposed to the trauma of violence develop psychiatric problems later in life. Girls who routinely see their mothers abused fall into the same scenarios. And truly, those boys who grow up with a battering role model may know of no other way to solve problems with their own wives.

Some of the behaviors you might recognize in children exposed to domestic abuse include poor impulse control, externalizing or internalizing of anger, sadness, depression, stress, and school delinquency. The abusing parent often distorts not only his victim's perceptions, but also those of his children. These kids are at higher risk and may act out with drugs, alcohol, and sex. They may even blame themselves for not being able to prevent abuse to their mothers. When this happens, it's best to let a child talk about his feelings, assure him that the abuse is not his fault (or yours), and help your child to dispense with any worry. "Mommy is going to be okay," or "I can take care of myself" are two phrases Lundy Bancroft, who also wrote *When Dad Hurts Mom: Helping Your Children Heal the Wounds of Witnessing Abuse*, suggests using. Because children witnessing abuse already have a heightened anxiety level, it's good to model responsible behavior, especially if you occasionally lose your own temper. Apologizing for your own mistakes sets you apart from an abusive father. In time, your kids will learn that despite the superficial apologies, he isn't truly working on improving his behavior, but that you are.

However, your children don't have to suffer. Many women's centers and shelters offer pro bono children's programs with trained counselors or group activities. Through the intervention of a shelter program, children can see males standing up against violence as well, and they can learn to be proud of their mothers for being strong.

By going to a group session with their peers, trained counselors, and volunteers, boys and girls will learn that they are not alone. Often, children feel singled out in a separated or divorcing family, especially if the other children they associate with come from intact homes. Add the component of being from an abusive home, and it merely compounds the loneliness. Help is available, and you owe it to your children to seek out such assistance. A pattern of abuse that may have lasted through generations can end.

After at least a year attending the pro bono children's program at our local women's shelter, my son and I were reading books about his new pet, a hermit crab named Freddie. We learned that when you have multiple crabs sharing the same environment, it's not uncommon that one fights the other to obtain custody of the shell. My son, who was eight at the time, got quiet for a moment.

"You know, Mom," he said. "If we get another crab and it's a girl, Freddie could get arrested for doing that."

In one brief moment, I realized how much my son had already learned about the appropriate and inappropriate ways of treating women. "Praise God," I wanted to proclaim. The effort of driving to the shelter and back each week really did pay off! If you find that your children, particularly sons, are troubled by what they have witnessed, or are hitting or verbally battering you, seek counseling for them right away.

State legislatures are also recognizing the effects of domestic violence on children, and many are passing laws that make it more difficult for the batterer to obtain custody. It's advisable that you inform your pediatrician and any other relevant professional in your child's life about the domestic violence in your marriage, whether it was witnessed or not. This can become a part of their records that can help others understand how to help your child, and it may strengthen your case if there are future custody battles. As I've stated previously, however, some courts are less inclined to see other behaviors as abuse, so in cases where a troubled man is causing negative emotional, social, or sometimes even physical health impact, they still err on the side of the man's "rights" to his children over children's rights to lead happy, healthy lives.

Finally, know that many shelters have an age range for the children that they accept, particularly boys. Sometimes, boys over age thirteen or fourteen cannot live with their mothers in shelter accommodations. If you feel that you need a shelter, then stay. It's better to make this move when your son is ten than wait until your options are limited.

Keeping Safe

Victims of domestic violence need to take added precautions to ensure their safety. Often dubbed "developing an escape plan," it's advisable to keep an extra set of keys, clothing, important papers, prescriptions, and some cash or credit cards with someone you trust. Identify a safe place for children to go during intense conflict, assuring them that their role is to be safe, not to protect you.

Call the police. Have the numbers of friends, family, and your nearest shelter available to you at all times. Arrange a secret distress signal with neighbors so that they can summon help if you can't. If you're injured, go to the emergency room, where physicians are trained to help you report and heal from your ordeal. Do not leave the hospital without a safety plan that's known only to friends and family.

Safety Measures and the Children

Up to 75 percent of all reported domestic violence assaults take place after parents have separated, with the highest risk involving the transfer of the couple's children, according to a study published in 1992 in the *Juvenile and Family Court Journal*. Be extra-vigilant during exchanges.

During the trials of the Washington-area snipers in 2003, investigators and prosecutors raised the theory (as reported in many leading publications) that John Allen Muhammad, having lost custody of his children, and desperately wanting them back, masterminded the shooting spree with the hopes of assassinating his ex-wife. He planned on walking in later, they asserted in their theory, to claim his children as the good father.

Think your estranged husband wouldn't lure his own children away? Guess again. Because children may not understand the cycle of abuse (with its predictable phase of contrition), and they desperately want to see parents in a good light, teach your children good safety habits. They should know, if they are old enough, what their regular and scheduled visitation times are with their fathers. This way, if the parent approaches them at any other time, they will know firsthand where they are to be.

Give copies of protective orders or your custody agreement to your children's school, youth group, scoutmaster, day-care center, doorman, or building manager. This way, if your estranged husband tries to take the children at times visitation is not specified, others will know not to release them to him.

And, teach children emergency contact numbers, such as your phone number, a relative's number, or the police department's number just in case they are left alone. As one mom who had a belligerent spouse put it, "Most kids ponder what clothes to wear, but our kids have to be prepared to be Columbo detectives." The kids' father got angry and left them stranded at a restaurant. Fortunately, these children knew what to do.

Securing Your Household

If you think abuse is likely, file for exclusive possession of your home. This helps when your spouse lords it over you that the house belongs to him as well. In situations where he shows up in a rage, the police can make him leave if you have exclusive possession of the marital residence.

Often, exclusive possession is granted as part of a protective or restraining order. But it can be placed into any agreements you devise with your estranged spouse. As I indicated before, visitation exchanges are often fraught with discord. Specify in your custody order, for instance, that the children's father is to remain in the car at all times. Or you can designate another, neutral location to exchange the children. Popular sites include your local police station or even within the courthouse—both places where there is surveillance.

But remember, an agreement is only a piece of paper. Your best bet is to remain cautious. Nasty behavior occurs when you least expect it. One woman reported that she and her husband had an agreement that he could let their children into the house and stay until she arrived. Weeks later, after one of her estranged husband's dropoffs, this woman reached into the wine cellar for a bottle to serve to guests. Only then did she discover that hundreds of dollars of wine had been literally poured down the drain. The note left behind stated, "You don't need to be drinking this."

Honestly, I can't understand why an estranged husband should ever have access to your home after you have separated. At the very least, there should be others present, besides you and the children. Such entries only bring on remarks about new possessions and changes you've made, or even roaming eyes that may be casing the place.

Beyond obtaining exclusive possession, here is a checklist of home security measures all women should take when separated:

1. **Change the locks** if you aren't certain you have all his keys to the property. If he has a key to get in, he will most likely pay you a visit when you are not home, and take any number of possessions and documents. Don't think he'd do that? It is not worth taking the chance. It happens in the majority of marital separations. In some communities, if you have a protective order, you might be eligible for assistance in changing your locks.

2. **If you don't have deadbolt locks, install these along with chains** on all outside doors. Steel doors are always better than wooden doors or those with glass panels that can be broken to gain access.

3. Install a security system in the residence, or change any access codes. Don't forget about garage door access. Retrieve his remote control device and the garage door key. Reprogram this entry if necessary.

4. Retrieve any hidden keys that you stuck under doormats or under rocks in the bushes in case of emergency. Don't forget about keys that might remain with friends or family. (If his family members or friends have keys, you must re-key the locks.)

5. Consider that kids and keys might not mix well, at least for a while. You don't want your ex to take a key belonging to your children. There isn't an easy solution to your children's access to your home. Until you've been granted exclusive possession or the marital residence is deeded to you in a divorce, the police can do little if your estranged husband shows up with a key, presuming the property is jointly held. If at all possible, try to keep the keys to yourself, and ask trusted adults to let children inside.

6. Instruct children that nothing leaves the house to go to dad's without your permission. Sometimes the kids are asked to retrieve objects that estranged husbands feel entitled to.

7. Inform neighbors of your situation. As embarrassing as it may seem, they will most likely be helpful and understanding. Neighbors are wonderful watchdogs, especially if they are at home during the day or are the vigilant type. Instruct them to call the police if they see your estranged on the premises when you aren't there to handle the situation (or any time if there's been a history of violence). Of course, they should never permit access to your residence by giving a key you might leave with them for emergencies.

8. Speaking of watchdogs, having a dog can be a great deterrent if anyone, including an abuser, wants to gain entry. Of course, if your estranged or ex-husband used to be co-owner of this pet, your canine guard may be easily charmed. But a dog's sense of smell and alarm—not to mention its bark—can alert you to criminal mischief immediately.

9. Keep a cellular phone handy for emergencies. Whether in your house or on the highway, a mobile phone works when lines have been severed or if you are not near a regular telephone. Don't be afraid to call a police dispatcher if you're ever followed, even if it appears to be the police. Call the police especially if you're pulled over by an unmarked vehicle.

10. If you experience telephone harassment, consult your telephone company. In fact, your telephone directory might help you through the steps of how to report such pranks, but in some cases if you proceed with the instructions, then you must also be willing to prosecute. After you hang up with a harasser, pick the phone back up and press *57 (or dial 1157). This reports and traces it.

11. Set your answering machine to record all incoming calls. This as well as caller ID can also deter telephone harassment. Keep a supply of extra tapes on hand so that you can save any messages of a harassing nature.

12. Since many answering machines have remote access to messages when you're away from home, **invest in a new answering system.** You don't want your estranged husband to listen to any messages or information conveyed confidentially to you. Never leave a message on your machine that you are away.

Other Home Security Measures

Your security measures will depend largely upon where you live. For instance, if you are in an urban or perhaps high-crime neighborhood, you might want to install grates or grilles on outdoor windows. Make sure that window air conditioners are properly secured. Sliding glass doors should be locked at the handle, secured at the top (with a latch you can purchase), and additionally protected with a piece of wood fit to the space between the frame and the inside panel.

If you have outdoor landscaping, prune any tree limbs that could allow a burglar's access to the second story, and trim shrubbery so that doors and windows are visible. Lock up any ladders you leave outdoors, and think twice about high wooden fences. These, like shrubbery, make it easy for criminals to hide.

You can purchase window stickers and signs at home building centers that warn intruders of electronic surveillance systems. In addition, you can purchase or borrow electric engraving pens to mark all items that would-be thieves (or your estranged spouse) might take. These include all stereo, television, video, camera, or computer equipment, expensive appliances, or anything else of value. Make a video of your household contents (including china, silver, and jewelry), and store this record of your belongings in your safe deposit box. You'll be better able to identify what you have (and it's a handy tool for filing insurance claims as well).

Hire house-sitters for funerals or celebrations when others might know you aren't home. Tell the police of your vacation so that they can enter you into their log book. Stop deliveries, and ask the neighbors to pick up any items left on your doorstep. Give your home a lived-in look by putting lights on timers, having the lawn mowed, and even asking neighbors to leave footprints or their cars in your driveway. Have them report any suspicious persons seen hanging around.

Personal Safety in General

Now that you are separated, you increase the chances that you'll be traveling on your own, not only on the highways but around the community and out of town.

Again, common sense dictates that you plan personal or business errands in daylight, that you travel with a friend, and that you don't drive or walk through the more dangerous parts of town. But crime can happen anywhere, at any time of the day.

Some women feel safer if they have pepper spray (Mace is illegal in some areas), a personal alarm (available at home supply centers), or a pendant alarm (given by some police departments to victims of domestic violence). These are added measures, but only if you use them or have them at the ready.

The best advice when traveling alone is to be vigilant. Know your surroundings. Keep an eye on others. Walk confidently and quickly to your car or destination. Don't limit your mobility with heavy packages or luggage.

When traveling away from home, insist on hotel security. Clerks should hand you your room key and number silently. If your accommodations do not seem secure, ask for a room change. Mark your luggage with just a first initial, last name, and office address if possible (or post office box). Don't be fooled by uniforms, either. Always ask for proper identification before admitting anyone to a hotel room or home, or even rolling down your car window.

A good resource for you to peruse is *A Woman's Guide to Personal Safety* by Janeé Harteau and Holly Keegel. You'll learn precautions to take that you may not have thought applied to you.

A Word about Firearms

When women are concerned about personal safety, they might be tempted to purchase a weapon, usually a gun, for their protection. But it's paramount that you receive proper training, and if you own firearms of any kind, that you keep them unloaded and locked away from children's reach (even teenagers).

The mere need to lock away protection and ammunition might deter you from ownership in the first place. If there was an intruder, it would take time to get to such a weapon. But your children's safety comes first here, as well as your own. Guns owned by the inexperienced are frequently confiscated by criminals and used against the owners.

Seek proper training if you choose to buy a gun. The husband of one of my friends offered to take me to a local sportsmen's club to learn to handle a gun safely. It was at first a little frightening, but overall a good step to know that even if I came upon a handgun, I'd know how to disarm it. It also brings about much self-awareness and recognition to take gun safety quite seriously.

Check with friends who have experience with firearms and ask how they learned to use a weapon safely. If you don't have anyone to ask, call your local police department for class referrals. Police departments also have literature on storing guns safely, and officers frequently lecture in schools and in the community.

Maintaining Confidentiality

We live in a technological world in which *anyone* can obtain access to privileged information. If you don't use caution, that anyone could even be your estranged spouse finding out information you'd rather keep to yourself.

For instance, did you know that anyone can look up your posts to Internet newsgroups merely by doing a search with the right Web site? That's right. It's great to find new cyberfriends and share online, but never divulge information you wouldn't want discovered. When you are litigating a legal separation or divorce case, you never know what could be used against you (such as job information, successes, personal struggles, etc.).

If you truly want to keep your address and whereabouts confidential, refrain from any deliveries, including newspapers, even pizza. Get a post office box and use that for mail. In fact, make sure the post office knows that your estranged husband has no business picking up mail or packages that might be held for you. When you travel out of town, or you are away for a day, have your mail held at the post office or ask a trusted neighbor to retrieve it. After all, you don't want your estranged spouse taking documents out of the mailbox.

Similarly, change your passwords or make them less obvious to others. These include passwords to your computer, e-mail account, ATM, or even utilities. Yes, without your knowledge, your telephone service could be altered unless you have protected your account with a password. Representatives will ask you for the magic word each time you make a change in service.

Victims of domestic violence should also inquire about getting a new social security number assigned to them if it's warranted. Contact the Social Security office near you, or ask for assistance with this at your local women's shelter.

Finally, having an unlisted phone number is advisable for many reasons, security being chief among them. Realize also that if your estranged spouse has caller ID, your number might be displayed unless you block it in advance. To do this, press *67 (or dialing 1167) before entering the phone number. Line blocking, available through the phone company, might be another option.

The best deterrent to crime, or even harassment, is prevention. This chapter was not meant to alarm you, but to prepare you for any threats. It's a good idea to review safety measures periodically since we all get busy and push prevention aside. If the ideas presented here make you feel more secure, or indeed prevent unfortunate occurrences, then this chapter has served its purpose.

Chapter Six

Your Financial Future

Immediate money matters plague many separated women. Some are left with literally no resources to support themselves. Others need encouragement on how to safeguard what they do have, and file the necessary paperwork to ensure spousal and child support. Many need to prepare a budget sheet for the first time. And as a separation continues, women who might not have been accustomed to managing money need to look out for their financial futures.

Does this sound like you? Well, even if you have the most cooperative and infinitely wealthy spouse, my guess is that you can learn a great deal from this chapter. Reading these pages, you'll discover money-saving tips to slash expenses. Proper financial planning can't be stressed enough. Your future peace of mind and quality of life depend upon it. Let me give you a scenario. We'll call our friend Barbara.

Recently separated from her well-off husband, Barbara continued to enjoy the lifestyle she'd been accustomed to in her marriage—country club memberships, weekly salon and manicure appointments, and shopping at exclusive stores, even for groceries.

Barbara didn't think she had a financial care in the world because her husband promised to take care of everything, and she knew he certainly had the means to do just that.

But as time went by, Barbara's husband resented that she continued to entertain extravagantly and volunteer her efforts rather than work for payment. The couple's three children were grown, with one in college and two in high school. Barbara's husband gradually diminished the funds she was used to receiving. And indeed when the couple divorced, Barbara was assigned an earning capacity. Needless to say, Barbara was dumbfounded. Soon she was in debt, and for a while, she struggled—a lifestyle she was *not* accustomed to.

Another woman—let's call her Melissa—was difficult and very self-centered, plus she was the master of setting up situations and then playing the martyr. If Melissa wanted something, she was accustomed to getting it—at least until her arrogance and passive-aggression, among other factors, became the proverbial straws for her husband, who then divorced her. Due to many different circumstances, Melissa's ex-husband retained custody of the couples' two sons, but a year after their divorce, his company transferred him to a major metropolitan area. Understandably, she was concerned with maintaining regular visits with her boys, but in her martyr style of conduct, she reinvented everything as a catastrophe.

Melissa's frequent pattern of spending had begun to catch up with her; however, after waging much litigation and demands, she could not possibly afford to relocate herself to this area with a higher cost of living. She'd spent tens of thousands of dollars trying to fashion a more favorable divorce settlement, and she spent even more in court complaining about anything her ex-husband did with the boys. Melissa told anyone that would listen that she would go anywhere to be with her two sons, but now when it really mattered, she couldn't afford to make that happen. Melissa clearly let herself spin out of control. If she had attended to her anger and other strong emotions, her behavior, decisions, and future may have been much more positive.

Financial Realities

I use these stories to illustrate that the financial situation you see yourself in today might not be the one you face in six months or in several years. You must think about your future, and what's truly meaningful to you. Don't continue to let a man do this for you.

Of course, your financial future does not have to be bleaker than the one you previously enjoyed. Sometimes it is bleaker, but in many cases, women find that they can manage better without a husband in the picture. How can this be?

Simple. Some husbands have bad habits. They might gamble, spend frivolously, even eat you out of house and home. Assuming that you aren't already in deep debt, and that you have an adequate amount of child and perhaps spousal support, it's conceivable that you won't feel as drastic a pinch as you might have expected. I found during my separation that the groceries went farther, I could keep the thermostat where I wanted it, and the water bill even went down!

Where money is concerned, we all have worries. Having been raised by Depression-era parents, I inherited their fears. But they taught me to spend wisely and live frugally, to research investments (even the simplest purchases), to control what I can, and to let go of the rest. That means having a little faith even where finances are concerned. You'll be okay, most likely, if you use common sense and caution. And as author Suze Orman often points out, the way you handle money is closely tied to your self-esteem. The deeper your financial woes, the more you probably need to work on your belief system. You can overcome your fear and misuse of money. First things first.

Safeguarding Assets

An important step is to safeguard assets you already have. Think your spouse won't raid bank accounts, sell off stock, or cash in insurance policies? Guess again. It's been done to unsuspecting wives who had made decisions emotionally, not practically.

When I discovered upsetting realities in my own marriage, I sought legal advice. I was told to safeguard assets by moving accounts into my own name. I felt my trust had been broken. It was only natural that I'd want some reassurance and more control over the finances.

Is this raiding? No. I can honestly say I did not pillage or plunder those accounts. In fact, they grew under my management and were safeguarded until equitable distribution.

Is it mean-spirited? Again, I don't think so.

After hearing several women share their separation stories, I've concluded that their situations are truly ironic. The same men who passively sit back enjoying their wife's financial prowess later claim that she was controlling with money. They can't have it both ways. And certainly if a husband uses funds illicitly, he shouldn't be surprised when his behavior hastens even more control of the finances by his wife. This ensures that assets aren't bled, paychecks drunk or gambled away, or funds used to furnish a mistress's apartment. As I've shared previously in this book, an estranged husband's anger and mental health concerns during separation and divorce also serve as an impetus for safeguarding many things, including your emotional and physical safety, and yes, even your financial picture.

My advice to any woman facing separation is to safeguard assets, transferring liquid accounts into your name alone. If your husband begs forgiveness, he may understand your resolve to protect funds. He might willingly sign any documents to affect this. But some banks will require only one party of a joint account to close it out and open another.

On the day my husband walked out the door, we had only one joint bank account and credit card. The checking had a low balance, and that night I closed the credit card account. Unfortunately, that left me without a credit card, and I learned quickly that every woman, married or not, should have a VISA or MasterCard held in her own name. Still, going without a credit card for a few weeks was better than being responsible later for any joint debt racked up. If your spouse is vindictive or addictive, believe me, you could be in for trouble if you don't close down any joint credit. So one last time—do not continue to share a credit line with your estranged husband.

Other assets such as life insurance policies, stocks, mutual funds, bonds, and other investments are usually more complex. Most will require both parties' signatures to liquidate. However, don't let too much time pass before you review these, and safeguard them as well. Your husband's new girlfriend just might show up at a brokerage firm trying to sign your name to release funds, or worse yet, you may have forgotten that power of attorney you signed years ago. Notify all financial institutions of your separation and require them to ask for identification before your signature is signed to anything.

For instance, to prevent a spouse from running off with the cash value of a life insurance policy, you might want to become the owner of that policy. Courts can sometimes mandate that your husband maintain a life insurance policy at least while you are separated. If you followed the guidelines of accumulating account numbers and balances outlined in Chapter One, you should be in pretty good shape with a paper trail. Make copies of these statements for your attorney. The real tragedy occurs when a wife hasn't a clue what accounts they hold and what her husband's pension looks like. Remember, knowledge is power. Knowledge also means less anxiety.

One last caveat here on the subject of safeguarding. If you are tempted to dip into any marital monies during your separation, just remember that you will have to account for these funds at equitable distribution. This isn't play money. It's not even a loan. It's merely money that you intend to protect until it can be divided equitably (not necessarily equally, mind you, but equitably). If support payments stop or fall behind and you need to protect a marital asset (such as your home) with this money to pay the mortgage, keep good records. And, of course, consult your attorney if you have one.

Filing for Support

Speaking of attorneys, many women have the misguided notion that you must have a lawyer to collect child support. This is partially untrue. I say partially because one of the first moves you should make in a separation is to file for child and spousal support. You do not need an attorney to do this.

It's paramount that you file as soon as possible because you will be assigned a conference date six to eight weeks away, when support will be decided. The longer you delay, the longer it will take. Also, the date of petition is the effective date, so it's best to do this quickly. File for support first and get a hearing date set. Then concentrate on finding an attorney (see Chapter Four).

To file for support, contact your family court division. Chances are good there will be a recorded message with instructions on filing for support or you may find the steps on the Internet. Or again, if you have already retained an attorney, follow that advice.

The paperwork that you need to fill out, including a budget sheet of living expenses and a statement of your income, deserves careful attention. Frequently this information will set the tone for all future support hearings and decisions. These sworn statements show the parties' need for and ability to pay support. Thus, the sleuth work you did gathering documents, pay stubs, tax returns, and paid bill statements will assist you in accurately filling out the required forms.

Some women frequently forget the incidental expenses any family incurs. This is a big mistake. Those items you generally pay cash for include newspapers, school lunches, babysitters, preschool tuition, haircuts, gifts (including those for children's birthday parties and holidays), entertainment (such as movie admissions, video rentals, or cable TV), household cleaning, and commuting or transportation costs (such as filling your gasoline tank or bus or subway fare to work). Your attorney, or perhaps the clerks present when you file for support, will give you a budget sheet with categories to jog your memory. Use this as a guideline, but brainstorm for any expense categories that are unique to your family. The parent who retains custody of the children always has higher incidental expenses.

Some states only consider the incomes of the parents when determining support awards. Others consider household income. Thus, if you or your estranged spouse is cohabiting during your separation, this could influence your support figure.

Of course, it's wise to reach an agreement on your own, called a consent order, rather than rely upon the discretion of a hearing officer or judge. The family court system is overloaded with cases and fraught with discord. Decisions rendered by third parties might be unfair, arbitrary, and difficult to overcome in the months and years ahead. Remember the expert advice in Chapter Four that the court only hears part of the total story, and then likely focuses on even less information to reach a decision.

You know your situation better than anyone, and you have a better chance of getting the level of support that you and your children require if you can discuss things rationally. Armed with the appropriate income data for each of you, ask your attorney (or go to the public library) to look at the support guidelines that many states publish.

Unless your case is complex, or you simply cannot get the other side to negotiate, try to reach an agreement outside of a hearing. Besides, support hearings are rarely run on time. Every minute your attorney waits in the hallway racks up your bill, sometimes by hundreds of dollars before you even begin presenting your case.

Some final words regarding support. It can usually be modified at any time, but you may want to pay careful attention to the language in your court or consent order. Federal law requires that all support orders issued after January 1, 1994, provide for wage attachment. It's more reliable; today wage attachment is common.

Also, beware of the income tax ramifications. It's best to designate a certain portion for spousal support (temporary alimony, which is taxable income) and another for child support (nontaxable). If support is awarded without being broken down, you may be liable for tax on the entire amount. In addition, it might be wise to use the term "without prejudice" in your document. Without such wording, one of you may have to prove a change in circumstance before any future modification.

Being as specific as possible eliminates future hassles and legal fees. For instance, your support order will likely state that one of you is to maintain the family's health insurance and reimburse for out-of-pocket medical expenses (copay amounts and prescriptions). Be sure to set a time limit for reimbursement, such as within thirty days. This eliminates one party withholding payment as a means of passive-aggressive control.

Tracking Down Deadbeat Dads

If either party fails to provide support as outlined in your order, the wronged spouse can present a motion for contempt of court. Your attorney will typically be the one to handle this, but anyone can present a motion before a judge. Alleged violators will have the opportunity at a hearing to explain why they have not complied with the order, and why they shouldn't be held in contempt. If the hearing officer or judge does find the party in contempt, assets can be seized, fines levied, or jail sentences invoked. Don't let too much time pass before initiating contempt proceedings because it may take weeks beyond the initial motion for a hearing.

Of course, if the father has skipped town, it might seem more difficult to collect child support, but there are ways of locating him. Your state's child support agency can do a parent locator search. Thanks to computer technology, it's possible to track down a deadbeat dad who has moved across state lines. In compliance with federal law, employers must turn in the names, addresses, dates of birth, and social security numbers of all new hires on or after January 1, 1998. This was designed in part to nab deadbeat parents. Here are other measures:

1. Many states also withhold from commissions, dividends, retirement benefits, and lottery winnings. Some revoke the professional or driver's licenses of deadbeat parents.

2. In many states, motor vehicle registration records are open to the public. Call the bureau with your husband's name, social security number, and date of birth to find out what vehicles are listed under his name, as well as his current address.

3. Visit your county's taxation department or deeds and property assessment office; these are all open to the public. If you have no luck, request that your county clerk of courts do a property search.

4. Allow the Internal Revenue Service (IRS) to intercept a delinquent payer's income tax refund. Your child support agency verifies the amount overdue and submits the case to the IRS.

5. Ask your agency's caseworker to obtain information from your estranged spouse's bank, mortgage company, or other financial institutions to determine his holdings. It's possible to put liens on real estate or personal property and to attach bank accounts to collect past-due support.

You can tackle all of these suggestions on your own and with no cost, other than your time. Advocacy and support organizations might offer additional ideas. One such agency is the Association for Children for Enforcement of Support (ACES), based in Toledo, Ohio (1-800-537-7072). Keep on top of your case, and if these measures fail, you can always hire a private attorney to investigate matters. However, this would be the most expensive route to go.

Credit—Establishing It and Getting Rid of It

As I've already stated, every woman should have a major credit card in her name alone. A credit card is important for many reasons. For starters, it helps you establish a good credit profile. It's handy in an emergency, and eliminates the need to carry cash. It makes ordering by telephone or the Internet or securing an airline reservation or hotel room a snap. Finally, it gives additional protection with life insurance (if, heaven forbid, you are in an airline accident and booked with that card), and it allows you to put an item in dispute if there is a problem with the merchandise.

However, while credit cards might lubricate the economy, they wreak havoc on people's budgets. So here I'll discuss how to establish and maintain good credit health, which is preferable to dodging creditors, declaring bankruptcy, or having a bad credit history haunt you. Bad credit is not only hazardous to your financial future but to your career. The Fair Credit Reporting Act permits employers to access your credit record, and some companies view the report as a sign of your fiscal responsibility.

For starters, if you have cancelled any joint credit cards with your husband, as I've already suggested, then you may be left without a card. Check with the bank where your checking and other accounts are held. Often, you're entitled to a major credit card, so all you need to do is fill out the application. Be certain when listing your income that you include spousal support in addition to your own earned income. This will help process the application without question or delay.

Depending upon your income (or lack of it), you might be turned down for a credit card. If that's the case, you can begin to build a credit history by obtaining a secured card, where you transfer money out of savings into a separate account that the credit card then draws from. Essentially, you can't spend money you don't already have.

Of course, it's great if you can get paid someway to use a card, as in frequent flier points, rebates, car discounts, or college savings through the Upromise program. But if you have to pay an outrageous annual fee, forget it. Budget-minded consumers shouldn't pay anything over $50 for the convenience of credit because there are cards with no annual fees available. These days every merchant seems to offer a major credit card. Therefore, the perk has to be pretty good to even consider paying any fee.

Establishing credit might be a whole lot tougher if you are trying to clean up a poor credit history. You might want to contact one of the three credit-reporting services to see what your history looks like. I'll discuss this in detail in the coming pages. You'd be surprised to find that charge cards you rarely use or thought you cancelled might still show up as available credit. This could work against you if a potential lender feels you have too much access to credit. Be sure to close accounts you don't use and refrain from opening too many charge accounts as well (no matter what the in-store give-away is that's tempting you). When determining whether to loan you money, creditors use a process called credit scoring. They even look at the number of recent inquiries into your credit record. So write to any companies whose cards you no longer use. Ask them to cancel the account and report that to the credit services.

While it may seem daunting, you do have several paths out of deep debt. If you're really in trouble, seek help from Consumer Credit Counseling (1-800-388-2227) or the National Foundation for Consumer Credit (1-800-284-1723). Both are nonprofit organizations with centers nationwide. Some are free or charge a minimal fee to consolidate your debt and deal with creditors. Beware of fraudulent telemarketers who promise to clean up credit reports for a fee. Third-party collectors often don't have the ability to remove damaging information previously reported by a bank.

Debtors Anonymous might not work with those you owe, but the meetings and support will help you rely less on credit and make sound financial choices.

Filing for bankruptcy, in which you ask a federal judge to repay creditors on different terms (often cents on the dollar), should be your absolute last resort. Such a move stays on your credit report for ten years, and future creditors will shun you for car loans, mortgages, and credit lines. Be prepared that a vindictive spouse may threaten to take this route. If you have joint assets, however, these usually can't be touched, at least not by the creditors. They'll go after anything that exists solely in your husband's name. Also, overdue taxes, alimony, and child support are not discharged through bankruptcy.

Some other avenues you can take to clear credit card debt include:

1. Call creditors on your own to work out a repayment schedule. This shows that you're taking responsibility. Individual creditors are usually willing to work with you; they know that they stand a better chance of collecting more money this way than if you proceed with a bankruptcy filing.

2. Ask the creditor for a letter of agreement that holds you responsible for half of the debt. Bear in mind that you may not get anywhere with this request. However, if you explain that you are in the process of a divorce and can't pay the entire debt, the company might listen. Offer that if they'll send you this agreement in writing, you'll find the money to pay off your half.

3. Pay off the highest interest rates first. For instance, pay off a balance that's growing at 20 percent before working on the 11-percent problem. Transfer balances to other low-interest charge cards while you use other strategies in this list to pay off debt.

4. Revamp your budget by trimming expenses.

5. Tap savings accounts, money market funds, or stocks. (If jointly held these are considered marital property and you had better consult your attorney). If an income-earning account is yours alone, you are better off using that cash in getting rid of debt that costs you an additional 18 to 20 percent each month.

6. Consolidate debt under a home-equity loan. (This would require cooperation from your estranged spouse if you jointly hold the mortgage.)

7. Borrow from family if all other options aren't possible.

The best investment you can make if you are in credit card debt is to pay off these balances and then charge only what you can pay in full each month. Life is 18 to 20 percent more expensive for those who carry credit card balances, and you don't need the additional anxiety.

If you have marital debt that technically you are both liable for, you need to be very careful with any promises your husband might make to handle that debt. Even if it is ultimately written in a divorce settlement that he will pay the debt, you might still be held liable from the bank's point of view. To protect your credit, ask for the amount in the settlement and make sure you retire the debt before you spend the money on anything else.

Throw away any new credit card solicitations you receive. I don't recommend cutting up all your credit cards; having at least one major credit card can be handy. However, if temptation and impulsive use of cards is a problem, try freezing them. That's right. Freeze your credit cards in a small bowl of water. By the time they thaw, you may have rethought the need for a purchase and decided you can live without it.

Obtaining a Credit Report

It's to your advantage to determine what the credit reporting services think about you. This way, you can correct any errors before you apply for important credit, such as a mortgage or car loan (sometimes applied for on short notice). Lenders and banks often use your credit score to decide how much credit they will extend to you and at what rates. A good score of 650 or higher usually insures quick answers and competitive rates. If you score in the 500s, you may need to seriously strengthen your credit situation before attempting major purchases or business ventures (even as a home-based business).

In most states, the fee for this report is $10 to $15 or less; however, in some states you are eligible for a free report each year. If you've been denied credit, employment, insurance, or housing, you are entitled to a free copy of your credit report within sixty days of the denial. Beware of too-good-to-be-true offers received via the Internet whereby you're offered a free credit report, only to find out that you must try out a trial credit monitoring service. After the first free thirty days, you may find an ongoing monthly charge of $40 to $80 subscribing you to the service. Since you can frequently obtain these reports easily on your own, responding to such pitches is generally not worth it.

Here are the major reporting services:

Equifax
P.O. Box 105873
Atlanta, GA 30348
1-800-685-1111
www.equifax.com

Experian
P.O. Box 2104
Allen, TX 75013
1-800-583-4080
www.experian.com

TransUnion
P.O. Box 390
Springfield, PA 19064
1-800-916-8800
www.transunion.com

What if you spot an error in one of these reports? Send a certified letter (return receipt requested) to the credit agency, dis-
puting the entry. Explain that the entry in question is not yours or
include documentation proving that you paid a bill (a reason that
good record keeping is an important task). If the agency doesn't
respond to you within thirty days, send a second letter, this time
asking that the entry in question be removed from your credit
report immediately.

Protecting Yourself from Identity Theft

In our era of credit card solicitations and Internet purchases, everyone has heard about and at times worried about
identity theft. Georg Finder of Fullerton, California, is an
authority on credit damage and identity theft. Identify theft certainly affects your credit report, which we now know can have
long-lasting impact, but it also affects your job and relationships
potentially. Vigilance is your best protection, according to
Finder, who offers these tips:

Check your bills monthly to verify charges as yours.

Do not list your full name on mailing labels, but use merely
your first initial and last name or have a subscription come to
"the ___ family." This prevents thieves from passing themselves
off as you.

Before tossing anything into the recycling bin, **tear up any correspondence that includes your name and address,** and likewise remove mailing labels.

Be certain that your **credit card receipts block out some of the numbers** of your account. If not, notify the merchant that it's putting you at identity theft risk.

Raising Quick Cash

Many separated women find that they need to raise extra cash because their spouse left them in a financial lurch. Others want to move on with their lives, perhaps physically moving households. Still others want to build a financial cushion.

In fact, if for no other reason than to boost your savings, reading the following tips could help build that emergency fund everyone should have. Financial planners encourage people to stash away six to eight months of living expenses in a money market fund. If you lose your job, or if your estranged spouse loses his and falls behind in support payments, you have money to fall back upon. Peruse the following list to raise quick cash:

1. Hold a yard or garage sale. Refrain from selling treasured heirlooms, antiques, or personal belongings that your estranged spouse may claim later. Concentrate on items that have little significant or sentimental value, or those belonging to you or your children. If you don't want the bother of a sale, take the items to an auction house or flea market dealer.

2. Remember the line in Disney's *Toy Story* where one toy, fearing replacement, says, "We're next month's garage sale fodder for sure." **Toys and no-longer-needed baby items are sure bets for clearing clutter and raising cash.** List popular items in your local advertising supplement where sometimes anyone can place a free ad for things $25 or less. EBay is certainly another popular option, but beware of the fees and shipping, and price items accordingly. It doesn't sound like major cash, but if you consider all the baby items you may have in the attic or basement, old bikes, outdated software, games, or videotapes, you'd be surprised how quickly you amass a few hundred dollars.

3. Return never-worn clothing or unwrapped items to stores for full credit, a cash refund, or an even exchange. Of course, this means clothing with the tags on, appliances and toys never used, books never read, or compact discs never taken out of the shrink-wrap. Again, you'd be surprised how much money is returned to you. If no cash equivalent is available, take a store credit to purchase items you or your children do need. It's like going on a shopping spree without spending any money. Or, take the credit and shop ahead for birthday or holiday gifts.

4. Cash in or borrow against certain policies you might hold, including life insurance or savings bonds. Weigh the long-term consequences, however, especially if you must pay a penalty and are not a good saver once you get your finances back on track.

5. Ask for refunds for products that didn't live up to the manufacturer's promise, or services poorly rendered. No one likes a constant complainer, but if you don't speak up, you don't allow others to produce a better product or service. So if a restaurant meal isn't satisfactory, call the manager. If an item has a money-back guarantee, save the packaging details. In past years, I've been refunded money from lawn-care products, diaper and pharmaceutical companies, and restaurants. My online service provider granted me additional hours because of problems with the service.

6. Refinance your existing mortgage if you can obtain a new mortgage at least one percentage point below your existing rate. Of course, if the mortgage is jointly held, this might not be possible until a divorce is final.

7. File amended tax returns if you forgot a legitimate deduction that could have saved you money or enhanced a refund. If you were accustomed to filing joint returns, this might require cooperation. But if you filed separately, it's a fairly painless and completely legal way of seeing some cash. You don't need to hire an accountant, either. TurboTax or Kiplinger's Tax Cut software make amending returns and preparing new ones pretty simple.

8. Change your withholding at work. If you traditionally receive a large income-tax refund, this could be a sign that you're paying too much in withholdings. So fill out the appropriate papers to effect the change.

9. Work overtime periodically, ask for a raise, or boost your rates if you're self-employed. These strategies impact your career, but often people procrastinate in seeking solutions with their current job. More income could be around the corner.

10. Track down lost money. It would appear I'm not the only one embracing the cash fast concept because attorney Richard E. Schell penned *Quick Cash: A Guide to Raising Money During Life's Planned and Unplanned Changes.* Certainly, you're experiencing this now, and his book yields many ideas for raising money in a pinch, including what things to eliminate from the budget such as cable, cigarettes, eating out, subscriptions, and much more.

11. Moonlight. As I said while promoting my book *Writing for Quick Cash,* writing is the one form of moonlighting that the boss is least likely to complain about. Thus, I'm a firm believer in moonlighting for many reasons. My book provides dozens of writing opportunities, some needing no prior experience, just creativity and drive.

For starters, moonlighting simply has a different cache about it. But you must choose your options carefully. If you told your boss that you were planning to work from 6 to 10 P.M. at the local Kmart, she might not be too thrilled, and in fact, may feel a bit threatened that you're giving your all to another employer.

But tell that same boss that you're going home to put the finishing touches on an article for publication, and she might surprise you with, "Oh, isn't that nice. When will it appear? How did you come to write for that magazine?" You get the picture. Moonlighting gives many a chance to turn a hobby into profit, and since we generally enjoy our hobbies, we tend to be happier doing the work. Therein lies another advantage.

Certainly as author of another book, *Working at Home While the Kids Are There, Too*, I have ideas for you to consider in your brainstorming process:

Administrative assistance—if you know how to type or maintain a database, you could find your services in demand by churches, small businesses, or entrepreneurs who cannot afford full-time personnel. You could advertise your services to job seekers who need resumes and cover letters as well.

Arts and crafts, including writing as well as making pottery, baskets, holiday crafts, gift packages, and more.

Computer consulting, if you know the technical aspects, allows you to teach others how to operate their systems and software. You might design Web sites for small businesses, individuals, or organizations that do not have large enough budgets to employ a firm.

Tax preparation is a seasonal way of making additional income if you're qualified to do the work.

Tutoring allows you to put that undergraduate degree or the skills you've acquired to work, helping others at the same time. You might even pick up extra money by teaching a noncredit class through a continuing education program near you, meeting new adult friends at the same time.

Ask for financial aid if you're a student. Ask the college's financial aid office for assistance or turn to your reference librarian for resources like *The College Costs and Financial Aid Handbook* (published by the College Board) or the books published by Peterson's including *Financing Graduate School*. In addition, the U.S. Dept. of Education has free pamphlets and materials: Call 1-800-433-3243. Ask about Pell grants (scholarships that aren't to be repaid), Perkins loans, and Stafford loans (both with low-interest rates).

Consider establishing a 529 Plan for your own education. In the event that you don't need it, you can usually transfer this to one of your children, and in the short-term, you're not only saving toward education expenses, but in most states receiving a tax advantage as well. Check out this book's appendix for resources on college funding, both for yourself and for your children.

Living on a Budget
Whether you dig out of debt, save for your own legal defense fund, or spend less to invest more, learning to live on a budget is helpful.

Some families put this in written form and live by the numbers each month.

While I've never committed my plan to paper, I do believe budgets are great, even in your head. For me, living on less is a challenge that can even be fun.

First, figure out where your money is going. Write down each expense as you pay for it. Keep a notebook handy or create a worksheet on your computer. Software programs such as Quicken can help you track your expenditures and balance your checkbook each month, too.

Cut out unnecessary expenses and resist impulse purchases. Often, you don't need these items. If you add up incidentals like coffee, snacks, and lunches out, you could save hundreds of dollars each year.

Direct depositing your paycheck means you're less likely to ask for cash back that you spend indiscriminately. Avoid overdrafts or have overdraft protection (though balancing your account and using self-discipline is best). Watch ATM fees by withdrawing from machines in the system to avoid surcharges. Never opt for deferred billing.

Use only one major credit card which should have a thirty-day grace period between the end of the billing cycle and the payment due date. Don't take out cash advances or use those convenience checks they provide. Treated the same as cash advances, they're one of the most expensive ways of borrowing money (without the protection or dispute resolution credit cards carry).

Drive a used (perhaps gently used) automobile. You can read more about car purchases and care in Chapter Eight. Never—absolutely never—shop when you're hungry! If housing is a concern, shared living arrangements are becoming a trend. Here, two single moms share residence with their children in order to cut back on expenses. Check out co-abode.com, a successful online roommate matching service designed for single moms.

Accepting Help When You Need It

Many women who go through a separation feel uneasy about accepting help from family, friends, or organizations. Often, they feel as if they need so much—from emotional support and caring for the children to legal and financial help—they are too proud to ask for assistance when it's warranted. Swallow your pride temporarily and do ask for the support that could make your life and your children's lives that much better.

I understand what it's like. When my now ex-husband left, I certainly faced a loss of household income, yet I still had two children with some special needs. It seemed that everything had to be haggled over by attorneys who billed hundreds of dollars per hour. Fortunately, helpers stepped forward. I've had some attorneys deduct items from the bill whenever they could. Friends pitched in to watch my boys whenever possible, and they never charged a cent. My oldest son's school gave us free turkeys at Thanksgiving. The preschool director assured me that scholarship funds were available since the developmental delays of my youngest made preschool paramount.

Sure it felt uncomfortable. Where preschool was concerned, I had to live with a small amount of humiliation; the preschool program was featured in local newspapers. My mother-in-law was credited in newspapers as founder of the program—a program that now supported her grandson, so of course I felt angry. But I got over it, and I realized that someday I'd be able to help someone else in need. In fact, my current husband and I made a charitable gift to that preschool the year we got married as a way of remembering them. Other women whom I interviewed accepted scholarships, received food pantry supplies, and did whatever else they could when their husbands bailed. We women are resourceful, but sometimes we do need to take people up on their offers to assist us. After all, it's only temporary.

Pinching Pennies

Have you ever noticed that certain well-off friends seem to be the best budget-minded souls around? That's no accident. You don't get wealthy by wasting money.

Similarly, you don't eliminate money worries or boost your savings by spending frivolously. For now, conserve your funds—whether you have to, or merely choose to. Let's begin our quest for eliminating unnecessary expenses.

Around the House

Obtain a free energy audit from utility companies. An energy auditor will reveal places in your home where you could make improvements, conserve energy, and save money. For instance, you could insulate the outside of your hot water heater, turn the water temperature down, and set the thermostat back when you aren't home.

Limit water usage by taking shorter showers or filling the bathtub halfway. Use mostly cold water for laundry. Refrain from watering the lawn, or avoid this when the moisture will evaporate quickly. Install low-flow devices on showerheads and faucets.

Use open windows instead of air conditioning unless it's absolutely unbearable. Landscaping shaded areas around your home may also reduce air conditioning costs.

Purchase your phones rather than lease them. Eliminate optional services on your bill that you don't need. Make long-distance calls at off hours or send e-mail instead. Buy phone cards from wholesale clubs. Dial direct. Look up phone numbers yourself.

Traveling

Pump your own gas and get to know where the lowest-price gas stations are in your community. Keep your engine tuned and your tires inflated to the proper pressure.

Shop around for the best rental car rates. Check with your auto insurance agent before paying extra for rental insurance. Your existing policy may already cover you.

Book airline reservations in advance or at the last minute using reduced-price Internet fares. A Saturday night stay usually reduces costs.

Look for nonstop flights if your children must travel unaccompanied to visit their father. Some airlines have doubled surcharges for unaccompanied kids.

If you belong to a motor club, ask for discounts. Give your frequent flier mileage number for flights, rental cars, and hotel rooms. Look for last minute travel bargains too.

Eating and Entertaining

Avoid convenience stores. Warehouse clubs and low-priced food markets often reduce your grocery bill.

Clip coupons and combine them with on-sale items. I once trimmed a grocery receipt from $51.46 to $13.97 using my frequent customer card, manufacturer's coupons, and a $10 gift certificate. If you don't have a substantial coupon, buy generic store brands.

Purchase items on sale, including some produce and meats, and freeze them for later use. The same goes for cheese, tortillas, coffee, and refrigerated cookie dough. Sometimes, buying a small standalone freezer pays for itself in convenience and the savings from on-sale items.

Find creative uses for things. Stale (but not moldy) bread can be frozen to make French toast or bread crumbs. Freeze unused milk if you'll be traveling, and use it to make milk shakes when you get home. A surplus of Halloween candy can go into the freezer and be doled out for school lunches.

Invite friends for potluck dinners or pizza made from scratch. Have relatives over for breakfast or simple lunches instead of fancy dinners. Or cut main courses and opt for dessert and coffee.

Staying Healthy

Take care of your health with preventative care, including dental cleanings and routine exams. If ill, go to the doctor before you get sicker.

When at the doctor, ask for prescription drug samples. Explain that your health plan doesn't include prescription coverage (or has a high copay). Often physicians have a stash in a supply cabinet.

When getting a prescription, ask for the generic alternative if it's available. Ask for your doctor to write this on the actual prescription.

Know where the discount pharmacies are, and call to compare drug prices. Consider mail-order or online pharmacies as well as warehouse clubs.

Use coupons for over-the-counter medications or vitamins, or buy generic store brands, comparing the ingredients and also watching for sales. Seek a refund if there is a guarantee on a product that didn't work well. Some prescribed medicines even have rebates. Or, stores with a pharmacy offer gift certificates if you fill your prescription with them. Thus, you might be $25 richer merely choosing their pharmacy.

Go to free health screenings and sign up for low-cost or no-cost health insurance (usually for kids) if eligible.

Participate in research studies if the subject matter fits and if you live near a major university, teaching hospital, or the National Institutes of Health (or Mental Health) in Washington, D.C.

Use the local dental school for cleanings, dental work, or orthodontia, often at less expensive rates.

Outfitting the Kids and Yourself

Buy clothes at end-of-season sales. This works for Christmas sweaters to swimsuits and beach towels. At a January clearance, I snagged a casual coat that was missing two buttons for under $10. Turns out, extra buttons came sewn inside the coat.

Keep an eye out at yard and garage sales for kids' play clothes and dress-up treasures. Browse the racks of secondhand clothing stores. I know of professional, middle-class families who purchase jackets, costumes, and clothing for recreation at thrift shops. Visit yard sales in exclusive neighborhoods. You'll find many selections for yourself, including suits for work or evening wear—even accessories at more affordable prices. Kids' clothing will often be the better brand names.

Choose next year's Halloween costumes at more than half off the day after Halloween. But don't wait too long because merchandise like this goes fast.

If you have siblings of the same sex, make use of **hand-me-down** items. They are new to younger siblings, especially if they weren't even born yet to see them worn!

Shop at stores where **merchandise is guaranteed** or **discounts** given. Sears' KidVantage program earns you discounts. And with boys, when the knees on jeans invariably rub through, the pants are automatically replaced in the same size.

Swap clothing with relatives or friends who have children the same genders as your own. If asked for gift suggestions from grandparents or anyone else, mention clothing that the kids might need.

Your Christmas tree isn't the only item needing trimming when you're separated. Chances are you can free up some extra money by making the holidays more affordable. And if conserving finances isn't a good enough reason, think of your sanity. Since you've already got enough stress, here are ways to simplify the holidays.

Trimming Holiday Expenses

Shop during sales throughout the year. I found Dilbert magnets, pens, and pencils on clearance in office and bookstores. One year, I stocked up on kids' wooden train tracks and accessories. These virtually never go on sale, but with a store's liquidation, I saved 30 percent plus an additional 10 percent with a frequent-purchase card.

Stash away small or token gifts by shopping early. Sometimes your employer or clients offer freebies. Save some of these to include in holiday giving.

Take advantage of after-holiday sales. Why anyone would purchase Christmas lights, garland, artificial trees, cards, and wrapping paper at full price is beyond me. All of these items are at least 50 percent off the day after Christmas. Throughout January, prices are slashed even further. The day after Valentine's Day, Easter, and other holidays, stock up on decorations or party supplies for next year.

Make homemade gifts for some relatives, friends, and teachers. Something as simple as homemade bread or cookies can be wrapped with festive ribbon tied around cellophane.

Stock up on baking supplies during the holidays when stores run sales. Watch your Sunday newspaper supplements for coupons too. With a sale and coupon combination, you'll have cookie and cake decorating supplies for other occasions throughout the year.

Create a grab bag with extended family to cut down on the number of gifts. Ship presents early so that you can mail packages at the lowest rates.

Send virtual greeting cards to those with online access. Or, use postcards and let your children create a family Web page that serves as your holiday newsletter. Send thank-you messages the same way.

Entertain simply with potluck dinners or merely coffee and dessert get-togethers.

Suggest items that you or your children need to those who ask for ideas. Often, relatives and friends want to help by providing toys or clothing that might strain your budget.

Settle on one large gift if your children are old enough to understand. For instance, if your kids could use a computer for schoolwork, such a purchase makes sense (and might qualify as a partial tax writeoff if you're self-employed or moonlight from home).

Combine giving, especially if you and your estranged spouse have an amicable relationship. No sense both of you buying holidays gifts for your children. Put both names on one set of gifts.

Donate with a little creativity. If you're conserving cash, you can still be generous with gifts of your time or gently used toys or outgrown clothing to food pantries and social service agencies.

Managing Your Financial Future

A marital separation often places women at a financial crossroads. Even if you master nothing else but your finances, I can assure you that you'll step into the future with a lot more confidence and security.

So what about that future? It's there, although at this juncture merely getting through today and tomorrow seems a challenge. The wise woman plans for her financial future and avoids the mistake of making emotional decisions versus practical ones.

Beating a Lack of Self-Confidence

Some women procrastinate, executing poor financial decisions because of their own lack of self-confidence where money is concerned. Particularly if they had husbands who were the primary breadwinners, managed their investments, and paid the bills, the thought of instantly moving into these roles is daunting.

Women who work in jobs that don't carry clout may also lack self-confidence. Mind you, I believe the day-care provider is just as capable of managing her assets as the vice president of a corporation. Unfortunately, as women we sometimes talk ourselves into a diminished role. Our self-esteem suffers in more than our career.

If this strikes a chord with you, just remember that most women, however, can double a dollar pretty darn fast—faster in fact than most men can dial their brokers!

College Concerns and Retirement Nest Eggs

As mothers, we are all concerned that our children obtain a college education, especially if we had that privilege. Few of us, however, can get the cooperation of our spouses or ex-husbands (sometimes the same ones we helped put through school!) to ensure this for our sons and daughters. Many states do not mandate that fathers help with higher education, even if they can afford to do so. Some states have legislation that makes child support available through college, and I know of courageous legislators who have proposed similar bills. That's some help, at least. It's painful to see your estranged run off, frivolously spending your children's college funds. However, financial planners can't emphasize enough the importance of securing your own retirement before financing a child's education.

"I can't do that," you might say, feeling as I did that the mere thought was selfish. But it's true. Your children can obtain loans and grants. They can also complete their degrees in intervals, over a period of years. No one else besides you will secure your retirement. And since many women lack pensions and live longer than men, don't think you're set if you plan to remarry. Often, if your new spouse has children, you won't be the only one inheriting his nest egg, and especially if they are minor children, he may choose to leave it exclusively to them.

Don't beat yourself up about boosting your own savings. Actually, it's better if assets are not accumulated in your children's names. When they apply for financial aid, they stand a better chance of obtaining it if they are poor and you have the money. Also, under the Uniform Gift to Minors Act, any money left to your children is theirs. They can spend it on college tuition or a sports car. This is another reason to seriously consider asset allocation. With the proliferation of 529 savings plans, you have more control over the money you invest for a child's education, making it less likely they can run off to buy a sports car at age eighteen because you can transfer the money to other family members, if necessary.

Interestingly enough, if you remarry you may find that a stepparent's income counts toward financial aid calculations as this is factored in under the student's family unit. "Applicants may not exclude stepparent financial information, nor does the need analysis methodology segregate custodial and stepparent data in determining eligibility for aid," says Dr. Margorie Engel, president and CEO of the Stepfamily Association of America. "This holds true even if you keep your money separate and use the 'Married, Filing Separately' form for tax returns."

Colleges have the potential to alter the federal assessment of your family's ability to pay for college by supplementing information about extenuating circumstances, says Engel. Once a student is admitted to a school, then a family can work with a financial aid officer on a much more personal basis. But it's important first to meet all of the application deadlines and financial aid requests. In order to claim extenuating circumstances, Engel advises that you be prepared to discuss who claims the child on their federal tax return, how long you've been divorced and remarried, any agreements regarding college funding, other children that the biological father or stepdad supports, or whether abuse may preclude involvement from a biological parent. Frankly, this seems like another area that those making our federal guidelines need to address because it adversely impacts more women and their children, since women are often custodial parents.

All hope is not lost, however. If your child really is determined to have an education, there is financial aid available. I learned of one high-achieving high school senior who grew up without a father's income, and after watching her mother struggle working three jobs, was inspired, not daunted by the odds. Against all advice, she applied to several colleges with varying tuition rates. She received at least two full scholarships to Ivy League schools, including room, board, and tuition. Check the appendix of this book for pertinent Web sites, and be sure to keep an eye on the annual college issue of *U.S. News & World Report*, in which schools are not only ranked for academics, but also for their financial aid generosity.

Using a Financial Planner

Years ago when newly married, one of the best decisions I made was to sit down with a financial planner to analyze my finances. Believe me, there wasn't much to analyze, and I'm certainly not making Danielle Steel royalties now! But the mere act meant I committed the time to studying where I was, setting goals for where I wanted to be, and figuring out what was important financially. It also established a pattern of regular saving and dollar-cost averaging (more on this later). The planner who helped me came from a personal referral, and while he did not charge a fee for advice given, he was making a commission on the mutual funds or insurance policies in which my husband and I invested. Financial planners are compensated this way, or else they charge for their counsel. Years later, I recognized the appeal of no-load funds. I transferred money into new accounts that I managed on my own through reading and investment education. Most important, I learned early on to set aside money. That lesson endures over time.

In the initial stages of separation, you probably aren't thinking of using a financial planner, or a certified divorce planner (CDP). You have an attorney giving you most of your advice. However, as you travel the litigation path and get closer to a financial settlement, you should analyze your finances, perhaps with professional help. Your attorney is trained to interpret laws, not tax regulations or long-term financial plans. Certified divorce planners charge an hourly rate similar or as varied as divorce attorneys, but some also commit to one lump sum to complete your case from start to finish.

Becoming a Savvy Investor

From the start, let's make one thing clear. Handling money isn't like brain surgery. No one will die, even if you make a few errors along the way.

Surprisingly, there are a number of truly simple steps you can take to increase your financial prowess. Reading is paramount. Read the business page. Peruse *The Wall Street Journal* at work or in the library. Read magazines devoted to personal finances, particularly for strategic end-of-year money moves. Don't just toss the prospectus you receive into the recycling bin.

By reading literature regarding the mutual funds or stocks you've invested in, you get a clear picture of how your funds are performing. For instance, if you own multiple mutual funds, review the stock picks chosen for you. It's possible that you're duplicating your efforts and might be paying unnecessary management fees. Consolidate your accounts, if that's the case.

In addition, it's wise to expand your understanding of personal finance. Attend financial seminars and bookstore discussions featuring financial authors. You might even try watching the financial channels. One year rather than football, I watched the "Money Bowl" on CNBC on New Year's Day.

Web surfers can take advantage of the Internet to learn about mutual funds and stock performance. Most investment companies provide a wealth of information to aid your decision-making. Just do a search with any of the major search engines. Quicken is a leading manufacturer of personal finance and small business software, and they have a Web site filled with tools and information. If you're in the market for better buys on insurance, mortgage rates, or credit cards, the Internet can help you as well. Here are a few more tips:

Call the Certified Financial Planner Board of Standards for the free booklet, "What You Should Know about Financial Planning." You can reach them at 1-888-237-6275.

In **"Social Security: What Every Woman Should Know,"** you'll read that if your marriage lasted ten years or more, you may be eligible to receive benefits on your ex-husband's record. Visit a Social Security office near you and ask for this information, free of charge.

Write for the Energy Savers booklet, c/o Post Office Box 3048, Dept. P, Merrifield, VA 22116, or call 1-800-363-3732. It's got money-saving tips, too.

Many continuing education departments have noncredit courses that teach you how to read the stock pages, understand bonds, or build a balanced portfolio. Each woman's situation is different, depending upon her age, earning capacity, goals, and needs, so it's nearly impossible to give blanket advice.

Having said that, however, there are a few tried and true investment strategies. For starters, set up an IRA, SEP-IRA, or Keogh if you're self-employed (or a 401(k) through your employer) and contribute to it at regular intervals. For instance, had you invested regularly throughout the worst decade of the twentieth century (1928–1938), you still could have averaged 7 percent per year in returns despite the Great Depression. That's the beauty of dollar-cost averaging—investing evenly over time for long-term gain.

In addition, reinvest all dividends and treat bonuses or found money as just that. Don't rush right out to spend a windfall. Sock it away into savings. Over time, the stock market has been the highest performing investment vehicle most people have. Of course, there is risk, but the object is to buy and hold. Do this when you are young and by retirement, you'll be in for quite a nice surprise.

Finally, focus on no-load mutual funds or direct purchase stock plans. Charles Carlson has written *No-Load Stocks*. As he explains in his book, a surprising number of companies offer stock to individual investors in what are known as direct investment plans (DIPs) and dividend reinvestment plans (DRIPs). Investors might only purchase a few shares, certainly a lot fewer than a round lot of one hundred shares that most brokers would require. Their money continues to compound thanks to dividends, stock splits, and very low investment expenses. As soon as you accumulate one hundred shares of a company stock, it's wise to request the actual stock certificates. This way, you can sell quickly if you need to by going to a brokerage firm (discount and Internet brokers would charge less than full-service firms).

An Important Rule for the Road

Before you set out on your investment journey, remember an important caveat. Make no quick financial moves for at least six months after your separation, especially those that lock you into an investment or carry a high amount of risk. Give yourself time to ponder your choices, educate yourself, and make wise moves. And, check out the resources in this book's appendix.

Affording the Great Escape

At some juncture during your separation, you or one of your children will likely remark, "Let's get out of here!" Indeed, new scenery allows you to recharge and see yourself as a work in progress.

But what if you're accustomed to vacationing with an extra set of hands, not to mention the added income a dual-career family often lends to the effort? Let's explore some options because they could be essential to your own mental health and to your children's sense of normalcy:

Take out-of-town friends up on offers to visit. Do you know anyone in a fun city your kids haven't visited?

Pool costs with another single-parent family, driving to a destination or renting accommodations.

Accumulate frequent flier miles, or if relatives ask how they can help and you know they won't use their miles accrued, ask them to transfer the miles to you.

Join an alumni tour, a church outing, or some other singles group. Use caution, but don't allow your single status to keep you from exploring the globe.

Combine a business trip with an extended stay. Sure, it might mean having childcare or asking another adult to accompany you to watch the kids while you attend meetings. But if you are going someplace fun with your expenses covered (and if an adult relative is willing to pick up her tab), this makes a lot of sense.

Learn how to do Disney on less. For starters, stay at one of their value resorts on the property, or choose to stay off-site at a budget-priced motel, though resort guests use Disney transportation free of charge. Decide which parks are most important and stay fewer days. Plan your arrival early one morning and your departure late at night if you are flying. This eliminates another night's lodging. Bring snacks and eat at food-court restaurants rather than sit-down venues. Two small children might split a children's meal, if the portions are plentiful. Purchase Disney trinkets at home (such as autograph books, clothing, and the like) when you spot these on sale. Stash them in your suitcase to present as alternatives to pricey merchandise.

If Remarriage Is on the Horizon

If a wayward spouse has jeopardized your financial position, think carefully before co-mingling finances again. I am not suggesting that you never remarry or take out a mortgage with a new husband. Prenuptial agreements are discussed in detail in the last chapter of this book. You should definitely look at that section if you are planning to remarry.

Chapter Seven
Carving Out a Career

What's a woman to do when she's been predominantly a helpmate, mother, and homemaker for at least the past several years of her marriage, and suddenly she's faced with the added responsibility of becoming primary breadwinner?

During a separation, some women answer this question with a sense of panic. This chapter will help you carve out a career path that's right for you, and move ahead in the work you currently pursue. It will deal with the necessary steps to finding work—creating resumés and cover letters, identifying companies and getting noticed by decision-makers, interviewing and following up, as well as career-boosting strategies.

When my own separation began, I had a career, but it sure was curtailed. When my youngest son, Alex, was born prematurely two years before, I had put everything on the back burner until his health improved. Finding myself alone was not what I had anticipated. I did panic a little, wondering if I'd be able to build my home-based writing business back and get the work accomplished while continuing to meet my children's needs. Or, should I opt right away for a full-time job? Of course, I felt pressured by my estranged husband. Suddenly the writing I did, which once brought him pride and a few nice perks, became "that hobby" I worked at.

But through it all, I held my head high. I always looked at the classified ads (though, as we'll learn, this isn't the best avenue for job searches). I went on several interviews, and mailed dozens more resumés and letters. In one instance, where I knew full well I was qualified for a special events position, I helped a good friend of mine write a resumé for the same company. Turns out that she got a job, and someone else was hired for the spot I coveted. But I did the right thing in helping her, and I'm convinced it was an indication I was still needed on the homefront.

In those initial weeks, another wise advisor put it bluntly. "The object here isn't to run to the nearest McDonald's and get hired. Give yourself time to find what's best for you." How very true! Time does have a way of lighting our paths, even professionally.

Time also grants us the opportunity to dream a little, to assess where we are and where we might want to be in our career, and to explore strategies of getting there. For some, this might mean a total assessment of employable skills, aptitudes, and personality traits that give us guidance. It might also mean going for a degree you never obtained or registering for the College-Level Examination Program (CLEP) whereby you demonstrate college-level achievement through a program of exams in undergraduate college courses. Nearly 3,000 colleges grant either credit or advanced standing for CLEP exams, and for the cost of the exam (approximately $50), it sure beats thousands of dollars spent on tuition for a class you may not need to take. Of course, your next educational goal might be a graduate degree, especially after you've had some work experience or exposure to other fields of study, which might enhance your career opportunities. As long as you explore all your options, you'll do just fine.

Starting from Scratch

Though that sense of panic is indeed very real for some women, I hope this chapter will help put your mind at ease. Even if you lack much formal education and have confined yourself to homemaking or volunteer work in recent years, you do have skills that will translate into the workplace. Career counselors call these "transferable skills." Furthermore, you have more options than women faced thirty or forty years ago.

The shelves of your local bookstore or library probably have dozens of resources to help you discover actual job titles, salary potential, and qualifications. If you're looking for a handy workbook to help you identify your skill set and talents, turn the pages of *101 Ways to Power Up Your Job Search*. Another favorite book of mine is *Do What You Are: Discover the Perfect Career for You Through the Secrets of Personality Type* by Paul Tieger and Barbara Barron-Tieger. This book is based upon a popular assessment used by career counselors called the Myers Briggs Type Inventory (MBTI). Though it is not as accurate as taking the formal test and having it interpreted by a career counselor, this book presents the concept in perhaps the least expensive way.

Career Assessments

There is a wealth of career assessments that you can take, often through adult education or women's career centers. Find these centers through your local community college, university, or women's center. Popular assessments include John Holland's Self-Directed Search, the Strong Interest Inventory, the Campbell Interest and Skill Survey (CISS), and the Position Classification Inventory. The MBTI is perhaps the best known, based upon Katherine Briggs' and Isabel Myers' study of Carl Jung's function type theory, measuring preferences, not skills. Through a series of questions, you discover your preferences for how you gain energy (extroversion or introversion), how you gather information (sensing or intuition), how you make decisions (thinking or feeling), and how you approach the world (judging or perceiving). Indeed, it's fun to discover this information about yourself, but if you truly wish to implement it properly, the feedback from a counselor or psychologist is quite useful.

Your MBTI can change over time while, interestingly enough, some of the other assessment scores (such as the Strong) may not shift dramatically but remain similar to your scores that you took while in high school, for instance. Some of these tests foster your dreams, scaling your likes and dislikes of current jobs against your ideal job. Also know that going through a life transition such as a separation or divorce can also influence your type. If you're planning your future on a number of fronts, the MBTI might be worth taking once more. Naomi Quenk explains this variance in your MBTI during times of stress in her book *Was That Really Me? How Everyday Stress Brings Out Our Hidden Personality*.

Next Steps: Spot Trends

Become a trend spotter as best you can when you begin a career makeover. This gives you a feel for what occupations are hot and which aren't hiring as well. Should you need to take additional courses or obtain another degree, you'll make wiser decisions. Read books, peruse the daily paper, and collect magazine articles. Some publications that I've found particularly helpful in spotting trends include *USA Today* and *The Wall Street Journal* as well as *Futurist* or *American Demographics*, which keep a pulse on consumer trends (these are also a bit pricey, so you might want to check out your local library's periodical holdings). Continue to spot trends by listening to talk radio, televised interviews, and newscasts. Many publishers offer fun books that explore the possibilities—*Changing Careers for Dummies®*, *Cool Careers for Dummies®*, *The Everything® Hot Careers Book*, and *The Everything® Alternative Careers Book*.

Of course, if you work in a particular industry, there might be trade journals to keep your eyes on. Use *The Gale Directory of Publications*, available at your local library, to help you find these professional periodicals. While there, check out *Standard & Poor's Register of Corporations, Directors, and Executives* as well as the *Encyclopedia of Associations* to find groups with membership rosters that might be useful. Your reference librarian might also have a copy of the *Occupational Outlook Handbook*, published by the U.S. Department of Labor, Bureau of Labor Statistics. This handy resource gives you an overview of jobs needed now and into the future.

That takes care of the marketplace, but now let's turn our attention to you. Richard Nelson Bolles brought us one of the best-selling job search books ever with *What Color Is Your Parachute?* It's a quirky title for sure, but it demystifies the job-hunting process. The author guides you in learning to look for signs of achievement in yourself. You consider profound questions like what type of work makes you happy and what you feel you have to offer.

Take a legal pad and list all your skills. Really think here. Have you paid the family bills for years and researched purchases (including home computers and software)? Have you juggled the schedules of everyone in your household? What about volunteer work at church or the PTA? Have you held positions of authority on church or civic boards? Have you ever volunteered for a political campaign? Are you comfortable getting up in front of groups, teaching, or soliciting a cause?

This gives you something to fuel your brainstorming. Describe these roles according to essential workplace skills such as organizational, research, and budgetary skills; multitasking; effective time management; and leadership responsibilities. In addition, you might have excellent promotion and sales skills—and perhaps creative talents—if you've produced newsletters, reports, or fliers.

Educational Training

I've already touched upon seeking an undergraduate degree or finishing one you may have started years before. It's never too late to apply to a college, university, or vocational school to realize your goals and dreams. Colleges and universities increasingly offer flexible schedules (such as weekend classes, or every other weekend schedules), online degree programs, and other options to help you earn a certificate, degree, or other necessary credential. Don't let certain obstacles stand in your way. Often as a single woman or single mother, you may find financial aid in addition to onsite childcare programs at many campuses. Some schools offer specific programs, which are funded by state grants such that there are no (or very minimal) costs involved. Career development workshops, whereby you learn keyboarding, medical or legal terminology, and specific software programs are also wise as these improve your skills, for more advanced education or the workplace.

Going back to school doesn't have to appear as daunting as it might seem. You can reframe this as an opportunity that will force you out of the house and into the company of new friends and business contacts. It will also help to take your mind off the negative influences you're currently facing, such as litigation or disagreements with your estranged or ex-husband. Frankly, it might be a breath of fresh air in your life, challenging your mind and opening many new doors to your future.

Going for a Graduate Degree

Now might be the time to contemplate graduate school. By furthering your education, you are increasing your earning potential and providing a new focus and a much-needed confidence boost in your professional skills. A study conducted at Stanford University School of Medicine shed light on one bright fact: Women with advanced degrees were often happier than their less-educated peers.

You can always take classes on a part-time basis. Thus, it may be wise to take the required standardized tests (GRE, LSAT, etc.) and do a little research. Peterson's publishes a wide range of guides that you can discover in the bookstore or at *www.petersons.com*. If financing graduate studies is a concern, be sure to check out *Financing Graduate School* by Patricia McWade.

Exploring Your Career Options

Truly, your options are diverse as you determine a new career path or consider altering the one you've already established. With a prepared resumé in hand, or at least drafted, you have a clearer vision of your skills. You still might want to revise and polish that resumé to tailor it to a particular job or work arrangement.

Full-time work might best serve your needs, especially if you depend upon benefits. Given your particular profession, you may find it difficult to work a reduced schedule. I know of a friend who, due to companies going out of business, mergers, and the corporate transfer of her spouse, has treated each search for a full-time position as a job within itself. But she's succeeded, after literally hundreds of informational interviews. I've also heard that for each ten thousand dollars in salary, it may take that number of months to locate the ideal position.

Part-time employment does give you additional flexibility, and actually can come with benefits, depending upon the company. If you have young children who require your care, this might be an option that appeals to you. While economics might be a primary concern and motivation in finding a job, you must also look at quality-of-life issues. Does your attorney feel that you are a candidate for alimony? If so, you may want to hold off on securing a hectic full-time position where you'll struggle to meet all of the family management tasks that fall to you.

One friend volunteered time in a school district that later offered her a part-time teaching position. Another established herself as a full-time employee, but later asked for a more flexible schedule with part-time hours. Because she'd proved her worth, she got the arrangement that she requested.

Temporary employment is no longer synonymous with secretarial work. According to Peggy O'Connell Justice, who wrote *The Temp Track*, the temporary service industry now includes engineers, accountants, writers and editors, computer programmers, paralegals, managers and executives, as well as medical professionals. By working as a temporary employee, you get an inside perspective of the company you're assigned to. Here you can become a known quantity and prove your worth. You try out jobs and fields before committing to a contract, you gain experience and contacts, and you add to your resumé. The work is flexible enough that you can often choose when and where you work, for a day, a week, or several months. Temping allows you to learn from cutting-edge companies and leaders who are going places. Finally, signing up with an active temporary service provides fairly quick cash.

Look to the employment section of your Yellow Pages, or use the help-wanted ads or trade magazines to see which firms are in your area, and which specialize in placing one sort of professional over another.

Of course other alternatives are telecommuting or working from home in your own business venture. Telecommuting is more accepted in some regions than in others, largely due to traffic concerns and lack of office space. Some employers, however, will want to see your work style before allowing you to work off business premises. To bring a boss around to this way of thinking, be prepared with a list of concrete examples of how you've made the telecommuting arrangement work in the past, or how you will now. Focus on how it's improved productivity, for you (or others in your organization) and what positive impact it's had on the bottom line. Initially, and then periodically afterward, you'll want to be visible so plan on making visits to your employer's office.

Perhaps you've always had the urge to be self-employed. A good idea ignites the entrepreneurial fire within a lot of women. As I found out while researching *Working at Home While the Kids Are There, Too*, there are myriad paths you can follow to pursue entrepreneurial ambitions and still manage your family. Many women who are happy in full-time or part-time careers begin a venture on the side, moonlighting in a sense. Just don't let any visions of the perfect workplace cloud your judgment, for as convenient as working at home is, it has its struggles and perils. You'll be your own boss, set your own hours, dress the way you want, start and end the day when you want. No more traffic. No more putting up with people you'd just as soon ignore.

However, you'll have the temptation to slack off and the very real need to discipline yourself. Casual clothes can wreak havoc on your confidence; home workers jokingly call it "the slob factor." And for some people, isolation can lead to loneliness. If you have a hard time with discipline and deadlines, then explore telecommuting and working out of your home only on occasion.

Before you set out on a business venture, do realize there are risks that go along with the opportunities. Nothing takes the place of doing your homework and research.

Networking Boosts Self-Confidence

The best way to shelve that panic of re-entering the workforce is to get out and mingle with other adults. Start putting yourself in settings where professionals get together. Look for a variety of networking and business groups comprised of women in your community. Some of these meet for breakfast or lunch, sometimes at restaurants or even the larger bookstores. Most of the time, you can join these meetings informally on a few occasions before you might be required to become a dues-paying member (if there is a fee at all).

Call your local chamber of commerce for luncheon dates and after-hours gatherings. Investigate professional organizations that apply to your career. In the field of public relations and communications, groups like Public Relations Society of America (PRSA) and International Association of Business Communicators (IABC) have local chapters. If you can't find listings for their meetings in the business pages of your newspaper, call the department chairperson at a nearby university. Many national organizations maintain Web sites with this information.

Adult re-entry or women's centers at community colleges have information and counseling, perhaps even testing, to help you objectively determine a proper career path. Don't overlook the career placement office of a school you once attended. Alumni groups might meet in your area, and through social events or merely telephoning fellow alumni, you can often find a very friendly and helpful network of professionals willing to grant you informational interviews or share contacts.

Search Methods

What do most people do when they are in the market for a job or career advancement? They browse the newspaper classified ads or mail a massive stack of resumés to potential employers. Unfortunately, only a small percentage of these efforts succeed. Of course, it only takes one great interview and subsequent offer to make a career move, and classified ads shouldn't be ignored entirely. Still, you need to broaden your job-hunting horizons.

Read *What Color Is Your Parachute?* to learn the practical lessons of job searching. You will gain strength and confidence when you realize that you aren't the only one trying to uncover the hidden job market. Thus, when you begin your search, knocking on people's doors, sending letters, or phoning to follow up your correspondence, you'll realize that we've all been along this journey at one point or another.

Depending upon your city, there might be books or directories pertaining to your region. Ask the reference librarian or do a search on the Internet. For instance, Adams Media publishes the *JobBank* series of books dealing with major metropolitan cities, listing contact names and addresses.

Professionally published directories are great, but you can create your own handy binder of information. As I've already indicated, I took time to learn about the job market, potential employers, and the qualifications they seek. While scanning the classifieds, I spotted interesting articles in the business section and often clipped out and dated materials.

The next step is to paste or catalog this information in a binder, sectioned off however you choose. Your organizational system could be alphabetical or categorized by industry. It could contain years' worth of classified ads and background material

Having such a resource compiled over time, helps you identify hiring patterns and qualifications. If you aren't currently ready to make a career move, you can hang on to this information. In some cases, you'll get a feel for courses you might need to take or skills you need to update. When you do decide to search, you'll have a company, perhaps even a name and a phone number, from which to begin. Call to update your information. Contacts move on to other jobs and companies merge or relocate. Still, you'll find this is not only a tool in your search, but it aids in the important step of obtaining informational interviews, meetings with decision-makers for the express purpose of picking their brains, gathering contacts, and learning about different companies. In addition, ask your alumni office at the college or university you attended for a printout of graduates working in your field. Approach them as an alum-made-good, asking them to share some insights on their success.

Use *The Adams Executive Recruiters Almanac* published by Adams Media to find search firms and employment agencies that might also help you in your job search. Typically, search firms handle higher-level positions than employment agencies, where you might be required to pay a fee yourself for the matching service. No matter if a search firm or an employment agency assists you or if you do the legwork yourself, searching for a new job creates a certain level of stress. Remember to schedule daily time for your search so that you feel productive. Keep up on industry developments and contacts, and considering temping to stay current. Do some of your searching away from home (like at the library or coffee shop) just to diversify your surroundings. Exercise regularly, get enough sleep, and generally take care of yourself, so that your mood and motivation stay high.

Writing Your Resumé and Cover Letters

With plenty of excellent books to guide you and show examples of successful resumés in your chosen field, I'm certainly not going to duplicate that advice here. Use this section to gather the data you'll need for your resumé, whether you do it yourself or rely upon the expertise of a professional writer or career counselor.

Using that legal pad, which already lists your job search notes, now list achievements such as dollar figures produced, funds raised, or percentages of sales and productivity you increased. Write down the job responsibilities or projects you initiated and completed. Employers like to see signs of self-motivation and accomplishment. If you self-financed your education, note this also. Don't forget military background, educational credentials, outside interests, and special honors or achievements, even in professional or volunteer organizations. (One caution: If you list too many pro bono activities, a potential employer might wonder when you have time to work).

When you finish listing, make a first draft of your resumé. Today using Microsoft Word is by far the preferred format because you're often asked to send an attached file to an e-mail. Producing an attractive resumé is fairly simple with *simple* definitely the integral word here. Unless you are applying for a job in a creative field like graphic design or advertising, it's best to create a conservative resumé. Less is more; leave the jazzy elements behind. You do, however, want to make it a quick scan for a hiring manager's eyes, and for a computer that will electronically scan the document. That means using plenty of white space, variations of type size, and some bold-faced type and bullets.

Today's resumés limit a lot of personal information that used to be standard. There truly is no need to list marital status or age, so don't worry that the separation will come up. In this litigious society, many employers prefer that you do not include this information. I also prefer a summary of skills and assets at the top of your resumé rather than an objective; an objective might needlessly disqualify you for a particular job.

Resumé writing requires a clear and tight writing style and effective use of action verbs. A potential employer will be impressed by your actions. Wording phrases in the passive voice with "is," "was," or "were" constructions doesn't give you the responsibility for your accomplishments. So brainstorm on yet another sheet of paper for appropriate action verbs or use the lists provided in resumé books.

The format you use is entirely subjective. Most formats work backwards, listing employment history and educational background from the most current position held. A functional resumé is best if you've worked on and off over the years. Shed as much positive light onto bad situations as possible.

Women concerned with a gap because they have been out of the workforce could call their document a professional briefing. Author Martin Yate told me this works best as you respond to classified ads or posted jobs. One side of the document lists the ad's requirements, and the other side showcases your qualifications that match. It's an innovative approach, but it should draw attention away from any employment gaps.

The same approach works for cover letters. Remember to use energetic language, not pompous prose. There is a line between taking responsibility and bragging. You definitely want to shine and have your self-confidence show through. Do focus on what you can offer the employer, not on what you like about them (at least until you've been asked this question in an interview).

Double-check and proofread obvious details, such as the name of your contact and company, addresses, and other data. From the employer's point of view, if you can't get these details correct, what will you let slip by on the job? Make certain that your materials are printed well. A commercial printer is probably your best bet, but if you do print them on your computer's printer, make certain you have a good toner cartridge.

The length of your resumé and cover letter depends on several things. A younger woman's resumé won't demand the length that an experienced professional's would at mid-life. Routinely, a resumé is best limited to two pages. I'd think long and hard before using three pages, unless you're applying for a high-powered executive position. If after two pages, you still have more to include, you might try a stand-alone sheet of accomplishments. This might look better than a mammoth resumé.

Do be aware that headhunters, personnel officers, and others check facts and credentials. Thus there is a difference between highlighting responsibilities and inventing fiction. Don't go down this path; it will surely haunt you.

Interviewing and Following Up

Entire books are written about acing the interview and being prepared for what a potential interviewer might ask you. Obviously you cannot memorize answers, but you want to come across as a professional with personality. Take the edge off that nervous feeling by being prepared and having knowledge of the company you interview with. Use your library and the resources in this chapter to prepare a short list of questions to ask.

Do dress appropriately, wearing conservative attire that's professional—not sexy. Leave the plunging necklines, flashy jewelry, black stockings, and stilettos in the closet (for future dates, of course). If you're just building a business wardrobe, you can get by with two basic suits in neutral colors (best without a pattern) that go together, another skirt, a separate pair of pants and a different jacket (this one could have a subtle pattern to it), four to six blouses, and at least two pair of nice black shoes. You really don't have to go broke.

During the interview, you may be asked some questions for which you don't have easy answers. But you can be your own spin doctor. Why do you have limited experience? Reiterate that they won't find anyone willing to work as hard or learn as fast as you would, no matter how many candidates they interview. Dismissed from another position? Tell them that you had fundamentally different views on what that job entailed. Why are you re-entering the workforce? Because you've had ample time to rethink your career and identify your own strengths and a new direction. Avoid saying, "I'm applying for this job because I'm separated and need the income." Everyone needs income.

And within a few days of the interview, do send a polite, handwritten thank-you note to the person who extended the courtesy of speaking with you. This cements a very favorable impression, and again puts your name in front of the decision-makers.

Balancing the Professional with the Personal

How do you cope in the workplace when it seems that the rest of your life is spinning out of control? This is a question many career women face as their personal lives are unraveling.

On one hand, you might be thankful for the distraction of having a job to look forward to and someplace to be each day. It sure beats burying yourself in legal battles and letting your mind fester with the escapades of your estranged spouse. Then again, it's difficult to hide your emotions and set aside time to attend to legal and personal matters involving your separation. A litigious estranged or ex-husband may also hope to derail your career or cause trouble with your employer because of time missed. This is another facet of legal abuse and passive-aggression, which I've mentioned in prior chapters.

Ask for flextime if your company offers this. Showing up an hour or two before the rest of the staff might give you more productive time, and an opportunity to work alone, without inquisitive coworkers. If you do feel on the brink of tears, go to the restroom for privacy or plan to take a long walk at lunchtime so you can have a good cry, get some fresh air, and exercise (which goes a long way to improving your mind's focus).

Don't make your boss your confidante in legal or personal matters. This just isn't a good idea, because some employers will think that you are too preoccupied to attend to work. It's best to limit the calls you make or take regarding your case. Try grouping these together, if you must, during a time you are alone in the office and can talk. Refrain from using your employer's e-mail to communicate with your estranged husband or ex-spouse. Instead, set up a free e-mail account that you can access from most any computer with an Internet connection.

It's also wise to settle issues out of court whenever possible, or see if your attorney can represent you on matters not requiring your presence. As I mentioned before, you're often paying for your attorney's time as he or she waits in the hallway before motions or hearings, and if you take time off, it may jeopardize your career and bottom line.

Of course, it's impossible to think that your separation won't pop into your mind throughout the day. You can improve your spirits by removing pictures or mementos of your husband and family as it was. Place new photos on your desk, along with an inspirational or humorous calendar that's guaranteed to make you smile. Stock up on healthy snacks, hot cocoa, or anything else that's a treat during the workday so that you can distract yourself as you start feeling down. Finally, enlist the help of a friend or an e-mail buddy whom you can call occasionally or send messages to if your workload permits. Little sanity breaks like this go a long way.

Career-Boosting Strategies

I'll bet there are some strategies you could implement to get noticed, get ahead, or get a raise. We'd all love that!

Only half of an author's job is actually committing words to paper. The other half is promoting projects, yes even ourselves. And since I've taught career-boosting strategies in a workshop, I've also learned what's worked effectively for other professionals.

It's important to consider these possibilities because you want your peers, colleagues, and bosses to notice what you can offer and what you've achieved. This makes everyone happy. It places you in the mindset of other decision-makers and potential employers. It even broadens your social circles. Sure, you need to be in the prover-bial right place at the right time in many instances. But did you ever think that you can create those right times and places yourself? Well, you certainly can. Here are a few strategies to start you on your way:

Keep your resumé current. You never know when it will be requested.

Learn to be your own publicist. Make friends of the media, knowing which reporters cover your industry or field. An editorial or broadcast mention reaps plenty of rewards, much more so than paid advertising. The only investment is your time and talent. Just be sure that you honor a reporter's deadline, and even offer to help out if they ever need an expert sound bite from someone in your field.

Practice word-of-mouth advertising. It starts with you! If no one is talking about what you're doing, then start telling others (within reason, of course). Ask your public relations office to release word of your promotions or accomplishments to local newspapers, or do this yourself. Ask satisfied clients or customers to tell their friends, family, or business associates about you. When you receive praise for a job well done, ask if you can use their endorsement if this is appropriate.

Reward your referrals with thank-you notes, gift cards, even tickets to events or performances if you can afford it. What comes around, goes around! Always mail a thank-you note after each interview that you're granted.

Offer to speak at school, charity, and professional venues. If you need to enhance your public speaking skills, join a group like Toastmasters. Then get out in front of groups like the chamber of commerce, a Rotary Club, alumni associations, and even bookstore gatherings.

Teach a class. Even if you only know a bit more than others about your particular subject, it might be enough to help them and boost their perception of you. Lifelong learning and continuing education programs are always on the lookout for top-notch ideas and people to present them. Besides, it can yield additional income and contacts.

Network. Then network some more. Though there are entire books written on the subject, you can begin doing this effectively by passing out business cards, writing notes to referrals, making full use of Internet newsgroups where people have questions, and offering to help others who may need a hand. After all, you never know when their stars will rise and they'll remember your kindness.

Dress for the job you want, not the job you have. Looking the part is pivotal.

Seven Steps to Higher Income

Even if you are happily employed, it pays to attract attention to your name and work. Nothing primes you for further opportunity like a solid reputation of excellent performance. Thus, pick up a few pointers here on how to get ahead in your chosen career.

1. Make yourself visible. Social extroversion is a predictor of higher income. Position yourself for a promotion. Champion your employment evaluations, showing how you've added to the bottom line. You just might see your numbers rise.

2. Become indispensable. Managers tend to give heftier raises to those upon whom they truly depend. Become one of those people by taking on projects that will reflect upon your boss as well as yourself. If you want the best, be the best that you can be.

3. Search for a new job, either in your current organization or in another. Trading up is the most significant way of increasing your salary potential.

4. Specialize and become the expert. Specialties exist in almost every career, and some are more lucrative than others. If necessary, obtain the required certification or additional degree to qualify for such status.

5. Change careers, even slightly. Moving your job title into a profit-performing part of the company can enhance your paycheck. Support positions generally pay less and don't offer bonuses and commissions like sales positions might.

6. Raise your prices if you're self-employed. Clients are unlikely to object to a reasonable price increase (say 5 to 10 percent) if you have a proven track record of satisfying their needs.

7. Negotiate a better benefits package. Whether it's better health or disability coverage, childcare, free parking, tuition reimbursement, stock options, more vacation or sick time, or the ability to telecommute, each benefit translates into value.

You Go, Girl!

Think of this unplanned change as a turning point and an opportunity. Perhaps you have untapped potential and strength you're only beginning to realize. One day when I was suffering from bronchitis, I visited my physician's office. They asked if I'd mind if the resident assisting them took care of me. I didn't mind at all. In fact, I was inspired.

This woman was just a few years older than me. When I shared that I was a single mom, I discovered that she was also. After her divorce, she decided to go back to school and obtain her medical degree. Now there's accomplishment. And determination.

"A job can go a long way toward repairing the self-esteem that got bruised through the emotional rigors of the divorce process," writes Esther M. Berger, CFP, in *Money-Smart Divorce*. "And having a place to go every day and knowing that you earn your own paycheck can give you a tremendous sense of independence and self-worth."

Indeed, one woman I spoke with in my research dubbed work "the glue" that held her together during this difficult time. Her job forced her to get out of bed, look good, and get on with her life. At first she was timid, but her confidence grew and further opportunities came right along.

Remember, any career worth having takes time to build. Be willing to put yourself out there, to risk having your ideas and all that you offer rejected. It only takes one potential employer to say, "Yes, you're hired!" Develop the patience and tenacity to keep moving forward. Wake up every day with a "why not?" attitude, and whether you learn to speak in front of a group, write for professional or commercial publication, obtain another degree, or merely enhance the way in which you perform your job, keep improving your skills.

Chapter Eight
Household Hints and Car Care

When I faced the fact that my prior marriage was unraveling, I felt an onslaught of anger over many issues, not the least of which was the house we'd just built four years prior. We had purchased the property, saved diligently to pay it off, and then proceeded with what was to be our dream house. How could my husband have committed us to these responsibilities, then walk away, leaving me the burden?

Well, it doesn't matter where a husband's mind was when such events transpired. Fact is, you're separated, and in many cases, you have the family home to manage all on your own. Before you feel tempted to cry a bucket of tears or sell outright, let's put things into perspective.

It doesn't take massive amounts of testosterone to tend to the lawn, fix the dishwasher, or shop for a new car—a few of the concerns some of us might have handed over to the men in our lives. If repairing leaky faucets doesn't thrill you, rest assured that I'm not trying to sway you with this chapter, merely assuage the anxiety associated with everyday repairs and decisions, and empower yourself by finding some fun in tasks you don't ordinarily tackle. When

I got remarried, I gladly handed over the lawnmower to my teenage son and new husband with an almost "here . . . have it!" grin. I must admit I'm glad that I can tend a lawn as well as some guys I know. More on that later, but if nothing more, ladies, you'll discover the sheer exhilaration of power tools. If you haven't tried any of these, trust me—it can be very therapeutic at times!

How You Can Be Handy

There were times when I'd find something in the garage, hand it to my father, and ask, "What's this thing's purpose in life?" Once the garage became my domain, you wouldn't believe how many tools I discovered we owned and I never saw used.

It might be the same around your house. If you don't have dad or some other male friend to ask about items, take them to your local hardware store or browse the aisles for something that looks similar. Perhaps its purpose in life will make *your* life a lot easier. So put the tools you already own to the task.

Another way to ease the burden of managing home maintenance is to rely upon your feminine instincts. Ask questions. Women aren't afraid to ask questions. We adhere to the old adage that there is no stupid inquiry. We stop and ask for directions.

We also aren't so proud that we won't call in help when we're clearly into a task over our heads. Barbara Kavovit (a.k.a. Barbara K, as she's known in the media) used to head a major New York construction firm before deciding to apply her skills to literally empower women in her new company of Barbara K Enterprises, Inc. Barbara provides women with comprehensive tools and the know-how to accomplish what they always feared they couldn't accomplish. Her Web site, *www.barbarak.com*, contains fix-it tips (how to hang, replace, and repair numerous items) as well as information about her line of tool kits developed exclusively for women. These are lighter weight and easier for many women to handle with ease.

The colors are great too, and the measuring tape is magnetic to help when you're measuring something solo. I especially like the handy guide to simple home repairs that comes inside each tool kit because it has diagrams and text to walk you through hanging curtain rods and pictures, installing showerheads and door knobs, patching small holes in the wall, and repairing a leaky faucet.

Overall, you'd be surprised how readily available household help can be. You merely need to know where to find the experts. Perhaps there is a handyman in your neighborhood or church. Hire these guys. In some cases, if they know you and the repair is minor, they might not even charge. That's because many men love helping out a woman. It boosts their ego. So go ahead and ask.

Others who can lend a hand include the contractor who built your home (or the superintendent in an apartment building). You can find handymen and repair services through a chamber of commerce, Better Business Bureau, the Yellow Pages, local advertising supplements, or even your insurance agent.

Repair or Replace?

If funds are tight, replacing a worn-out appliance is the last thing you need. It's always a tough call. For instance, the washer breaks and the repair tech says it will cost $285 plus tax to get it spinning again. However, if you're willing to spend just under $600 you can buy a brand new one with a manufacturer's warranty. Unless an extended warranty already covers the expense, what do you do?

First determine the age of the appliance in question. Something that's less than ten years old makes more sense to repair than its ancient counterpart. If you're dealing with hot water heaters, microwave ovens, or computers that are over twelve years old, seriously consider replacing them. These items just aren't made to last that long; computers that old are probably technologically outdated.

Next, look at the relative replacement cost and usage. It might take $2,500 to replace your central air conditioning but only $800 to repair it. This would make sense to repair versus replace. Central air conditioning, refrigerators, ranges, and furnaces are big-ticket items you don't want to replace unless you absolutely must. And if you are considering a move, that's another reason to conserve cash and go with the repair. Furthermore, when an item qualifies as a business expense, the tax deduction may sway you. For computers and office equipment that boosts your bottom line, sometimes it takes money to make money.

Before you authorize a repair, ask if labor is charged by the hour or at a flat rate. If there is an estimate fee, make sure this is applied to any subsequent repairs. Always get a claim check with the company's name, address, and phone number, plus the technician's signature and your product's serial number. If your item is under warranty, be sure the receipt is marked "no charge." And ask for the replaced parts to ensure that the defective part was indeed replaced.

Household Maintenance Checklist

There are a number of household items that will last a lot longer with an ounce of prevention than if you hadn't tended to them. Here's a sampling:

Heads or lenses of video equipment and audio components can easily be cleaned with inexpensive cleaning units you can purchase.

Dishwashers require hot water to dissolve soap. Thus, turn on the hot water before starting your dishwasher. Too much detergent causes etching on glassware. Rinse dishes before loading since food particles clog filters and impede water flow. Believe it or not, experts say dumping a jar of Tang into the dishwasher each month and running it through a regular cycle cleans the dishwasher's parts by its acidic content.

Clothes dryers need to be kept lint-free. Wash the lint screen periodically with mild soap and water, and vacuum the vents and inside panels to prevent a fire hazard from forming from excess lint.

Washing machines can be cleaned with two quarts of white vinegar poured into a machine full of hot water. Let it agitate for ten minutes, then let it sit for an hour before finishing the cycle. This cleans the buildup of lime, magnesium, and other deposits.

Refrigerators are best served by vacuuming the condenser coils. Failing to do this can ruin the coils over time. Get a condenser brush, remove the front lower panel, and brush and vacuum the gunk. By unplugging the unit and removing the cardboard that protects the condenser coils, you can clean even more of the grime. It's best to do this once a year.

Furnace filters and air-cleaning unit filters should be replaced or cleaned annually. This improves efficiency and air quality.

Defrost your freezer once ice accumulates a quarter of an inch.

Unscrew drains periodically to clean out hair and soap that has accumulated. If your washer empties into a laundry tub, attach an old piece of pantyhose (use a rubber band to secure firmly). You'd be surprised how much lint this collects. Always use extreme caution when using liquid drain cleaners. Wear goggles and be certain not to breathe in the noxious vapors. A safer alternative is the homemade mixture of one cup baking soda, one cup salt, and one-fourth cup cream of tartar. Shake this well in a jar and pour one-fourth cup directly down the drain, followed by two cups of boiling water. After letting it sit one minute, flush it out with cold tap water.

Clear gutters in the spring and again in the late fall. Sometimes the window cleaning crew can do this.

Hire a chimney sweep at least every few years to clean and inspect your chimney, sealing any cracks and insuring the safety of your fireplace.

Apply a water sealant to your wooden decks or outdoor railings.

Keep up with exterior painting tasks before the paint peels. Do this when weather permits and before harsh weather sets in.

Conduct an energy audit. See Chapter Six for tips on insulating, improving your home's energy efficiency, and saving money.

Consult Chapter Five for ways to **secure your home properly.**

Prune shrubbery to keep it looking nice and growing well. If you don't own a hedge trimmer, you might be able to borrow one on occasion from a neighbor. Do use extreme caution if you aren't used to power tools. Install deer fence or other protective mesh so that the deer or rabbits don't feast on your rhododendrons or other plants.

Cut off no more than one-third of the grass at a time. Scalping the lawn will weaken turf, cause it to burnout and bring on disease. Use a mulching mower when possible. Never mow wet grass. It's bad for the lawn, the mower, and you.

Lessen That Lawn Art

Time to rev up the engine and mow that grass. A rite of spring-time. And actually, a welcomed change after sitting indoors for months.

As a writer, I do my share of sitting, and much of my work might not see print for months, even years, after I've completed it. So lawn care, once I was suddenly single, became an outlet where I could immediately *see* the results of my labors. Only I had no idea what a creative outlet the results would be.

To start, I tackled the job like any good journalist would. Have a half-used bag of Scotts something-or-other. Call the 800 number listed on the bag. Get that free booklet. Next step, e-mail a few male friends: "I know you're incredibly busy, so I've designed this survey with only one question, requiring a one-word answer. All right, at what age did you, all on your own, use a lawn-mower?" Now I realize that this was a thoroughly whimsical, yet selfish approach. Instead of wondering when these two sons of mine could safely push the Black & Decker, I should have asked for bulleted lists complete with Power Point charts. Mistake number one.

This lapse was evened out soon enough. Another journalist's gem: Go to the experts (in this case, the guy in my neighborhood with the best lawn) and ask copious questions. Keep at people until one of them tells you to go get a hobby.

Okay, for a while, all was just swell. It's amazing what sun and a little rain does to dirt. Then came mistake number two. I used that blasted spreader for the fertilizer application. It was painfully obvious that its previous owner hadn't taken care of it. Imagine pushing a rotary device that needed to be oiled—five years ago. But I wasn't smart enough to see my zebra lawn as being the spreader's fault. I still thought it was me.

In time, the stripes disappeared, but the lawn still had a few pesky weeds. On comes mistake number three. I got out *that* spreader, filled it, and pushed. And pulled. Pushed. And pulled—cursing with each effort because it wasn't working well.

You pretty much have to live on my street to appreciate this, but within a week's time, there it was. Voila, lawn art. Patches and lines of brown in a pattern that only a two-year-old with a crayon might be able to depict.

One neighbor (a guy) smiled and asked if it was part of a writing assignment. Another (female friend) said no, I *had* to write about this. And the man with the great lawn? Well, he was too polite to comment. It was so horrendous that I just hoped no emergency would necessitate visits by family and friends from afar. No, I didn't even want the minister to see this fiasco!

But what turns out and looks ugly has potential with that sun and rain factor. Throw on some topsoil and seed, and wait. And pray. Weeks later, when the growth appeared, I just shook my head. There were these psychedelic puffs of light green amid the blades of a more normal nature. Obviously, the turf color wasn't a great match!

Worse yet, they kept growing well into December, which leads me to tell you what no free booklet ever will. Lawn care ceases to be fun if you can't say goodbye to the task in October! And for the mildly curious seeking a cheap thrill again this summer, don't worry. That spreader is now hopefully six feet deep. In the landfill!

Selling Your House?

If you're living in the marital residence that is jointly owned, you will need your estranged husband's cooperation to sell the property. But say you've been remarried, or you owned the home before your marriage. If the deed is still in your name, you're free to move if you choose.

With the other stress in your life, it's probably wise to use a real-estate agent. You'll be too preoccupied to list your house and deal with prospective buyers. Still, while you'll rely on your agent's advice, there are things you can do to hasten the sale of your home.

If you truly need to sell quickly, price your home realistically. Sure, you'd like to list it at the higher end of the fair-value range, but you'll get more traffic if you price it for quicker sale. The longer your house stays on the market, the lower its position becomes when agents punch up the computer printouts.

Do ask your agent if there is anything you can do to help. Certainly word-of-mouth advertising helps. When I sold the house that had been my marital residence, I used the same strategy that worked when I sold an apartment-sized condominium. I developed a flier using my desktop publishing capabilities. It listed all the advantages, a little about the neighborhood camaraderie (including annual holiday parties and picnics) as well as resources the community offered. Distribute fliers in apartment houses, libraries, and other gathering spots that attract attention. Make sure your agent has a stack to hand out to interested buyers and consider putting them in a covered box attached to your realty sign.

Make any cosmetic improvements you can afford. Repainting rooms to neutral colors and putting a fresh coat on the exterior lends curb appeal. So does keeping the lawn and shrubbery trimmed. Other subtle messages include setting a pitcher of lemonade on the patio set, arranging plants, having a fire in the fireplace, and simmering potpourri on the stove.

Fresh flowers are nice; lots of light adds appeal. Set the kitchen or dining room table for a meal, or just have a bottle of wine, glasses, and napkins set out. This helps others visualize themselves entertaining or enjoying the home. Put out your best towels in the bathroom. Keep pets outside. Also try as best you can to clear closets and keep children's toys from view. Rent a storage locker if you must, at least while you are trying to show your home.

Car Shopping

When the time came to replace my ten-year-old car (appropriately dubbed "Schlep" among friends), I dreaded car shopping. That was until I realized that in all car purchases my husband and I had made together, I was always the one who haggled the price anyway.

Still, I had reason to be hesitant. I didn't know as much about cars as most guys did, and let's face it, who usually sells you your new set of wheels? Guys. So we women need to do our research before we're caught off guard or sold more of a line than a car.

Try not to fall in love with what you picture as your ideal car. That is, don't be married to a make or model. (Having said that, your comfort level *is* important.) Reading is the best way to increase your auto knowledge and car-shopping prowess.

Call the National Highway Traffic Safety Administration for an informative brochure on buying a safer car. Dial 1-800-424-9393 and request operator assistance. Look up the annual *Consumer Reports* auto issue at your library or newsstand. This issue reviews current car models and gives buying tips. Besides, getting a feel for the repair records of used models is important even if you're buying a brand-new vehicle. *Edmund's New Car Prices & Reviews* gives invoice prices on new cars, trucks, and options. *The National Automobile Dealers Association (NADA) Used Car Guide* offers current trade-in and retail values. Borrow these resources at your local library. In addition, you can obtain the *Kelly Blue Book* value for automobiles you're buying or selling from your bank or directly off the Internet at *www.kbb.com.*

This gives you plenty of information, but your thinking is far from over. Analyze your needs. Safety and reliability are obviously paramount. If you have children or other passengers (say you sell real estate), then four doors are necessary. If you use your car for work-related or recreational hauling, a spacious trunk or rack storage is handy. For those who live in a snowy climate, four-wheel or all-wheel drive helps, and if you traverse a hilly region you should consider a larger engine with six or eight cylinders.

Now that you have assessed what kind of car you need and can afford, next comes the actual shopping stage. Sure, you'll be visiting auto dealers, but you can also find vehicles at auction or from individuals you trust (so that you know the history of the car). In addition, call rental car companies to see if they are parting with any models. Then follow these tips:

Don't buy based on monthly payments. Know the full cost. In fact, know what the dealer paid for the car (using the resources I named above).

Keep quiet about a trade-in, since dealers sometimes raise the price they quote you on the newer car. If you are trading in, figure this at the end.

Consider where you will have the vehicle serviced but don't be swayed by this entirely. Should you find a model that your dealer or trusted garage doesn't sell, chances are good that they can still service the car.

Never take the first price you're quoted. Make the salesperson march back to the sales manager, several times if necessary. Get a written quote so they can't back out of it later. Hold your ground on your bottom-line price. Be ready to get up and walk out of the showroom as that usually puts the salesperson on notice of "deal or this is over."

Take any used vehicle to a third-party mechanic you trust. They'll look for signs of repainting, poor performance, and other red flags. Often for as little as $25, you can get a knowledgeable opinion. This small investment is comfort insurance that you've made a good decision.

Make sure any money down is refundable, and get this in writing. Stipulate that the deal is contingent upon a successful outside inspection. Usually a dealer will only hold a vehicle for a few days this way, but it gives you time to investigate further.

Remember that cash is king. If you can afford it, or if you've been saving to replace an older car, go ahead and deal in cash—for two reasons. In your litigation, a large cash sum in the bank might be used against you. Secondly, you increase your bargaining power tremendously with a cash purchase.

Realize that **an extended warranty is one of the most expensive options** you can tack on to the price, and it's a major source of profit for dealers. Therefore, don't allow yourself to be talked into options you do not need or want.

Time your car purchase, if at all possible. Some say the best months to buy a car are the slow months of January through March. Others, however, swear that fall and into December are best. You might begin your research early in the month and conclude as you near the end when salespeople are eager to meet their quotas. The absolute best time to strike a deal is an hour before closing when the dealer is more willing to make a last-minute sale.

Consider a "no haggle" model that many auto manufacturers have introduced if you truly can't fathom negotiating the price of a car.

Basic Car Care

If you used to defer all car-related matters to your husband, the responsibility of your automobile's maintenance now rests with you. A lot of us women also become accustomed to having a second car in the family (his car) to reply upon in emergencies. Now that you're separated, you probably don't have that steady backup plan.

For starters, revisit your insurance coverage. You may want to increase your deductibles on older cars, and take advantage of low-mileage discounts that could reduce your premiums. Since you don't want to be without transportation, inquire to see if your coverage has a rental car provision should your vehicle become involved in an accident.

Three immediate moves you should take are to (1) read your car's manual for suggested maintenance schedules and other tips (ask any dealer servicing your model for a schedule if you can't find yours); (2) enroll in an auto-care course especially designed for women; and (3) read *Lucille's Car Care*, written by transmission mechanic Lucille Treganowan and Gina Catanzarite. No joke, Lucille built her own successful repair shop, and her book includes everything from understanding the difference in oil labels and selecting a quality repair shop to emergency repair tactics and tips for your teenager's first car.

Keeping your car in top condition comes down to following a set schedule for such things as oil changes and other service. My mechanics always put a handy sticker on my windshield with the date and mileage at which I should have the oil changed next.

Have your mechanic rotate your tires every 5,000 miles for even wear (don't forget the full-sized spare if you have one), and always keep them properly inflated. Check the condition of your tires, replacing them when they reach 2/23-inch tread depth. When in doubt, use the penny test. Insert the top edge of a penny into the tread groove. If the top of the head shows, replace the tires. Replace belts on the recommended schedule and get a tuneup also.

As Lucille says, you need to rely upon a sound-effects checklist and trust your common "scents." Listening for knocks and pinging is as important as looking for leaks, sniffing overheated elements, and inhaling a whiff of burnt rubber.

While you can always rely upon a trusted mechanic, you can learn to add windshield wiper fluid, test and add oil, and check antifreeze levels on your own. This is not rocket science.

Your Car's Emergency Kit

Pack the following in your trunk for emergency use:

- Small throw rug for kneeling on and work gloves
- Bread wrappers, rubber bands, roll of mechanic's wire
- Large standard screwdriver, pliers, rubber hammer, and spray can of oil
- Jumper cables and four-way tire wrench
- Wheel chock, emergency flares, jug of water, funnel
- Flashlight, batteries, first-aid kit, blanket, nonperishable food (if stranded)
- Old scarf, old belt, cigarette lighter, small shovel, some sand or cat litter

Defensive Driving

When I was first separated, I was amazed at how many people told me to be careful driving. It wasn't just my mom, mind you! I understood that friends and family were concerned about my safety on the highway.

Accidents easily occur when your mind is elsewhere. And let's face it, when you are emotionally upset, preoccupied by a dozen different details, groggy from sleepless nights, or adjusting to medication that you might be taking, you and your passengers are at greater risk. Review this checklist just to be safe:

Change car door locks or make certain you have all sets of keys your estranged husband may have had to your car. Again, don't let him rationalize that the car might be titled in his name also. Secure your vehicle.

Consider a car security system or at least a steering wheel lock, particularly if your wheels are valuable, new, or one of the frequently stolen models (*Consumer Reports* often lists these annually).

Become an auto club member (AAA) for added security. If you ever break down, you can call the number and receive free or discounted towing within the vicinity.

Consider purchasing a cellular phone for emergency calls (see below) and if you get any accessories to go with it, hands-free gadgets such as speakerphones or earpieces and microphones give you added safety on the highway.

If you live in snow belt states, **stash emergency items in your trunk.**

Keep at least a half tank of gas in your car at all times.

Use caution. Sure, you'll probably be frazzled for a while and chronically short on time. But don't hurry, especially when you could harm yourself, your children, or innocent others in an accident.

Selecting a Cellular Phone

These days, cellular telephones (cell phones) are so common that you may have already investigated the best options for ownership. There are some, however, who have not opted for one, but perhaps now being separated or divorced, they'll want to consider the purchase for safety's sake. Anyone stranded on the highway can benefit from having a mobile phone, especially women who might be less willing to change a flat tire or tackle some other car repair.

If you're unfamiliar with cellular phone service, start with a plan that doesn't require a long-term commitment and one that carries no early termination penalty should you decide to opt out of the service.

The phone itself might be less expensive, but the airtime is costlier. Fancier handsets aren't guaranteed to work with another carrier if you switch service, so stick with something plainer and more universal.

When shopping for the whole package of phone and service, freebies might look good, but beware. They can lure you with the promise of free airtime or a free phone, but you're probably paying for those items somewhere in your contract. Ask your provider to show you a map of its coverage area, and then determine if this suits your needs. In your quest for seamless coverage, you may find it frustrating because your favorite places where you need a phone are dead zones, meaning that your carrier's network of coverage simply ends. Log onto *www.cellphone.homestead.com,* an Internet site inviting cell-phone users to report coverage gaps. Search the database, and it may help you decide upon the best carrier and plan. Most companies charge a penalty if you opt out of your contract before it comes to an end so investigate your options carefully.

Cellular phone thieves listen for people to give their credit card numbers and other privileged information over the air. Also, be conservative about giving your cell number out. You have the phone for your convenience and safety, but if others use it indiscriminately, you'll be the one charged. If your estranged husband is the vindictive type, you might be wise to keep the number from him. Know what emergency numbers to call using your cell phone as well. Some women have contacted police dispatchers when they were followed, even by what appeared to be unmarked police vehicles. Calling the dispatcher can verify if it's truly the authorities or a ruse.

Chapter Nine

Learning to Lighten Up

Right when I faced several unpleasant realities about my first marriage, my minister gave a thoroughly inspirational sermon one Sunday. In relating how we all walk difficult paths, including those of separation and divorce, he came to the conclusion that "you can become bitter, or you can get better."

No doubt about it. A marital separation, especially when you least expect it, ranks up there as a horrendous life passage. I can now look back at those first few months, even years, and see that I was angry. I harbored a lot of negative energy. With all that had happened outside of my control, I had every right to feel anger as well as every other negative emotion in the dictionary. So do you perhaps, but you also need to learn to let it go.

This chapter is about letting out the anger and allowing in the laughter that may be sorely lacking from your spirit. In what I hope is lighthearted text, I'll relate incidents that many women have shared with me, all true and all too grand not to laugh at. That's the whole point here—learning to laugh again.

Bitter Versus Better

So how do you know what qualifies as bitterness and when you're getting better? The truth is, you won't always know the distinction. This is a very subjective matter. Time helps. So might friends who can see things a little more objectively. The path your life takes may reveal a lot also.

For instance, your take on the following story will most likely reflect where you are in the journey of your separation or divorce. One woman struggled since her husband ran off with his coworker. She ran into another jilted woman at her daughter's school, and the two got to talking about these "other women."

Now, every time she feels the betrayal, the anger, and the hurt, she focuses on one profound, perhaps funny thought. During her chat at the school, the new friend she'd made summed up the situation.

"Let's call these other women what they really are," her new friend shared. "Bimbos."

Now, this scenario may make you think these women weren't letting go. But in a sense they were. Friends have certainly added even more pejorative terms to my vocabulary, and I think any female facing infidelity can relate to the word these two women laughed at. I don't think it's bitterness unless it's a constant state of mind (rather than an occasional laugh).

When you're with trusted friends or those who can empathize, let go a little. Call that other woman a bimbo behind her back, or tell your best friend how happy you are that the bottom feeder you used to live with swims in someone else's aquarium. Unless you wake each day breathing fire or you air these sentiments in front of your children, an occasional verbal stab among friends can elicit a good laugh.

Why Move On?

I placed this chapter toward the end of the book on purpose, because as you progress through the weeks and months of your separation, you'll find it easier, as I did, to move on. And if you think it's not even a conceivable goal, then realize the alternatives—a life of bitterness, anger, and depression. I've seen far too many women allow this painful journey to color their futures, whereby they become jealous of other women's happiness, passive-aggressive, or openly hostile. Then they set their sights far too low so that they create a downward spiraling self-fulfilling prophecy.

Furthermore, think of the effect on your children. In collaborating with my friend, psychologist and author Dr. Tim Murphy, I've learned a lot about anger's power and the reasons to rein it in. In *The Angry Child,* we try to raise awareness about anger.

Tim has shared with me that in all his years of practice, the moments he most wanted to pull a parent aside and lay into them has been over issues of divorce and its effect upon the children involved. Most therapists probably would love to shout, "Grow Up!" because many divorcing people are blind to their own anger and emotions. So the lesson here for you, as an individual and as a parent, is to try as hard as you possibly can to manage your emotions, purge the anger in a positive way, and accept a new direction in life, even if you don't want to. If you're like me, you'll realize that while you never anticipated this passage, you have become stronger, and you'll continue to be.

Reframing Your Past

Another friend was also employed as a therapist years ago. Throughout my separation and divorce, I counted on her for a quick reframing lesson. So now I'll share the technique with you. It works!

Reframing occurs when we take a scenario that looks bleak and unappealing and shed new light on the picture. We can choose to wallow in uncertainty and hurt, or we can move to higher ground and a brighter outlook.

So regardless of who initiated your separation, you've had to cope to preserve your sanity and survival. Sure, you might have additional responsibilities, loneliness, and mixed emotions. But look at it this way. The bathrooms probably aren't as dirty, the food lasts longer, and the laundry might be a genuine snap. And if you have children, sure you must continue to deal with the father, and yes, you'll miss the kids when they're with him. But visitation can also equal time to lounge in bed on Saturday morning, time to date, or moments merely for yourself.

I'm not saying reframing your situation will be easy. Far from it. What has happened in your marriage is history, and I know the temptation well to beat yourself up about what transpired. Could you have seen signs of trouble? From where you were standing at that time, probably not. Even if the wife in us may have had an inkling, the mother in us was most likely steadfast in wanting to make the family unit work. I know I had two children that required extra efforts. I could have used help. I understand *exactly* how you might feel trying to salvage a bad situation.

Frankly, meeting the needs of children with special concerns is taxing. I really feel for women who are left with primary responsibility of learning disabled, mentally handicapped, chronically ill, or physically challenged children because another set of adult hands in the home is such a relief. I've aligned dozens of doctors, specialists, physical therapists, speech clinicians, school nurses and counselors, plus teachers over the years, to team with me in helping my children. It's like having a part-time job with a lot of juggling, and a lot of phone calls, driving to appointments, and believe me, a lot of paperwork. A lot of sadness along the way, too, when seemingly I couldn't convey to other adults in my sons' lives the importance of what doctors and others were trying to achieve. But I had to let it go, allowing the problem to rest where it belonged.

Though the time commitment has weighed on my schedule and career the most, it's my ability to find the joy and accomplishment in this responsibility that allows me to reframe. I have made things happen for these two boys. My priorities were and still are right. People I've met, even men I used to date (and for sure the one I married), have told me I'm doing a great job. Not that I'm the perfect mother (oh, just ask my boys!), but my children are indeed my two greatest accomplishments, and I choose to focus on this whenever the other negative stuff starts to pull me down. It sure helped the day when my youngest son told me that he had to pick a hero to write about in third grade. He picked me. My son pegs the E on extrovert as I do, so there was more! He explained his choice because in his eyes, I take care of him, have always been there for him, and have taken him for medical care, and to karate.

I hope you'll join me in learning to look at the cheerier side of things. I'm not dismissing your circumstances or making light of them. I know what it's like to be devastated, afraid, lonely, troubled, and then some. From here on out, however, I'll take a much more humorous tone. At times it might be sarcastic, occasionally flippant. But these are all coping mechanisms as we heal. And heal we must.

The Work of Reframing and Relaxing Your Mind

I know that what I wrote in the earlier chapters, especially with some distance from some of those situations, and now remarried, may seem easy. When you're thrust into a new situation, with much stress at bay, it's anything but easy. It's real work. A good lesson, too, because we can often apply these techniques to future struggles.

The first, best step that you can take is to catch your negative thoughts. Stop them. Thought stopping is a cognitive-behavioral technique that will help you to achieve happiness. Replace the negative thoughts with something more calming such as "Now is not the time to dwell on that; I'm too exhausted (too busy, whatever). Tomorrow, I'll figure it out." It's not procrastinating unless you never tackle the problem.

Another way, which I discussed above, is finding something positive, even small, in disappointment, loss, or anger. Even after my remarriage, I spent thousands of dollars in family court. In one September hearing, we put an important December date in our schedule proposal. It was the bar mitzvah of my son's best friend—something he really wanted to attend, like any other teenager with an invitation to a special event. That bar mitzvah has made it into court documents more than once because we were captive when it came to scheduling. What an embarrassment—to make new friendships in a community and rarely be able to commit to anything. The flip side? This boy's mom is probably my best friend in Maryland, especially when I faced hassles waged over my own son's confirmation event. She understood, once again, exactly what I was going through.

Reframing is no guarantee that you'll recover what you lost (in this case money and mental agony), but if you remain open to secondary gains in any situation (such as this friendship) they might add a lot to your life in a way you never imagined (remember my decision to go to graduate school when faced with a chunk of time each summer—another example). When not reframing, try distracting yourself with relaxation techniques. If you're driving along the highway and you feel yourself beginning to ruminate, listen to a book on CD or tape, turn on some energizing music, and maybe even sing along. Deep breathing using your abdominal muscles is another great distraction and relaxer. Mindfulness or focusing through meditation, helps to heighten perception and improve your spirits.

Plan time in your day for purposely created diversions to calm, relax, or distract yourself, such as taping a favorite sitcom or *Saturday Night Live* and viewing it some night after the kids are tucked into bed. Or, do something profoundly silly, such as a picnic on the floor or watch a movie (make it a comedy) in the middle of the day.

Getting Over Those Non-Events Transitions

Nancy K. Schlossberg and Susan P. Robinson wrote about transitions pointing to life's non-events—hidden, rarely observed transition events that no one rallies around to help us to grieve, but that we grieve nonetheless. Their book *Going to Plan B: How You Can Cope, Regroup, and Start Your Life on a New Path* went into much greater details, but typical non-events for divorced women might be never having had children you'd wanted to have, family relationships that didn't materialize, missing an educational opportunity, or not being that "All-American couple" any longer. It might be another disappointment. Something that did not happen externally has made quite a difference internally, for you. Sure, you might get people's support because you're separated or divorced, but those same people rarely acknowledge, "Gee Sally, I'm sorry you never had the chance to have a baby."

As I learned of this concept in graduate school, I thought about my own non-event, which for me, was probably never having had a daughter. While I love my boys tremendously and they've sure taught me a lot in life, I had hopes of also having a daughter, buying dresses, playing Barbies, picking prom dresses. Some non-events are out of our control. One could argue that my record of problematic pregnancies made it unwise to have more children, but I also looked upon the dissolution of my first marriage as definitely ending that dream. By the time I got remarried, it just didn't seem right, and I had come to some peace about it. Reframing helps with these non-event transitions, too. So I won't ever build a Barbie house for my own daughter; but maybe for a granddaughter, and I can certainly shop in the pink aisle, as my son jokingly calls it, when we select a child each Christmas to purchase toys for, through our church.

As you learn to let go of that which has bothered you, think carefully about these lost dreams in your life. Could it be merely a delayed event as in the case of returning to school, only at a later age? If not, acknowledge it, label it, feel it, share it, and let others comfort you. Determine how you'll cope and move forward. As Nancy Schlossberg tells it: All of us have scripts for our lives that are interrupted and do not go according to plan. All of us have surprises—some positive, others negative. Part of life is having alternative plans—from A through Z.

A Heavy Heart Isn't Healthy

If you listen to the experts, you'll realize that lightening up aids more than our mental health. Published studies indicate that wealth doesn't really buy true happiness. It only tips the scale ever so slightly above the satisfaction level of the average American. So what, then, has the power to make us happy, and healthy?

Norman Cousins, who wrote the book *Anatomy of an Illness*, detailed recovery from pain and terminal illness using humor therapy. While somewhat obscure, this work has become a specialty for some therapists. Laughter not only reduces muscle tension, but it also stimulates the heart and lungs. When we laugh, we give our bodies the same benefit that a deep breath allows, increasing the oxygen levels in our bloodstream. We raise our endorphin level, and we increase the number of disease-fighting antibodies. That's why chronically depressed people are often the sickest people. Sure, they have a virus or a disease that has struck them, but their mood certainly hasn't helped their health. We know that stress drives up blood pressure and triggers stress hormones making it harder to process insulin, putting you at greater risk of diabetes, and then heart disease. Stress fat also accumulates as we reach out for comfort foods that boost our mood (i.e., natural serotonin levels) while adding pounds to our waists, hips, and midsections. Refined, white flour or simple carbohydrates add weight but also boost mood; thus the recent awareness that curbing all carbs can lead to feeling blue (see Chapter Two for a list of healthy carbs). Watching your weight is reason alone to lighten up, quite literally, and adopt healthier habits overall.

Some experts have theorized that we are born destined to be happier or sadder based upon our genetic makeup. But even if this is so, we can often adjust our contentment level by acknowledging what gets us down and keeps us happy. We can steer clear of the former and lean toward the latter.

Life is indeed filled with obstacles. That's a given. How we deal with these openly determines the satisfaction we derive out of life. Others who have written about the habits of happy people note that most contented individuals think highly of themselves. Thus, they have higher self-esteem. Happy people tend to feel in control of their lives. Right now, you may still feel that your future is out of control, perhaps even at the whim of the court. This will get better and indeed you can exercise greater control over day-to-day details of even small segments of your life.

Perky people tend to be optimistic as well as extroverted. If you find yourself battling pessimism, a good cognitive therapist may help you to reframe matters much as I demonstrated earlier. Limit your relationships with negative people, a surefire way to push away pessimism. Surrounded by negative people, it's pretty impossible not to become like them, so choose positive companions. Brainstorming for mood elevators is another tactic. Music can be upbeat in more ways than one. If you're trying to become more extroverted, use the healing power of the pen to help you get there. Journaling your way through a painful ordeal purges those negative emotions onto the page. It also helps you to perceive difficult situations as blessings when viewed through a gratitude lens. I'll address strategies for journaling next.

Finally, you can make yourself happier by filling your life with laughter. Former *Good Morning America* host Joan Lunden, herself a survivor of separation and divorce in a prior marriage, chronicles her own laugh track in her best-seller *A Bend In the Road Is Not the End of the Road*. After interviewing an expert on trauma and grief counseling, Lunden learned that it takes three to five years to fully recover from divorce and even begin to think about rejoining life. Lunden writes, "When we can no longer change a situation, we are challenged to change ourselves."

Joan is right. Change frightens us all, and one of the best action strategies she presents is to write down whatever it is that scares you or causes you to feel negative. Then write the complete opposite. For instance, she says, write "change is scary" followed by "change is exciting." To follow up this exercise, Lunden suggests that you continually remind yourself of these positive thoughts. Put sticky notes on your mirrors and bulletin boards. Do this and you'll fill your mind with warm, wonderful images as opposed to the old ones that got you so down and depressed.

Writing Your Own Prescription

When you were a little girl, did you pen your deepest secrets, hopes, and dreams, then keep them under lock and key? As an adult woman journaling her way through separation or divorce, the results are similar because sometimes our concerns are tormented; other times our spirits soar with expectation and wild abandon.

Experts credit writing or "scriptotherapy," as it's sometimes called, with lowering inhibitions and alleviating stress-related diseases. The National Science Foundation and National Institutes of Health funded research by James W. Pennebaker, Ph.D., who found that people who wrote about their deepest feelings evidenced heightened and persistent immune function. Pennebaker described his research in *Opening Up: The Healing Power of Expressing Emotions*.

The joy in journaling comes in many forms—a gratitude journal that boosts morale; a memory or log book to keep track of progress producing change or to use as a decision-making tool; a scrapbook of original thoughts and pasted in mementos; a worry ledger where we commit stress and anxiety so that we can put it out of our minds to sleep at night; and a story book, filled with experiences having a beginning, middle, and end so that we might gain insight from these narratives and avoid similar stress in the future. Therapeutic journaling generally has a purpose. We heal by using intentional writing to obtain a desired goal. In this situation, it's often closure or understanding. Journaling also brings about awareness. It puts distance between the writer and the problems that people struggle with, allowing them to see multiple facets until a new perspective emerges.

Start with disposable pages in a spiral notebook if it's less intimidating than committing thoughts to a bound journal that you buy in the bookstore. Start simply by writing an intentional statement or desire as one of your first entries. Think about what you wish to accomplish and let that guide you. If your mind is simply too cluttered to be creative, some days write lists as this helps you to mentally gather and organize. In this chapter, we discuss anger, so if bitterness consumes at the moment, list feeling words or phrases that better delineate your mood. Are you aggressive, cranky, displeased, enraged, frustrated, hateful, indignant, provoked, resentful, or seething?

Sentence stems are another journaling technique where you finish the rest of the sentence such as "the strongest emotion I've felt so far in this experience is _____; I remember feeling it (when), (where), (how), and (with whom)." Once you've identified these missing parts, then you can write about how you'd take better care of yourself should that emotion strike again. *In the Meantime* author Iyanla Vanzant says, "Write out what you fear, what you think could happen, what you would feel if that happened, what would happen to you if that happened, and anything else you can think of that keeps you in fear. End this exercise by writing, 'I do not choose to have this experience. I choose to _____.' Complete the sentence by writing out what you want."

Another journaling technique: The letter you never send or the imaginary conversation, which you have between yourself and your worst enemy (gee, who might that be?). Just be aware that while the written word can be cathartic, it can also lead to obsessive rumination, impeding any therapeutic goal you hope to achieve. It's never a substitute for a friend or a therapist if you're truly troubled.

Don't fret if you don't commit journal entries to the page each day, for unless you're tracking a physical process like food intake for weight loss or reactions to medication, write when it feels comfortable, or sometimes uncomfortable, as that's a sign that maybe you ought to purge powerful thoughts or feelings. If you do choose to write daily, setting aside the same time each day helps form a habit. Date your journal entries so that you can chart your progress, your chronicle of events, or your reflections as you overcome difficult moments.

Developing Other Happy Habits

What makes one woman happy might make another miserable. That's life. It's entirely subjective. Nonetheless, there are additional remedies to swing your mood in a more positive direction.

For starters, know what *not* to do. This includes obsessing and ruminating, which we women tend to do, and I addressed a bit already. Try not to spend excessive time thinking about the husband who walked out the door. The more you think of and discuss this man and what impact he's had on your life, the more connected you will feel to him. Thus, the more controlled you'll be by *his* actions, not your own.

Instead of coming home to an empty house or apartment, get yourself out among people. It's a lot harder to sit and think about unpleasant events when surrounded by other people, their conversations, and their distractions. It's also a great way to meet new friends so that, again, you aren't reminded of what you did as a couple. You begin to redefine yourself as a single woman with a bright future.

Treat yourself to a restaurant meal. I know it's not easy to take yourself out for dinner, but do it. Who cares if others look at you in the booth with your book? It's a meal you don't have to cook, scenery different from your own four walls, and at the very least, a diversion. Someone else might not have treated you well, but you can darn well give yourself permission to treat yourself like a queen if you see fit.

Embrace the chance to learn about yourself and what makes you so very unique. Create a list of things you've always wanted to do but never did fit into your married lifestyle. Maybe it's taking up ceramics or enrolling in a writing class. For me, I'd always wanted to learn more about investing money, and I needed to develop a Web page to promote my books. Noncredit, lifelong-learning classes provided insights and new interests. Later, when my sons were away for longer stretches, I went to graduate school and made the most of my workdays. I got a dog, enjoying walks and all the quality "nonverbals" a devoted pup provides.

If you don't reorganize your life, you'll continue to feel your spouse's absence, or that of your children, if they are with their father. If necessary, literally reorganize your life by moving the furniture or clearing closets. Eradicate the negative noise from your life. When I spotted unnecessary e-mails popping up that just kept some sort of battle brewing, I blocked my ex-husband off my e-mail account and set up a free e-mail account, just for him, only to hear more grumbles about Yahoo! not being legitimate. Oh, please!

Volunteer commitments are wonderful opportunities to give to worthwhile organizations at a time in your life when you feel least able to write a check. During my separation, I joined the crusade to educate others and eradicate domestic violence. A very courageous family lost their daughter in a domestic violence standoff. They turned their grief into good by establishing a task force that visited schools, put up displays, marched in parades, met with law enforcement officials, and ultimately worked to create a safe house for women and children in their first few days fleeing abuse. I lent my writing talents to help with brochures and written material, and though I couldn't always attend meetings, I felt good about being a part of this group.

Lessons in Lightening Up

I still remember the time I was lamenting to a friend that my computer printer died—a travesty to us writers! I was telling her that my ex-husband seemed surprised when I replaced it so quickly since I'd always deferred to his guidance on computer matters.

"Loriann, you don't get it," my friend told me. "You're supposed to be lying at the bottom of the steps begging him to come back. But the house is still standing, the lawn isn't three feet, and by God, you did the ultimate—you went out and got computer literate." This newfound independence brings to mind another lighter moment—observations my first husband made during the holiday season when we were first separated. He wondered who put up the Christmas lights (as well as the deer fence protecting the shrubbery). Weeks later, we got together for the boys' gift exchange. When I gave him some of my traditional rum balls, he seemed surprised I'd even made them.

Well, who did he think put up the lights and deer fence—the elves? I did, and I told him as much, ignoring the stunned look on his face. As for the rum balls, I did all the work on these most other years, so why would I break tradition?

Honestly, I think many men believe wives will just shrivel up and die without them. Hello! We have lives. We have interests. We have traditions. Husband or no husband, life goes on.

All right. You get the idea of what it takes to lighten up, even if it's between you and your friends. Again, I'm not suggesting that you try these tactics out on your estranged or ex-husband. Certainly anything you put into writing can and probably will be used against you.

Just learn to reframe things for yourself or between friends, making jokes out of even the worst scenario, and you will feel your body and mind relax.

Seriously though, I believe that many men (especially control freaks) define themselves through their interactions with spouses. Without their wives to push around, they are nothing. If this fits the description of your interactions, merely refuse to play the game. Set limits. Demand to be treated well. Hang up the phone if you must. I'm always amazed by men who can't control their rage, particularly on the telephone. You'd think these guys would have grown nodules on their vocal cords by now from screaming. It's hard to figure them out. But alas, I don't believe the Environmental Protection Agency has declared good single men an endangered species. At least not yet!

If It Acts Stupid, It Probably Is Stupid

Wasn't there a line in *Forrest Gump* that said something about "stupid is as stupid does?" Well, plenty of estranged husbands make some absolutely bonehead moves. Honestly. Instead of asking their doctors to write a script for Viagra, these guys need brain-potency pharmaceuticals.

In researching this book, I collected many stories. And each woman has a gem to tell. One husband, upon separating, promised to live cheaply with soup and canned goods. So his wife helped him pack up pots and pans (old ones mind you!), and she threw in a can opener. "Gee, I hadn't thought of that," the guy remarked.

The next guy attended his son's school play. He knew his estranged wife would also be there each night they performed because their son had a lead role. Each performance, Studly walked in with a different woman on his arm. Finally, one of the wife's friends shook her head and said, "What's WITH him? Can't he even get a second date?"

Another man called his estranged wife at six o'clock while she and the kids were trying to eat dinner. He had forced her to considerable expense in court to affect their divorce, such that when he greeted her with, "Would you like to save money?" she didn't recognize his voice, thought he was a telemarketer, and hung up.

In my own separation, I needed to replace my ten-year-old car. My then estranged husband refused to sign the title for a trade-in. But I'd found exactly what I needed, and fortunately that save-for-a-rainy-day mode served me well. I just went out and bought what I wanted before it got snapped up. Of course, my little one spilled the beans to his dad one night. Oh, how I wish I could have been there to see his face when he was told, "Mommy got a new car." I'd have added, "You didn't REALLY think I thought you'd sign that title, did you?"

One woman's cheating ex-husband got a promotion, a post that demanded his presence all over the globe. During an exchange he prided himself over his jet setting. "Aren't you sorry you didn't stick with me?" he asked. She was thinking, "I'd rather go to Alcatraz with a faithful guy than Australia with a louse who hasn't a clue what monogamy means."

Another man insisted on a separation despite the pleas of his wife and children to stay put. He claimed he needed peace and quiet, but the room he rented was next door to a fast-food drive-through. Each morning and late into the night he was awakened with, "Would you like fries with that?" Two divorced friends cheered each other on when their lazy ex's couldn't solve problems but instead resorted to game-playing at every opportunity. Only the court began, finally, to figure one guy out. "He's like a rat in the river, and the water is rising," one woman assured her friend. The visual elicited a few laughs.

Even if your marriage was a rocky road, there will come a time when another man shares your life. You'll get to savor the moment when your ex meets Mr. Right. It's only human nature to enjoy this a little bit. One woman dubbed this meeting the "who the hell are you moment," because indeed that's what her ex belted out seeing her new beau reading the newspaper, sipping a martini, and sitting in his old chair!

Being Better Off

Sooner or later, women facing divorce learn to look at their future with a positive glow. At first, the one-phrase sentences outsiders offer may make you even angrier. "He wasn't your type anyway" or "You'll be better off without him." These lines sound trite. Indeed they probably are, because in many cases, the people trying to cheer you up have never ventured down this path themselves. If you take care of yourself and work through the negative emotions productively, you will reach a lighter point.

So I asked women who have taken the journey. Here are some thoughts, mixed with my own, when I asked them to complete the phrase "you know you're better off divorced when . . . ":

- You find yourself exploring your hobbies, not his.
- You can forget which night Al Michaels hosts football.
- Your basement isn't a graveyard of broken gadgets, rusted tools, or thingamajigs.
- Your mother can visit anytime.
- Your garden consists of rosemary and lavender rather than beefsteak tomatoes and jalapeño peppers.
- It's goodbye deer hunting and trout fishing. Hello art classes and book discussions.
- You don't have to deal with dirty socks, discarded underwear, or his mother.
- Your food lasts longer, costs less, and means half the work.
- Each day brings a little victory versus a defeat.

After reading that list, go ahead and display your old Barbie collection on the mantel. Talk to your girlfriends on the phone all night long, or like me, keep the TV tuned to CNN. Spend Super Bowl Sunday at the ballet. One woman reported how blissful it was to enjoy a night out that didn't involve wings, beer, and Hooters! Commandeer the recliner, the remote control, and the hot water supply.

Have you ever rolled your eyes at your coffee table magazine collection that rivals the waiting room of the urologist's office? Well, deep six the swimsuit issue and make six stacks of *O, Oprah's* magazine, if you want.

Freeze the lasagna leftovers, and sneak a few pieces of the kids' Halloween candy. When you go on trips, near or far, you pick the destination, and get this: You'll know you're better off divorced when you don't have to ask for *his* directions, and frankly, you don't even care if he's lost on his journeys. You'll travel your way—the whole way—and you'll know where you're going from the get-go!

Imagine the days of having your estranged husband show up in your driveway with a brand new SUV, each time he got the kids. When the troops came marching home, you heard it belonged to his perky new girlfriend—reminding you of "mine's better than yours is!" Dream a little here, that someday—maybe sooner than you think—when you pull into his driveway, there he is peeking out from behind the ruffled curtains, drooling a puddle because you're driving a sporty new Lexus, a gift from your incredibly generous—not to mention well-enhanced—new husband. If you think that it can't happen, guess again. From the anecdotes I've gathered, this and much more could be in store for you.

View his midlife crisis as your opportunity. Taking the higher ground is so much more pleasant than his dirt path, in many respects. Say something breaks. Hire a handyman, albeit a handsome handyman, to fix it. Okay, if that's not in the budget, try fixing it yourself. Women can often do more with a can of WD-40 than he ever did with his entire toolbox. Another thing about being in charge of repairs is that you can discover the sheer exhilaration of power tools. And, isn't it nice when there's no engineering treatise offered over the most mundane snafu.

Man watching is a wonderful way to pass the time. Dating can also be fun. Men can be both supportive and friendly. And, sex is even more sensational the second time around when you know you're loved and respected for who you are.

When it's all over, and the legal papers are filed away, the only person you'll seek to improve is yourself. And if you have children, all of your decisions from this day on focus on your bright future and theirs. It will shine. And so can you!

Having the Last Laugh

Indeed, few people emerge unscathed from a separation and divorce. It takes a bit of moxie to brush yourself off and steam forward. But good things can result.

Remember that choosing to be lighthearted doesn't mean that you don't care about the difficult path you've walked, nor does it make that path fade into the landscape. If you lead with a lighthearted approach, you make the conscious choice to be empowered by all of your struggle and survival. This alone will carry you during the days ahead. When life gets you feeling low or your estranged lives up to the "strange" component of that word, just say to yourself, "Well, there's something to be said for consistency!"

Chapter Ten
Exploring New Horizons

Though you're beginning the last chapter of this book, with some decisions determined and others still left undecided, there are enormously positive possibilities that await you. This chapter explores some of those, realizing that if not today or tomorrow, someday you may face any number of these events. Some marriages surviving separation will reconcile. This possibility should not only be explored but particularly celebrated if the two of you can grow from what has gone wrong. Hopefully, any counseling you've received has helped you determine whether reconciliation would be a positive step forward versus a halting step back.

In other separations, it's clear that the marriage will end in divorce. One of you may have made the choice and informed the other. In cases where behavior is not corrected, is denied, or is indeed dangerous (abuse or serial infidelity), then divorce becomes necessary. I know there are many pro-marriage advocates out there who would say that even in these cases, a couple might still be able to salvage their commitment, but I'm talking about unions where perhaps a husband's behavior is not changing despite his wanting the happy family façade. Most women would agree that he cannot have both. Though I've never viewed this book as pro-divorce, my intent has always been to provide support whenever women realize themselves that their marriage is over, or sometimes, when that choice has been handed to them.

Even if divorce results against your will, what lies ahead can indeed be exciting, with time and the proper perspective. Sure, there are bound to be challenges, changes, some loneliness, and other adjustments, but in time you can learn to see these as opportunities, not setbacks. For instance, facing the newly single crowd can be daunting, but it can also be fun, leading you to new activities and friendships. I'll use myself as the example here.

When I wrapped up writing the first edition of this book, I had been meeting a few eligible men who fit the standards I'd created and began dating one of them on a steady basis. You probably know where this is leading (unless you've been snoozing with book in hand) because I married him, moved my life to another state, formed a stepfamily, and embraced some new professional goals as well. This chapter will cover new territory, for life can indeed bring further journeys we'd never imagined.

Lingering Questions

If you're still undecided about which direction your marriage should take, there is a book that may help. *Should You Leave* by Peter D. Kramer, M.D., explores personal autonomy versus interpersonal intimacy, and the question of whether to stick out a troubled relationship. It's got good information. Kramer writes, "When you ask whether you should leave, what is at issue includes fairness. Is it disloyal for you to bow out? Is the commitment made to you being honored? Are you being taken advantage of? Is an isolated instance of betrayal a sign of abuse, or is there a level at which your partner remains trustworthy? Is your implicit bargain corrupt or honest?"

Those are the questions you will have to face when you decide to reconcile or divorce. If there is blaming or refusal to change a major issue (like infidelity or abuse), is the marriage worth saving? Or does the quick escape route (usually another partner) look particularly appealing? Most people mistakenly think that a quick flight into another nest will solve their problems. Not so, say the experts. If you don't deal with your difficulties now, they will haunt you in other relationships.

You don't have to answer these questions immediately, for marital separations sometimes last many years until the parties have compelling reasons to move beyond them. Time has a way of showing us our path. The goal is to arrive at a new contract that works for you, possibly for the two of you together.

Attempting a Reconciliation

Remember the famous Ann Landers' question: Are you better off with him, or without him? There are some unions where escape is simply the easy out, and in all sincerity, you might be better trying to save the relationship.

I have seen marriages put back together. For couples who separate and then reconcile many months later, their separation served as a marital time out, a chance to reflect upon problems, feelings, and goals. If you do reconcile, be certain that you're doing so because both of you are committed to one another, not one of you returning out of fear. Few of us want to be alone, and no one looks forward to single parenting or financial adjustments. However, if you reconcile prematurely, you risk splitting up permanently, and those are the adjustments you will indeed make.

Hopefully, you have sought your own therapy, especially if there has been domestic abuse or if a partner's affair has shaken your self-esteem. Assuming it's safe and wise to contemplate getting back together, your next step may be couples counseling, though even here there is debate. William J. Doherty, Ph.D., is director of the University of Minnesota's Marriage and Family Therapy Program, and has published in professional journals that not all marriage therapists help couples. Indeed some may impede positive progress because their therapeutic strength rests with individual counseling, and they may undermine a couple's commitment to their marriage with a value system that reflects "if it's not working, get another one." For this reason, Doherty encourages couples to ask a potential marriage counselor to declare his or her value system, and to avoid those whose values differ from your own. Check also that any prospective marriage counselor has been adequately trained and supervised in working with couples. A properly trained counselor can help you realize the distorted thinking patterns that may have led to misunderstandings and hurt feelings. All relationships go through phases, and all have some conflict. It's a matter of how you handle that conflict, and how you strive for equality in the marriage. Communication and conflict resolution skills can be acquired through couples therapy.

Counseling can also help determine your list of emotional needs. Everyone has them. In fact, couples who make a point of meeting their partner's top five needs stand a better chance of building a healthier marriage. Even focusing on the top two puts you ahead of the game. Doherty is also the author of several books including *Take Back Your Marriage: Sticking Together in a World That Pulls Us Apart*. In his chapter titled "Preventing Unnecessary Divorce," Doherty writes, "I see more people nowadays whose only admission of responsibility for marriage problems is that they chose the wrong person, or maybe put up with that person's failings for too long." He likens a marriage to a car when the owner hasn't bothered to change the oil yet blames the manufacturer for poor performance. Truly when our emotional concerns go unmet, we tend to feel empty, and we're willing to sacrifice just about anything to have them met, even our spouses, children, careers, or core beliefs.

Many self-help books list typical needs for men and women. For instance, most men give highest priority to sexual fulfillment, recreational companionship, physical attractiveness, domestic support, and admiration. Women, on the other hand, rank their top needs as affection, conversation, honesty and openness, financial support, and family commitment. The only way you'll know your husband's needs is to ask, and the same goes for him. As adults, we are responsible for understanding our own feelings, integrating that knowledge for useful purposes, and indeed communicating that perspective to our spouse. As one woman shared with me, "If you go to the dentist and you don't understand the procedure, it's his or her job to explain it in whatever language until you do understand. The same goes in a marriage. Don't expect me to just figure out what you mean. Tell me. Give me examples until I clearly get it."

Not that you should keep score, but experts agree that compliments, hugs, and positive interactions absolutely must outweigh criticisms, blaming, exasperated sighs, and the like. If you aim for five positive to every one negative, you're doing well. Learn the language of reconciliation by overcoming the anger and resentment that led you to separate in the first place. One step to take in removing the negativity from your life is to eliminate it from your speech and tone. Which request sounds easier to acquiesce to?

"Don't put the dishes in the rack that way." Or, "When you load the dishwasher, could you please be careful not to bang the dishes."

The first sentence is demanding and negative. The second states your request in the positive adding a little information that explains your meaning, and ultimately may get cooperation with the dishes. When asking questions, refrain from starting with the word "why" in favor of "how" or "what." Sure, it takes a little extra thought to rearrange what you intended to say, but it's much less likely to put your spouse on the defensive, and it elicits feeling (as well as thoughts). That's what you need to share in order to succeed.

John Gottman, Ph.D., a prolific author and researcher at the Seattle Marital and Family Institute believes he can predict which marriages last and which may falter based upon certain factors. Those who avoid conflict, or go at conflict with great volatility (like two lawyers in a courtroom) don't fare well, and sometimes you've got a great debater married to a chronic avoider. Thus, nothing ever gets resolved. No surprise that Gottman has found the stable pattern of validating one another to be a positive predictor of marital success. Each partner respectfully listens to the other, and thus each keeps arguments to a minimum.

Perfect Timing

It takes time to meet each other's needs so don't expect overnight success. Most important, it takes time alone, time without friends or family (including your own children), and time that's truly earmarked for attention, as you did when you first dated and fell in love. Doherty writes about the importance of following rituals in your marriage, whether it's a cup of coffee and conversation following dinner, long walks with the dog, or some other means of keeping the two of you connected with events in each other's lives. An important ritual could even be recreation—something fun that the two of you enjoy.

Time was a shortcoming in my first marriage. I felt pressured by others to vacation with in-laws and extended family. Without childcare, there were few options available for a reprieve, just the two of us. Even after the toughest year of our marriage, when we'd brought our preemie to relative health and needed to do something special, I felt brutally chastised. I was told by an extended family member that I didn't belong, all because I'd dared to plan an escape for the four of us at a resort that had excellent childcare onsite. Certain (wrong) assumptions must have been made about our priorities, and that stung. To this day, I'm jealous of those couples that escape together with relative ease (and relative support).

That vacation we took, ironically a year before we separated, did wonders to renew us as a family and rekindle romance, at least in my mind. My husband's coworkers even urged me to take him away again because they'd never seen him so relaxed.

If you can't leave the children behind, choose a vacation with excellent childcare. Boscobel Beach, a SuperClubs resort in Jamaica or the Disney Cruise Line are two examples of vacations where couples can delight in one another while making sure their children are happy and safe. Search for a vacation option that appeals to your needs and budget.

To really reconcile your differences, of course, other tasks need to occur, but these can't happen unless you dedicate those precious moments. Spending time with a spouse shows him, or shows you, that there is respect, especially if you are overcoming infidelity. A woman who doesn't feel respected outside of the bedroom will rarely feel that way in it. Time also affords the chance to actively listen, paraphrase back to our partners what we've heard, and make sincere attempts at two-way communication. Time gives us the opportunity to learn new things together—to take a class, become familiar with our partner's favorite pastimes, or merely make new memories. Taking even a minute here or five there allows us to have fun, for it only takes a second to scribble a funny note tucked inside a briefcase, send a sexy e-mail or pager message, or reach out to offer a much-needed hug.

Other Steps

The other necessary ingredient toward successful reconciliation is an open mind. You need to be able to understand the world as your partner sees it. This doesn't mean that you necessarily must agree with it, just take that emotional leap.

How often have you looked objectively at a friend's marriage and wanted to shake her into reality? Perhaps she has what you yearn for, only she stubbornly refuses to make minor changes. Sure you don't walk in her shoes, and you don't want to coerce her into something she's personally uncomfortable with. But I'm talking little things here—like being open to new recreational pursuits, taking a different kind of trip, engaging in playful conversation if there has been too serious a stance, or even splurging for Victoria's Secret merchandise when she's shunned it before. Again, the way to determine which changes—major or minor—in your attitude require focus is to ask your spouse what he thinks, and consider the possibilities with an open mind. The results might just surprise you.

Overcoming Infidelity

When spouses promise to be sexually and emotionally faithful, and then aren't, their betrayal is wrenching. Often if you can understand why the infidelity occurred, you feel more in control. Having no clear answers allows confusion to reign, and it's harder to overcome.

Of course, we've all heard various definitions of what constitutes sex, let alone infidelity. My feeling is: If in doubt, the tempted partner should ask the spouse if it constitutes infidelity. Of course, some partners consider flirting as being unfaithful. While the excitement of a crush is transferred to the marriage, it can be dangerous if you're tempted to share emotional intimacy with this person rather than your spouse. *Psychology Today* in August 1998 ran a cover story on overcoming infidelity during the Monica Lewinsky scandal. It pointed out that if unfaithful partners treated their spouses the way they approached their lovers, the spouses would probably be ecstatic. The report also concluded that yes, oral sex counts; infidelity is more serious the earlier it occurs in a marriage; and if you think you were unfaithful because you weren't getting enough in the marriage, you probably weren't giving enough to begin with, as some experts shared earlier.

If you've been the spouse who was cheated on, then you know the trauma. You'll act a little crazy, almost hypervigilant, until you can start to manage the scar tissue that's resulted in the relationship.

If you're the spouse who did the cheating, realize that your husband will feel that everything has been a lie. Your marriage has lost its innocence. In fact, the deceit is sometimes harder to bear than the actual sexual images. Traitors who commit treason against their country have been sentenced to death. In the minds of most betrayed spouses that seems too mild a punishment to fit the crime.

Oh, there will be anger. And the hurt will run deep. Occasionally, the debt is too big to pay off. But some woman will likely overlook a man's transgressions, giving the husband a second chance. Will that woman be you?

The betrayer also goes through an emotional gamut, feeling ashamed, guilty, anxious over adverse consequences (loss of reputation, job, income, assets, children). Personally, I don't have much sympathy for betrayers who compound secrets because they don't want to deal with the destruction left behind. With disclosure, there can be hope. With secrets, there is shame.

I firmly believe that there is no excuse for infidelity. Therefore, you shouldn't blame yourself if you're the victim. One husband rationalized that by hiring hookers, he never forced anyone, as if that made up for breaking his vows, lying to his wife, risking everyone's health, and quite possibly corrupting minors (since many prostitutes are runaway teens).

Some betrayals are deliberate passive-aggressive attempts to hurt the innocent spouse, and many others are committed to avoid intimacy. By placing one's attention and energy outside the marriage, one runs away from emotional involvement in the family instead of dealing with it. When this happens, infidelity serves as a barometer that indicates that something else is going on within the person seeking escape. Does this sound like you or your estranged spouse?

Though it's the common perception that infidelity is all about sex, it rarely originates there. In order to overcome infidelity, it's important to gauge what the affair meant (or whether the pattern of one-night stands constitutes an addiction) and whether there is sincere remorse and responsibility taken for the deed. In addition, all extramarital activity must end, and the betrayer needs to make restitution and reparations. Without such, it's impossible for one party to find forgiveness. (Mind you, that's not forgetfulness, because many betrayed spouses cannot completely erase it from memory.) The offending party needs to deal attentively, with great empathy toward one's spouse and with frequent reassurance to resolve infidelity or the possibility of it in the future. Another way of summarizing this hurdle is to know why the infidelity occurred, have assurance that it won't happen again, and state what consequences will occur if it does.

Marriages can recover from betrayal. Trust can be restored, for infidelity is often a wakeup call. Recovery will take a great deal of work, but if both parties are willing, the indiscretion can lead to greater ground as a married couple. The late Shirley P. Glass, Ph.D., spent more than two decades researching infidelity. Her book, written with Jean Coppock Staeheli, *Not "Just Friends": Rebuilding Trust and Recovering Your Sanity After Infidelity* is a must-read if you're facing this crisis.

Some of Shirley Glass' insights include: A happy marriage is not a vaccine against infidelity. Therefore, a troubled marriage, we can assume, may even be a greater risk. Emotional affairs, characterized by sharing secrets outside the marriage, enjoying emotional intimacy, and sexual chemistry, can be more of a threat to a marriage than a brief sexual fling. Yet surprisingly, men and women both rationalize these behaviors. If you experience this, see it as a sign that your marriage needs help. Glass advocated that you keep private issues between the two of you (or with your therapist), and resist the urge to rescue an unhappily married person who pours out his or her soul to you.

Accepting Divorce

Some marriages can't be fixed. This is especially the case when there are multiple issues fraught with broken trust and a pattern of fight or flight.

Though it's hard to accept the demise of your union, which may have brought into this world beautiful children who never asked for this, accept you must. There will still be sentimental times, even if you don't want him back. Indeed, most women admit that they can't fathom ever being intimate with their ex-husband again, even if the world's population depended on it! Some sentiment stems from the broken dreams—the vacations never taken, the holidays never had, the school events never attended together with pride. It comes from what could have been, instead of what truly was.

With so much negative press that divorce receives at times, *For Better or For Worse: Divorce Reconsidered* by E. Mavis Hetherington, an emeritus professor of psychology at the University of Virginia and New York writer John Kelly, challenge the bleak generalizations. Some families, they say, have emerged with fewer problems, showing resilience and resolve. Another source of encouragement is *Cutting Loose: Why Women Who End Their Marriages Do So Well* by Ashton Applewhite. If you find yourself having to accept divorce, where is your compass pointing? To whom will you most listen because if you only read a litany of pessimism then your mind will go there.

Real and Imagined Losses

Managing the memories and the necessary losses will surely tug at your heart. But when I'd start the wistful thinking, my friends would quickly step in, reminding me that now I felt safer, healthier, and happier, set free in a sense. One male friend, hearing that my estranged husband asked to move back, implored, "Listen to what you're saying. If he wants the garage remote, the security code, and access to the boys, those are conveniences. Not a marriage." My friend was right.

Just as time helps reconciling couples, it also helps those divorcing. You must travel through the pain, not around it, to get to the other side. Don't worry about the marriage, and certainly not about your soon-to-be-former spouse. As mothers, we're supposed to figure out our children—when they need to go to the toilet, when they are hungry, when they need sleep, etc. But as wives and ex-wives, we're *not* our partner's mother. Your ex-husband must be responsible for himself and his future. If his poor choices impact his relationship with the children, then let him make or break that relationship of his own accord. Pick your battles wisely, and only where the children's welfare matters. Otherwise, stay out of his life, his decisions, and his future.

The Blame Game

While it takes two parties to dance, one partner can really miss the beat. Only you know the energy and commitment you contributed to your marriage, but my guess is that you did the very best you could at the time. There is absolutely no sense beating yourself up over past mistakes.

In fact, thinking about your marital missteps can become obsessive and lead you into deeper distress. Your life is a continuum, and your marriage was only a stop. Try as best you can to focus on the future, to reframe things in a positive light. Much of the time, what you think determines how you feel. Quit asking "why me?" or "what could I have done?" Ruminating over this loss will keep you shackled by it.

If you're feeling continually lost without the framework of your marriage, it's time to seek professional help, and perhaps to begin something of your own (such as a new job or a new academic program) to force a refocus. Remember: You are your greatest gift to your own happiness and successful future. As the famous writer Joseph Campbell once shared, "We must be willing to get rid of the life we've planned so as to have the life that is waiting for us."

Learning to Be Single

One woman I spoke with articulated the common feeling of socially not fitting in anywhere. Used to moving in a circle of couples, you might feel as if you're wearing a neon sign, hesitant to reveal your circumstances or making up excuses why you can't join others. Sooner or later, however, you'll want and need to venture out. Believe it or not, you don't need a man by your side to do so.

A friend described this as the "putting yourself back together" phase, a time when you make new friendships, begin new traditions, and even decide you might like time to yourself.

"I revel in having the house to myself," another woman told me. And that is so true after you've shared living space with another adult. You can eat potato chips and sip iced tea for dinner, at midnight if you want. You can invite the dog or cat into the queen-sized bed, watch television in the middle of the night, or turn on the light to finish your novel!

Indeed, it's perfectly fine to go it alone, for a while or forever. But the word *alone* does not mean a life destined to complete solitude. "Remember, you may be on your own, but you don't have to be alone," write Keith Anderson, M.D., and Roy MacSkimming in *On Your Own Again*. They stress that quality friendships are vital; friends act as mirrors that help us see ourselves.

Admittedly, some women have a larger appetite for solitude than others. There are women who can't take themselves to a restaurant with a good book, or attend a social function without a date. I'll admit that it's different being single, and some events are easier than others. I'm glad that I pushed myself a little. I attended my neighborhood Christmas party solo, years before I brought a guest. I went to church and graduation parties unaccompanied. And the thought of having a king-sized bed to myself in a wonderful hotel was a luxury, not a lament.

I did these things because I've learned to treat myself well. I've seen some women postpone their dreams because they figure Prince Charming is on his way. There may well be a gentleman who will capture your heart and render you silly. But why wait? Create your own future, even if it's uncomfortable for the moment. Who ever said growth and change were easy?

One simple way to navigate the world independently is to do it with a friend. A girlfriend, a relative, even a platonic guy friend can accompany you when the thought of going solo is too troublesome. If you and a friend agree to have dinner, force yourself to take two cars, arriving alone and having a few moments to yourself. Each time you venture out, take gradual steps at social independence.

The same holds true for vacations. I'd traveled solo for business, but there were other small victories I had to create. I'd never rented a car on my own. I'd never single-parented a vacation nor explored different parts of the country completely solo, but I did those things too, stretching beyond my comfort zone, and feeling so good because of it.

If you're still leery of setting out solo, look at it this way. We unattached women combat the perception enough that we're supposedly missing out on life. However, women often outlive men. Face the fact that you will be on your own for a few years regardless of your present circumstances. Would you rather learn to be independent now when you're younger and relatively active? Or would you rather wait until you need assistance in a wheelchair? I think you'll enjoy it now, and later too. My point: Be happy now. Embrace the opportunities before you.

Dare to Date Again

I've found that women re-entering the dating scene fit into about three categories. First, since there is no law that says that you must date, these women are perfectly happy being single and self-sufficient.

Second, there is a set damned determined to date *now*. Often, these women are reacting to sadness, anxiety, anger, or guilt, and dating serves as a quick fix, or so they think. Entering into this arena too fast nearly guarantees that you'll fall into a rebound relationship, which can lead you down another path of misery. This life transition often requires time to heal, and you won't be in a better position to do that after surrendering time and energy to someone else. Or as someone so cleverly put it, "Why would you want someone else's butthead if you already had one?" Watch for this temptation to soothe yourself with a too-soon companion especially during holidays, important anniversaries, or birthdays.

Third, there are women who have waited, yearning for companionship, only they don't know how to go about it or they need to fine-tune their rusty dating skills. It helps if you set the goal of meeting new people, rather than looking for Mr. Right or even Mr. Right For Now. Dating doesn't have to be all that daunting, with an approach that protects you from disappointment. Be thankful at this stage in your life that you know more of what you want, and that you realize what you have to offer another person. These assets far outweigh any re-entry fears.

If you've experimented with the journaling exercises in a prior chapter, here you might write out your life as you'd like it to be in three, five, fifteen, or twenty-five years. Who is by your side? What has this man added to your life? How does he treat you? Does he have emotional intelligence? How does he leverage his education and life experiences? Okay, don't write a fairy tale here, for in case you haven't noticed, no man is perfect. But now that you've set some standards, go out there and find it. We teach people how to treat us, so this exercise will help you to seize a successful match.

Setting Your Social Worth

I'm sure you've heard the cliché "once burned, twice cautious." Nowhere does that apply more than dating again after a failed, perhaps hurtful, relationship. So what do I mean by setting your social worth? Very simply, I'm referring to the social pricing (or worth) that you establish for yourself. I ventured this way when I encouraged you to journal about whom would be by your side in future years. If you craft a picture of how you'd like it to be, even if you must fine-tune any too-perfect expectations, you place a higher worth on yourself and your future. The higher the worth you have to offer, the more you can expect to receive in return.

Some women set their sights too low because they inaccurately assess their social worth. Fear of rejection factors into this, as does a lack of your own education, past emotional wounds, and all or nothing thinking. One woman admitted years too late that she'd been prejudiced by her husband's success. Though she enjoyed the lifestyle they shared, the minute he cheated on her she referred to him as "the suit," or the professional, college-educated man, and to hear her say "I had that once," made it quite clear she was eliminating this type of gentleman from her life ever again. That's her right, I suppose, but she based that opinion upon an irrational belief that most professional men would treat her as poorly as her ex-husband did. Her own lack of a college education may have contributed as well to any bias and sight setting. Thus, she limited her search, and did find a caring, kind man, but one who brought less financial strength to their subsequent marriage. This created other long-term struggles that perhaps could have been avoided had she really worked on those irrational beliefs, and affirmed what she really wanted, in terms of the larger life-planning picture.

Social worth is certainly something to ponder, especially in an age where many available men gravitate toward a peer marriage—one in which they find balance, if not financially, then in terms of other assets a woman brings to the marriage. These are often the intangibles like great compassion, honesty, commitment to one's children, things that can't be quantified by a dollar sign but are valued nonetheless.

Spotting Other Singles

Not too long ago, I heard my son's basketball coach yell to the boys, "Find your man." I smiled, realizing I felt like that at one time! Seriously though, where do you find available men? Sure, clubs or bars are obvious choices, but many women prefer an atmosphere that offers more substance. Look at outings with other single parents, classes at community colleges, religious or volunteer activities, or chance meetings at your favorite hangouts like bookstores or bowling alleys. You may form new friendships at professional meetings or parties hosted by friends. There are singles groups and volunteer associations designed to foster introductions. Some are free to join; others charge a fee to match you with compatible partners. Of course, the safest dates are those you know through friends who can vouch for character. Even men you meet at work might mask what they don't want you to see. There is a calculated risk in any dating. I'd advise against dating any married man, including a recently separated man who uses lines like "my wife didn't understand me." These guys, desperate to reattach, should use their energy to heal, grow, spend time with their children, and figure out what went wrong in their marriages *before* getting involved with you or any other woman. Besides, until his divorce is final, he could always go back, and where does that leave you and your emotions?

Expect that you may have to part with some of your existing notions and perfect portraits that you have created. I'm not suggesting that you lower your standards, by any means, but that you open your mind to new possibilities. I never thought I would date a man with more than a ten-year age differential, but when presented with maturity, how refreshing and wonderful it was. This is what I mean about giving things a chance.

Online Dating

Those knowledgeable about cyberdating report that one-third of online friendships result in face-to-face meetings. While I don't have any statistics to vouch for the success of those encounters, I do have my own success story to share.

After three years in which I got myself, my life, and my children together, I felt the urge to become more social. I laugh now, because when I got engaged and had to ask the court to relocate my children, the opposing counsel's tone was unmistakable, at least to me. I can't do it justice here, but I invite you to read into "You met him on the *Internet* . . . correct?" It left me wondering how other venues would have been reduced for effect!

Where else was I supposed to meet this plethora of eligible men, especially as a work-at-home mom? Not that I cloistered myself in my basement office, mind you. I participated in church events, lived much of my spare time in bookstores, and ventured to a few nightspots, realizing these just weren't my setting. I set my own social worth by realizing I wanted someone who enjoyed culture, travel, good conversation—someone caring and kind to my children—and well, he had to appreciate books. A quick browse through various personal ads and Web sites showed the field, and I felt that I had better chances of meeting my criteria if I limited my search to professional men. I pretty much steered clear of Perry Mason types, and now that you're in the last chapter, I'm sure you understand why! There, online, I met a man named Bob, a dentist, whose ad was titled "Life is a journey." It sounded intriguing, and so was the correspondence back and forth. A dental meeting conflicted with our scheduled first date so we met three months after numerous e-mails and exchanging photographs.

If you decide to venture online, realize, girlfriends, that you're only a mouse click away from Mr. Married who makes no apologies about his search for a good time! You will have to set standards, and you'll be tempted to give up Internet service a time or two. I met Mr. Mensa who was intelligent all right, and fully conscious of that genius. As a writer, how men crafted ads caught my eye, for some had traces of thinly disguised anger. No thanks! Of course, photographs did matter. One man sent me a photo of himself in a tux, only standing by his estranged wife at their daughter's wedding. Some inner voice just told me that he surely could have found a better photo representation. Then, Dr. Psychiatrist sent me a photo of himself in scrubs, which seemed odd given his specialty, but when I met him, I realized the picture had to have been taken twenty-five years prior. Trust me, he was no stand-in for the docs on NBC's *ER* when we did meet. I couldn't wait to get out of that restaurant though a restaurant meal went pretty well for a first meeting with another man who worked in sales.

My first date with Bob was at Starbucks early one evening. We sat there for hours talking and sharing bits of our lives. It felt incredibly comfortable, and as he walked me to my car, we made plans for dinner the next weekend, again each driving to a neutral destination. On our third date, Bob picked me up for a picnic in the park, which I had orchestrated. Then we went shopping for a bike I wanted to buy. In hindsight, I can't believe I took this man to Toys "R" Us to look at one model, and it didn't deter future dates. I could be myself and be accepted, even when the pizza dough recipe I'd used since eighth grade home-ec class finally failed me. Mind you, Bob is Italian, and little did I know what skill he mustered in the kitchen himself, but even then, it didn't matter. He hit it off with my boys immediately, so much so that when we were walking out of the stadium after a baseball game that summer, my then ten-year-old son reached out his hand—for Bob's.

I'll end my personal story there at such a tender moment, but as you can surmise, the Web is a prime place to look for love. Should you decide to place a personal ad, start with a great attitude and select positive words, writing that first sentence to really grab a reader's attention. Keep your profile to 100 to 150 words, and be sure to proofread it. I remember spotting sloppy writing and spelling errors, wondering if that translated into other habits. Be honest about yourself, accentuating the positive, and of course, be prepared to answer questions should your ad spark some interest in some man's mind.

First Date Jitters

I shared the good and the not-so-good there to demonstrate reality in dating. It's hard not to purposely want a first date to be magical, but you really must adjust your attitude and expectations to calm the jitters. Refuse to obsess about what you'll wear, what your date will think, or any other aspect of this first meeting, for that's all it is—maybe a cup of coffee and some conversation.

The art of revealing your personality is gradual, both for you and the other person. If you try to impress, you'll surely fail. Thus, put yourself in your date's place. Doing so keeps you from wondering how you're coming across. He's feeling anxious too. He wants to make an equally good impression.

I can see logic in choosing a venue where there is no alcohol served, but in either case, expect to pay your own way. Meet at a neutral, public location where you have driven yourself. This is for safety and sanity's sake. If you find that the date is a disaster, you can politely cut it short. It's also a safe bet to stick with subjects like work and recreational interests, as opposed to personal inadequacies or failings in a marriage. You don't want to seem as though you're sizing up your date. Similarly, too much unloading comes across as bitterness. We all have the proverbial baggage, but we don't necessarily need to advertise that fact. If there is a future, the rest will reveal itself.

Discuss things with kindness and compassion, and maintain good eye contact when listening and speaking. This means that you're focusing on the other person, which is always flattering. Also, consider each other's expectations. As a guy friend confided, women tend to like a guy first, then find him attractive. Men, being more visually inclined, are physically attracted to women first. Then they fall in love.

Next Steps

If you're fortunate enough to form a connection and a friendship, you'll wonder where this new relationship might lead. The majority of divorced women do remarry, in time, but that doesn't mean you must rush into a new union. You want to make sure that this is the right move, and the only way you'll know is to proceed a bit cautiously.

As Dr. James C. Dobson has written, "Remember that respect precedes love. Build it stone upon stone." That's why it's wise to postpone sexual relations as long as possible. When the endorphins are raging is not the time to size up your relationship. Indeed, those love hormones will mask all the red flags and warning signs that this might *not* be the man for your future.

Additionally, know that what you see is indeed what you get. If you think you care for this man, but hope your love will change this habit or that peccadillo, think again.

Also, realize that every relationship is tested in due course. There's a natural pulling-back process that each of us does when we feel things getting too serious. John Gray often says men are like rubber bands—they stretch before springing back. They might do this because they are scared. It could be that they feel their independence threatened. Or, for many men, it's the fear that we women will indeed want to change them. Again, part of the excitement of dating and falling in love later in life is the journey of exploration.

If your efforts are successful and the relationship is meant to be, you'll be well on your way to that one very satisfying moment. No, I'm not talking about sex. I'm not even talking about walking down the aisle. It's the moment when you revel in sheer delight as your former mate meets your current love or finds out that you have one. I believe it was Ivana Trump who claimed living well is the best revenge.

How Do I Know?

Whether you happily reconcile with your husband or form a new relationship with a future partner, only you can come to that place in your heart where you know it's the right decision. But a lot has gone on in your life if you're reading this book. Take some time to think.

If time tells us certain things so does a sense of maturity. It reminds me of the famous Ann Landers "Maturity has many meanings" column that I clipped years ago where Ann said that "dependability is the hallmark of integrity," and that three important little words were not "I love you," but "I was wrong."

I do think that maturity reveals itself in the ability to see the larger picture and to persevere instead of going for immediate gratification. I think a man also reveals his maturity in how he interacts with his children and his ex-wife. If you find that the man you're dating, for instance, never has a kind word for the mother of his children, I'd dig deeper for answers. Does he offer to work with her (and don't just take his word at this), or does he run straight to court when problems arise? How does he treat his children? Does he nickel and dime everything because he's paying child support, or does he freely give of himself, especially meeting any obligations or requirements his kids might have? Does he put himself in their lives or compel them to become a part of his? If he makes demands of them, his ex, anyone, what's that behavior about? These are true tests of maturity as well. Hopefully, this list will incite some additional answers, though all questions may not apply to each scenario:

- Can you be yourself with the man in your life?
- Are you treated well or mistreated in some way?

- Do you feel safe, both physically and emotionally, in this relationship?
- Is there absolute trust or do you feel that pieces of the puzzle are missing?
- Do you feel a sense of support (that is, not usurping your authority but complementing it) in your parenting efforts?
- Can the two of you fight fairly? Or do disagreements never get negotiated?
- How does this man manage anger? Does he explode? Keep it in? Act it out in passive-aggression? Problem solve for a solution?
- Do you still wonder if you could click with other men? Mere curiosity is a red flag that you might not be as grounded as you should be in this relationship.
- Does your husband (boyfriend) respect you? Experts say that when the respect goes, the marriage (relationship) is pretty much over.
- Does your man of the moment have female chums? Most women don't form platonic friendships with jerks. Besides, men learn valuable insights about us from spending time with other women.
- Is the man you're dating separated? If so, are you enabling him to flee rather than work on his marriage and keep the commitment to his family? Where will you be if he does reconcile?
- Are you frequently reminded that you're thought of and loved?
- Is staying in this marriage a worse fear than venturing out on your own?

Remarriage and Second Weddings

There may come a day, even when you least expect it, when you know that it's the right time to merge your life with someone else's, learning from the past, yet creating bright hopes for a new future.

Researchers have come to understand the dynamics of remarriage, and the trend has actually spawned an industry of magazines, books, and services devoted to couples planning another wedding—an event that incorporates not only a bride and a groom, but also the couples' children.

Sharon Naylor, author of *1001 Ways to Have a Dazzling Second Wedding*, discusses the mix of excitement and anticipation blended with the reality of anxiety as you take this next special step in your life. The good news on wedding planning is, just about anything goes. Repeat brides aren't criticized if they wish to wear a white gown, and you're free to have an elegant sit-down dinner or a barbecue in your own backyard. There are plenty of decisions, and since each family is unique, these are best left to you to ponder and have fun choosing. At my own wedding, I wore navy blue because I loved the dress and wanted something I might wear again. We got married in the late morning at a historic church in the town where I used to live. We hosted a luncheon at a local country club with piano music in the background. It was elegant yet more laid back and exactly what I'd envisioned for the occasion.

Merging two families can be stressful though, and that's where marriage education as well as stepfamily workshops can help at the outset. As I learned in a group counseling class, group cohesion is hard to establish if the leaders aren't working well together. With all the changes in your lives, it's a wise idea to check in with one another, and allow other trained professionals to share potential roadblocks you might encounter along the way. Good marriage education programs cover communication, conflict management, problem solving, and empathy building skills, according to Smartmarriages.com.

Francesca Adler-Baeder, Ph.D., is a certified family life educator and director of family life education for the Stepfamily Association of America (SAA). She developed a curriculum called Smart Steps, which is taught through cooperative extensions, land grant university human development and families studies departments, and at the Smart Marriages conference annually. "We've been really advocating for the use of stepfamily life education as 'remarriage preparation,'" she says. "Raising awareness and building skills at the onset is clearly an advantage for stepfamilies. Involving the children in education and preparation is clearly key as well because children have more 'power' in stepfamilies, than is typically seen in first families." Adler-Baeder also reports that the U.S. Department of Health and Human Services lists Smart Steps as one of the two recommended programs for remarriage education.

The SAA and Smart Steps prefer not to use the term "blended families" because that gives people the impression that this newly merged group ought to gel quickly, and that's just not realistic. Still, if you find that you and your spouse are divided over issues related to your children, consider this to be a red flag and seek help. "Research tells us that poor stepparent-stepchild relations can 'undo' a remarriage," says Adler-Baeder. "It seems clear that strengthening the marriage should also be given equal attention."

According to Bill Doherty, Ph.D., "Remarried couples are a minefield even for experienced therapists, because the partners almost always come with parenting issues, not just couple problems, and because many therapists miss the nuances of stepfamily dynamics." So again, choose wisely, but do seek help if you need it. You can find help not only in couples counseling, but also in group counseling devoted to couples and with educational groups as well.

Preparing a Prenuptial Agreement

If you have gained assets, and if there are children involved, you *must* look out for their interests as well as yours. A prenuptial agreement often calms many fears merely stating that what has been yours will remain yours. This alone is important. In cases of considerable wealth or inheritances, it's even more appropriate. It just does not make good sense following a divorce to co-mingle all of your assets. If you've worked hard to build a portfolio for yourself, keep it in separate funds. After your wedding, you can jointly title certain assets or share household funds at the bank, but this way you have in reserve what you entered the marriage with.

Several months before your remarriage, hire separate attorneys to draft an agreement and sign it. The more distance you can put between signing the document and walking down the aisle allows you to enjoy the excitement of planning your nuptials more fully. Furthermore, if you sign under pressure (i.e., on the way to the altar) the agreement may be rendered null and void if ever disputed. That's why some attorneys videotape their clients signing the document to have as evidence that neither was coerced.

Don't underestimate what you own. Take time to list everything that's important to you and your children, including those personal belongings you wish for them to have someday. The added perk here is having a complete inventory for insurance purposes should you ever need to make claims on account of fire, theft, or other disasters.

Of course, prenup agreements can go into greater detail. Outlining the disposition of certain assets is one thing; spelling out who does what, who makes this or that decision, or where you'll live or visit for the holidays are all daily decisions that seem unnecessarily silly to declare ahead of time. Read *How to Write Your Own Premarital Agreement* by Edward A. Haman. Even if you draft your own agreement, it's wise to seek legal counsel to make sure it's notarized and binding in your state.

Forming a Stepfamily

The SAA reports that 75 percent of those divorced do remarry. According to the Stepfamily Foundation, 1,300 new stepfamilies are created every day, and 50 percent of U.S. families are re-coupled.

Even the best-laid plans don't account for emotions running high for young and grown children alike. While your remarriage represents a moving forward for you and your new husband, it may stir feelings of loss, jealousy, and anxiety for children. Many adult children of divorce have strong emotions when a parent remarries, particularly if they've never fully grieved the loss of their first family. Brace yourself because you, or your new husband, may be the target of some unkind words or actions that clearly express disapproval, even anger. These acts might even occur in the context of your own wedding where children might refuse to attend or do so grudgingly, letting their disdain show. Since passive-aggressive behaviors are often aimed at retribution, don't be too surprised to see sarcasm, withholding, and other covert displays of their true angst.

New marriages threaten established rituals and family dynamics created years prior. Here, there are no shared memories acting as the glue, which bonds you all together. Some children, young or old, may wonder what will happen to the past? Will these treasured times with the sense of belonging merely vanish? How can everyone's rich history be renegotiated?

Other concerns include the fear of abandonment, the dashed hopes of parental reconciliation, or favoritism that you might show to your new spouse or new stepchildren. Finances or lack thereof enter the equation when fears of your having more children threaten any anticipated inheritance, or when your fully grown and adult child asks for funds and upon receiving a negative reply, immediately assumes your new family ranks a higher priority. You might be refusing to enable or have already given generously. It doesn't matter. This just goes to show that virtually anything your new spouse and you do can be packed with emotions. Something as simple as land-scaping the front yard might be seen as an attack because you dared to remove the damaged tree that mom planted years ago.

Of course, a child who has worked through negative emotions is now free to accept new life passages and the new people he or she will now call family. Kids who have made healthy transitions feel less tied to their past and freer to explore the future. They don't feel obligated to watch out for the other parent in the case of a divorce, or that parent's memory when death preceded remarriage. Be mindful of what might lurk in a new stepchild's heart. Some only know the myths, which have been perpetuated by media images of the wicked stepmother or the notion of dad's silly new (sometimes younger) wife.

It's also best not to push new titles of stepmom or stepdad on children unless you truly know a child is okay with it. Stick with first names, and introduce stepchildren as "Chrissy, my husband's daughter" until you know that stepdaughter is safe. Should one of the kids say or do something mean or unkind, just speak honestly that unkind statements or certain events hurt your feelings. Avoid finger pointing or it begins a downward spiral. If you allow younger or older children to see the hurt, they can often make their own judgments, and if you know anything about group dynamics, some of this resistance is likely to occur before things smooth out.

As I indicated in my dating, my boys accepted Bob with open arms, literally, but as we began sharing a home, they did realize that with the fun came responsibility, chores, and even discipline meted out at times. If I gave them an answer they didn't like, whom do you think they went to next, proving how important it is to form a united front? In that first year especially, new stepparents need to honestly step back some and support the decisions of the biological parent. We made fun memories though from the start with bike rides, outings to explore our new area, and family dinners. Just weeks after our wedding, my then eight-year-old son snuggled next to Bob as they watched a movie proclaiming: "Look Bob, just you and me. Two pals."

Similar adjustments must be made with adult children, or kids who are off at school. Age and geography can pose barriers to connections everyone needs. It's harder because these kids often don't have as many interactions from which to cement a new start. I'm sure Bob's adult son and daughter had much uncertainty as we got remarried, but in time, I think they came to see that he was happy and they didn't lose their dad to a new family. In fact, when we can all get together, given schedules and distance, it's especially nice to see connections form. With Bob's grandchildren, it's fun to watch my boys relate to and care for children much younger. My youngest loves to play with his nephew, but when "his pal" started gushing over a new little grandson, I remember seeing signs of jealousy. This is all very normal for birth order shifts may mean the oldest son isn't the oldest any longer, and the youngest must shift rank also. Imagine being the only girl in a family of boys, then suddenly having two new sisters.

The good news is that though it takes five to eight years to attain family cohesion in some cases, in others, it's attained much more quickly. According to Margorie Engel, SAA president, children in stepfamilies learn valuable skills of interpersonal interaction—skills that they will need later in life. They become sensitive to others' emotional states and they become more adept at reading people, interpreting tone of voice and body language, as well as fighting fair. Just be attuned to the changes occurring within your family. It's simply not the same as couples starting out at earlier ages. They could focus on the fun of being newlyweds. You can't forget the dynamics of parenting, good communication, time, and patience.

Onward Bound

Though some use successful dating or remarriage as the end marker of your marital journey, these are outer markers. What counts rests on the inside where if you haven't fully worked through these troubled relationship experiences, you usually aren't as free as you might think. I suggest that you'll know you're healing when you feel calmer and better able to focus on the tasks of work, daily living, and parenting. You'll recognize a pattern of wellness that is reflected in your ideal weight, a good night's sleep, and a more pleasant demeanor. You'll smile. You'll laugh. No, not all the time, but you won't wake up every day consumed by feelings of change, loss, or panic. In essence, you'll be back to being your own best friend—with less angst, self-criticism, and blame.

New friends, new goals, new attitudes will take hold in your soul, and others will notice the shift in your life. In fact, I'll end with these two recollections—one from my own separation and another years later. It was merely weeks since my husband had walked out when I found myself in a parent-teacher conference, feeling wounded, overwhelmed, and distraught. I imagine I looked just the way I felt, and what an embarrassing moment that was.

Cut to two years later. I was still separated, but not yet divorced. One of the teachers I'd met with during that initial conference spotted me in the school hallway. She'd always struck me as being a little on the quiet side, so I expected that she'd smile and keep walking. Our eyes met, and this time I held my head a lot higher than I did during that initial conference. To my surprise, she stopped me that day.

"You look great," she said with a broad smile. In that instant, I felt proud, no longer embarrassed. Seven years after that, remarried and going on my third anniversary, I traveled back to my community in Pittsburgh as the guest speaker at the local library. I was heartened to spot so many familiar faces, several former writing students, and others. Many came up to chat after my remarks just to say "Welcome back." Two librarians who had supported me as a writer and researcher, but also as a mom and community member, declared—and I'm not making this up either—"You look great!" They knew of my journeys, and let me tell you, I felt very good that night, too.

Everyone goes through tough times, I thought when I wrote the first and subsequent edition of this book. We don't relish when others see us at our low points, but when we perk back up again, what a wonderful feeling that is!

Afterword

Most assuredly I do feel wiser, and fortunately a lot less weary than I did through those initial days and months of my marital separation, during my divorce litigation, and even during the struggles beyond. I hope that by sharing some of my own personal hurdles and feelings about them, that you realize you're not alone, and I can only hope that learning others' stories and expert opinions have made some difference for you as well.

I'd like to summarize the top twelve things (in no particular order) I've learned while researching this project and walking the path of separation, divorce, and new journeys:

1. Never assume your friend's, sister's, or neighbor's marriage is perfect, for there very well could be cracks you don't see.

2. Many among the married ranks don't realize what a safe harbor a warm, loyal spouse can be until it's way too late.

3. It's better to be alone, relying upon good friends for communication and validation, than miserable in a silent, but bitter union that wears you down.

4. No woman should live with fear and intimidation. Ever.

5. Family court is a complete waste of your emotional and physical energy let alone precious monetary resources. Limit

your time there. If you're forced into court or the system keeps you locked in step, keep trying to extricate yourself from the mess. Remember that the only good reason to argue anything is to solve a problem. If you can't, a little prayer might help ease your way.

6. Helping children through adolescence is plenty of work. Navigating it for a husband is hopeless.

7. Single parenting isn't a picnic, but the bond you form by sticking with your children is irreplaceable for later in life, if not sooner. You will become their hero for having looked out for them.

8. Yes, some dates can be disasters, but flirting and meeting potential partners is fun. And believe it or not, men and monogamy *can* coexist in the same sentence. Who would have thought?

9. You get out of any post-divorce agreement what you put into it. Conflict resolution and problem solving are two of the best gifts you can grant your children. If you don't have them, attain them through good parent education or counseling services.

10. The men who left their wives—for whatever reason or whatever person—often did them the biggest favor of their lives. Most of us women are stronger and more resourceful than we ever imagined.

11. If you work hard, live right, and trust in God, there will be opportunities for you.

12. The future is so much more pleasant to ponder than the past.

Resources

Some of the following resources were useful to me as I traveled various paths in the separation, divorce, and post-divorce process; others I've found during my research and graduate studies in counseling. I hope you'll find them helpful to you as well.

Chapter One: Suddenly Separated

McGraw, Phillip C., Ph.D. *Life Strategies: Doing What Works, Doing What Matters*. Hyperion, 2000.

Rogers, Fred M. and Head, Barry. *Mister Rogers Talks with Parents*. Pittsburgh, Pa.: Family Communications, 1983.

Chapter Two: Looking after You

American Medical Association's Complete Guide to Women's Health. Random House, 1996.

Barbach, Lonnie Garfield. *For Yourself: The Fulfillment of Female Sexuality*. New American Library, 1991.

Beattie, Melody. *Codependent No More: How to Stop Controlling Others and Start Caring for Yourself*. Hazelden, 1987.

Boston Women's Health Book Collective. *Our Bodies, Ourselves for the New Century*. Touchstone Books, 1998.

Breathnach, Sarah Ban. *Simple Abundance Journal of Gratitude*. Warner Books, 1996.

Browne, Dr. Joy. *Dating for Dummies*. IDG Books, 1997.

Dodson, Betty. *Sex for One: The Joy of Self-Loving*. Crown Publishing, 1996.

Glass, Shirley P., Ph.D., with Staeheli, Jean Coppock. *Not "Just Friends": Rebuilding Trust and Recovering Your Sanity After Infidelity*. Free Press, 2003.

Gordon, Lynn. *52 Relaxing Rituals* and *52 Ways to Mend a Broken Heart*. Chronicle Books, 1996.

Hallowell, Edward M., M.D. *Worry: Controlling It and Using It Wisely*. Pantheon Books, 1997.

Kantor, Martin. *Passive-Aggression: A Guide for the Therapist, the Patient, and the Victim*. Praeger, 2002.

Kennedy, Sheila Rauch. *Shattered Faith: A Woman's Struggle to Stop the Catholic Church from Annulling Her Marriage*. Henry Holt, 1998.

Lerner, Harriet G., Ph.D. *The Dance of Anger*. Harper & Row, 1985.

Lunden, Joan and Morton, Laura. *Joan Lunden's Healthy Living*. Crown Publishing, 1997.

Nelson, Miriam E., Ph.D., with Knipe, Judy. *Strong Women Eat Well: Nutritional Strategies for a Healthy Body and Mind.* Perigee, 2002.

Nelson, Miriam E., Ph.D., with Wernick, Sarah, Ph.D. *Strong Women Stay Slim.* Bantam Books, 1998.

Northrup, Christiane, M.D. *The Wisdom of Menopause.* Bantam, 2003.

Nuckols, Cardwell C., Ph.D., and Chickering, Bill. *Healing an Angry Heart: Finding Solace in a Hostile World.* Health Communications, 1998.

O'Brien, Mary E., M.D. *In Sickness and in Health.* Health Press, 1991.

Schlessinger, Dr. Laura. *How Could You Do That? The Abdication of Character, Courage and Conscience.* Harper Collins, 1996.

Snyderman, Nancy L., M.D., and Blackstone, Margaret. *Dr. Nancy Snyderman's Guide to Good Health.* William Morrow & Co., 1996.

Vanzant, Iyanla. *In the Meantime: Finding Yourself and the Love You Want.* Simon & Schuster, 1998.

Vaughan, Peggy. *The Monogamy Myth: A Personal Handbook for Recovering from Affairs.* Newmarket, 1989.

Wetzler, Scott, Ph.D. *Living with the Passive-Aggressive Man.* New York: Fireside, 1992.

Chapter Three: Coping with Your Children

Ackerman, Marc J., Ph.D. *"Does Wednesday Mean Mom's House or Dad's?" Parenting Together While Living Apart.* Wiley, 1997.

Allen, Marvin with Robinson, Jo. *Angry Men, Passive Men.* Fawcett Columbine, 1993.

Bienenfeld, Florence, Ph.D. *Helping Your Child Through Your Divorce.* Hunter House, 1995.

Bodnar, Janet. *Mom, Can I Have That?* and *Dr. Tightwad's Money-Smart Kids.* Kiplinger Books, 1996 and 1997.

Brown, Nina W., Ed.D., L.P.C. *Children of the Self-Absorbed: A Grownup's Guide to Getting over Narcissistic Parents.* New Harbinger, 2001.

Childcare Aware 1-800-424-2246

Farmer, Steven. *The Wounded Male.* Ballantine Books, 1991.

Gardner, Richard A., M.D. *The Parental Alienation Syndrome.* Creative Therapeutics, 1998.

Gottman, John, Ph.D. *The Heart of Parenting: Raising an Emotionally Intelligent Child.* Simon & Schuster, 1998.

Heatherington, E. Mavis and Kelly, John. *For Better or Worse: Divorce Reconsidered.* W. W. Norton & Company, 2003.

Hendrix, Harville, Ph.D., and Hunt, Helen. *Giving The Love That Heals: A Guide for Parents.* Pocket Books, 1997.

Krementz, Jill. *How It Feels When Parents Divorce.* Knopf, 1988.

Lansky, Vicky. *Vicky Lansky's Divorce Book for Parents.* Book Peddlers, 1996.

Lyster, Mimi E. *Child Custody: Building Parenting Agreements That Work.* Nolo, 2003.

Murphy, Timothy F., Ph.D., and Oberlin, Loriann Hoff. *The Angry Child: Regaining Control When Your Child Is Out of Control.* Three Rivers Press, 2002.

Murphy, Timothy F., Ph.D., and Oberlin, Loriann Hoff. *Overcoming Passive Aggression: How to Stop Hidden Anger from Spoiling Your Relationships, Career and Happiness.* Marlowe, 2005.

The National Association for the Education of Young Children (NAEYC) 1-800-424-2460

Neuman, M. Gary with Romanowski, Patricia. *Helping Your Kids Cope with Divorce the Sandcastles Way.* Times Books, 1998.

Ricci, Isolina, Ph.D. *Mom's House, Dad's House: A Complete Guide for Parents Who Are Separated, Divorced or Remarried.* Fireside, 1997.

Rogers, Fred. *The World According to Mister Rogers: Important Things to Remember,* CD Version. Audioworks, 2004.

Segal, Judith, Ph.D. *Dealing with Difficult Men.* Lowell House, 1993.

St. James, Elaine. *Simplify Your Life with Kids.* Andrews McMeel, 2000.

"Talking with Families About Divorce" a booklet, published by Fred Rogers & Family Communications (Call 412-687-2990 to order).

Thase, Michael E., M.D., and Lang, Susan S. *Beating the Blues: New Approaches to Overcoming Dysthymia and Chronic Mild Depression.* Oxford University Press, 2004.

Thomas, Shirley. *Parents Are Forever: A Step-by-Step Guide to Becoming Successful Coparents After Divorce.* Springboard Publishing, 2004.

Wallerstein, Judith; Lewis, Julia M.; and Blakeslee, Sandra. *The Unexpected Legacy of Divorce: A 25-Year Landmark Study.* Hyperion, 2001.

Zimmerman, Jeffrey, Ph.D., and Thayer, Elizabeth S., Ph.D. *Adult Children of Divorce.* New Harbinger, 2003.

Resources for Children

Deaton, Wendy. *A Separation in My Family.* Hunter House, 1994.

Rogers, Fred. *Let's Talk About It: Divorce.* Philomel Books, 1996.

Rogers, Fred. *Let's Talk About It: Stepfamilies.* Putnam, 1997.

Swan-Jackson, Alys. *When Your Parents Split Up: How to Keep Yourself Together.* Piccadilly Press Limited, 1997.

Chapter Four: Navigating the Legal Landscape

Ackerman, Marc J. *Clinician's Guide to Child Custody Evaluations.* Wiley, 2001.

The American Academy of Matrimonial Lawyers, Chicago, IL; 312-263-6477.

Berger, Esther M., CFP. *Money-Smart Divorce: What Women Need To Know About Money and Divorce.* Simon & Schuster, 1996.

Bergman, Paul and Berman-Barrett, Sara. *Represent Yourself in Court: How to Prepare & Try a Winning Case.* Nolo, 2003.

Eddy, William A., Attorney, Mediator and Clinical Social Worker. *Splitting: Protecting Yourself While Divorcing a Borderline or Narcissist.* BPD Central, 2003.

Everett, Craig and Everett, Sandra Volgy. *Healthy Divorce.* Jossey-Bass, 1998.

Haman, Edward A. *How to File Your Own Divorce.* Sourcebooks, 1997.

Krantzler, Mel, Ph.D., and Krantzler, Pat, M.A. *The New Creative Divorce.* Adams Media, 1998.

Lovenheim, Peter and Guerin, Lisa. *Mediate, Don't Litigate: Strategies for Successful Mediation.* Nolo, 2004.

Oberlin, Loriann Hoff. *Working at Home While the Kids Are There, Too.* Career Press, 1997.

Samenow, Stanton E., Ph.D. *In the Best Interest of the Child: How to Protect Your Child from the Pain of Your Divorce.* Crown, 2002.

Smith, Gayle Rosenwald, J.D., and Abrahms, Sally. *What Every Woman Should Know About Divorce and Custody.* Perigee, 1998.

Stahl, Philip M., Ph.D. *Complex Issues in Child Custody Evaluations.* Sage Publications, 1999.

Woodhouse, Violet, CFP, and Collins, Victoria Ph.D., with Blakeman, M.C. *Divorce & Money: How to Make the Best Financial Decisions During Divorce.* Nolo, 1998.

Chapter Five: Abuse and Safety Awareness

Ackerman, Robert J., Ph.D., with Pickering, Susan E. *Before It's Too Late.* Health Communications, 1995.

Bancroft, Lundy. *When Dad Hurts Mom: Helping Your Children Heal the Wounds of Witnessing Abuse.* Putnam, 2004.

Bancroft, Lundy. *Why Does He Do That?: Inside the Minds of Angry and Controlling Men.* Berkley, 2002.

Bancroft, Lundy and Silverman, Jay G. *The Batterer as Parent: Addressing the Impact of Domestic Violence on Family Dynamics.* Sage Publications, 2002.

Betancourt, Marian. *What to Do When Love Turns Violent.* Harper Perennial, 1997.

Brown, Lou; Dubau, Francois; and McKeon, Merritt, J.D. *Stop Domestic Violence.* St. Martin's Griffin, 1997.

Brown, Nina W., Ed.D., L.P.C. *Whose Life Is It Anyway: When to Stop Taking Care of Their Feelings and Start Taking Care of Your Own.* New Harbinger, 2002.

Dutton, Donald G., Ph.D. *The Abusive Personality.* The Guilford Press, 1998.

Dutton, Donald G., Ph.D., with Golant, Susan K. *The Batterer: A Psychological Profile.* BasicBooks 1995.

Eddy, William A., attorney, mediator, and clinical social worker. *Splitting: Protecting Yourself While Divorcing a Borderline or Narcissist.* BPD Central, 2003.

Engel, Beverly. *The Emotionally Abusive Relationship: How to Stop Being Abused and How to Stop Abusing.* Wiley, 2002.

Evans, Patricia. *The Verbally Abusive Relationship* and *Verbal Abuse Survivors Speak Out.* Adams Media, 1996 (revised) and 1993.

Harteau, Janeé and Keegel, Holly. *A Woman's Guide to Personal Safety.* Fairview Press, 1998.

Hawker, Lynn, Ph.D., and Bicehouse, Terry. *End the Pain.* Zinn Communications, 1995.

Jacobson, Neil, Ph.D., and Gottman, John, Ph.D. *When Men Batter Women.* Simon & Schuster, 1998.

National Domestic Violence Hotline: 1-800-799-SAFE (7233)

NiCarthy, Ginny, M.S.W. *Getting Free.* Seal Press, 1997.

NiCarthy, Ginny and Davidson, Sue. *You Can Be Free.* Seal Press, 1997.

Quigley, Paxton. *Not An Easy Target: Paxton Quigley's Self-Protection for Women.* Fireside, 1995.

The Refuge Project, Charlotte, NC: *therefugeproject@yahoo.com*

Walker, Lenore. *The Battered Woman.* Harper Collins, 1980.

Wilson, K. J., Ed.D. *When Violence Begins At Home.* Hunter House, 1997.

Resources for Children

Paris, Susan and illustrated by Labinski, Gail. *Mommy and Daddy Are Fighting.* Seal Press, 1986.

Chapter Six: Your Financial Future

Association for Children for Enforcement of Support (ACES), Toledo, Ohio: 1-800-537-7072

Carlson, Charles B., CFA. *No-Load Stocks.* NorthStar Financial, Inc., 1997.

Chilton, David. *The Wealthy Barber.* Prima, 1998.

The College Cost and Financial Aid 2004: All-New 24th Annual Edition. The College Board, 2003.

Dunnan, Nancy. *Never Balance Your Checkbook on Tuesday.* Harper Collins, 1997.

Energy Savers booklet: P.O. Box 3048—Dept. P, Merrifield, VA 22116; 1-800-363-3732

Hannon, Kerry. *Suddenly Single: Money Skills for Divorcées and Widows.* Wiley, 1998.

McWade, Patricia. *Financing Graduate School.* Peterson's Guides, 1996.

National Foundation for Consumer Credit, 1-800-284-1723

Oberlin, Loriann Hoff. *Working at Home While The Kids Are There, Too.* Career Press, 1997.

Oberlin, Loriann Hoff. *Writing for Quick Cash: Turn Your Way with Words into Real Money.* Amacom, 2003.

O'Neill, Barbara. *Investing on a Shoestring.* Dearborn Publishing, 1999.

Orman, Suze. *Suze Orman's Protection Portfolio: The Forms You Need Today to Protect Your Tomorrows.* Hay House, 2002.

Orman, Suze. *The 9 Steps to Financial Freedom.* Crown, 1997.

Orman, Suze. *The Courage to Be Rich.* Riverhead Books, 1999.

Peterson, Ann Z. and Rosenberg, Stephen M., CFP. *Every Woman's Guide to Financial Security.* Career Press, 1997.

Quinn, Jane Bryant. *Making the Most of Your Money.* Simon & Schuster, 1997.

Schell, Richard E. *Quick Cash: A Guide to Raising Money During Life's Planned and Unplanned Changes.* Sphinx, 2004.

Singletary, Michelle. *7 Money Mantras for a Richer Life: How to Live Well with the Money You Have.* Random House, 2003.

"Social Security: What Every Woman Should Know." Contact your local social security office.

Sparks, Robert A. and Vaddi, Mamatha. *Debt-Free College: 79 Secrets for Successful College Financing.* Perigee, 2002.

Stanny, Barbara. *Prince Charming Isn't Coming.* Penguin, 1999.

St. James, Elaine. *Simplify Your Christmas.* Andrews McMeel, 1998.

Streamer, James. *Wealth on Minimal Wage.* Berkley Publishing Group, 1998.

U.S. DEPARTMENT OF EDUCATION, 1-800-433-3243

The Wall Street Journal Guide to Understanding Personal Finance (series also includes *Money & Investing* and *Planning Your Financial Future*)

"What You Should Know About Financial Planning." Booklet from Certified Financial Planner Board of Standards, 1-888-237-6275.

Chapter Seven: Carving Out a Career

Bolles, Richard Nelson. *What Color Is Your Parachute?* Prima, 2004.

Buck, J. Thomas; Matthews, William R.; and Leech, Robert N. *101 Ways to Power Up Your Job Search.* McGraw Hill, 1997.

Frank, William S. *200 Letters for Job Hunters.* Ten Speed Press, 1993.

Frishman, Rick and Lublin, Jill. *Networking Magic.* Adams Media, 2004.

Goleman, Daniel, Ph.D. *Working with Emotional Intelligence.* Bantam, 2000.

Holcomb, Betty. *Not Guilty! The Good News About Working Mothers.* Scribner, 1998.

Kerr, Cherie. *Networking Skills That Will Get You the Job You Want.* Betterway Books, 1999.

Mannion, James. *The Everything® Alternative Careers Book.* Adams Media, 2004.

McWade, Patricia. *Financing Graduate School.* Peterson's Guides, 1996.

Oberlin, Loriann Hoff. *Working at Home While the Kids Are There, Too.* Career Press, 1997.

Oberlin, Loriann Hoff. *Writing for Quick Cash: Turn Your Way with Words into Real Money.* Amacom, 2003.

Reis, Ronald A. *The Everything Hot Careers Book.* Adams Media, 2001.

Tieger, Paul D. and Barron-Tieger, Barbara. *Do What You Are: Discover the*

Perfect Career for You Through the Secrets of Personality Type. Little Brown, 2001.

Tullier, Michelle. *The Unofficial Guide to Acing the Interview.* IDG Books, 1999.

Quenk, Naomi L. *Was That Really Me?: How Everyday Stress Brings Out Our Hidden Personality.* Davies Black, 2002.

Yate, Martin J. *Knock 'em Dead 2005: Great Answers to over 200 Tough Interview Questions, Plus the Latest Job Search Strategies.* Adams Media, 2004.

Chapter Eight: Household Hints and Car Care

Barbara K Enterprises, Inc. *www.barbarak.com.* 1-800-803-5657

Better Homes & Gardens New Garden Book. Meredith Corporation, 1990.

Carrell, Al. *1000 Questions About Home Repair & Maintenance.* Summit Publishing Group, 1997.

DeJulio, Beverly. *Handy Ma'am.* Dearborn Publishing, 1999.

Great Health Hints & Handy Tips. Reader's Digest, 1994.

Green, Mark. *The Consumer Bible.* Workman, 1998.

Household Hints & Handy Tips. Reader's Digest, 1995.

Jeffries, Yvonne. *The Everything® Fix-It Book.* Adams Media, 2004.

National Highway Traffic Safety Administration booklet on buying a safer car, 1-800-424-9393

New Complete Do-It-Yourself Manual. Reader's Digest, 1991.

Schnaser, Gene. *The Home Repair Emergency Handbook.* Galahad Books, 1992.

Treganowan, Lucille with Catanzarite, Gina. *Lucille's Car Care.* Hyperion, 1996.

Chapter Nine: Learning to Lighten Up

Baker, Dan, Ph.D. *What Happy People Know: How the New Science of Happiness Can Change Your Life for the Better.* Rodale, 2002.

Brodie, Deborah and Applewhite, Ashton. *Untying the Knot.* Griffin, 1999.

Buckhorn, Dean and Merril. *The Perfect Man.* Andrews McMeel, 2002.

Cousins, Norman. *Anatomy of an Illness.* Bantam Doubleday Dell, 1991.

Doyle, Laura. *Things Will Get As Good As You Can Stand.* Fireside, 2004.

Garner, Cindy. *How Are Men Like Noodles.* Andrews McMeel, 1995.

Jones, Merry Bloch. *America's Dumbest Dates.* Andrews McMeel, 1999.

Lunden, Joan and Cagan, Andrea. *A Bend in the Road Is Not the End of the Road* William Morrow, 1998.

Meyers, Marc. *How to Make Luck: Seven Secrets Lucky People Use to Succeed.* Renaissance Books, 1999.

Murphy, Timothy F., Ph.D., and Oberlin, Loriann Hoff. *The Angry Child: Regaining Control When Your Child Is Out of Control.* Three Rivers Press, 2002.

Newman, Amanda. *Women Are from Venus, Men Are from Hell*. Adams, 1999.

Pennebaker, James W., Ph.D. *Opening Up: The Healing Power of Expressing Emotions*. The Guilford Press, 1990.

Reivich, Karen, Ph.D., and Shatte, Andrews, Ph.D. *The Resilience Factor: 7 Essential Skills for Overcoming Life's Obstacles*. Broadway, 2002.

Salmansohn, Karen. *How to Make Your Man Behave in 21 Days or Less, Using the Secrets of Professional Dog Trainers*. Workman, 1994.

Salmansohn, Karen. *I Don't Need to Have Children, I Date Them: 23 Child Psychology Techniques to Use on Boys of All Ages*. Workman, 2001.

Schlossberg, Nancy K. and Robinson, Susan P. *Going to Plan B: How You Can Cope, Regroup, and Start Your Life on a New Path*. Fireside, 1996.

Smith, Richard. *101 Uses for an Ex-Husband*. Warner Books, 1997.

Vanzant, Iyanla. *In the Meantime: Finding Yourself and the Love You Want*. Simon & Schuster, 1998.

Zobel, Allia. *The Joy of Being Single*. Adams Media, 1992.

Zobel, Allia. *101 Reasons Why a Cat Is Better Than a Man*. Adams Media, 1994.

Zobel, Allia. *101 More Reasons Why a Cat Is Better Than a Man*. Adams Media, 1997.

Chapter Ten: Exploring New Horizons

Amador, Xavier, Ph.D., and Kiersky, Judith, Ph.D. *Being Single in a Couple's World*. Simon & Schuster, 1998.

Anderson, Keith, M.D., and MacSkimming, Roy. *On Your Own Again*. McClelland & Stewart, 1998.

Applewhite, Ashton. *Cutting Loose: Why Women Who End Their Marriages Do So Well*. Harper Collins, 1997.

Barash, Susan Shapiro. *Women of Divorce: Mothers, Daughters, Stepmothers—The New Triangle*. New Horizon Press, 2003.

Berman, Eleanor. *Traveling Solo*. Globe Pequot, 1999.

Bilicki, Bettie Youngs, Ph.D., and Goetz, Masa, Ph.D. *Getting Back Together*. Adams Media, 1990.

Bushong, Carolyn. *The Seven Dumbest Relationship Mistakes Smart People Make*. Villard, 1997.

Culligan, Joseph J. *When in Doubt, Check Him Out*. Hallmark Press, 1996.

Dale, James and Schapiro, Alex Beth. *Step Wise: A Parent-Child Guide to Family Mergers*. Andrews McMeel, 2001.

Davis, Michele Weiner. *The Sex-Starved Marriage: A Couple's Guide to Boosting Their Marriage Libido*. Simon & Schuster, 2003.

DeAngelis, Barbara, Ph.D. *Are You the One for Me?* Bantam Doubleday Dell, 1992.

Deida, David. *It's a Guy Thing: An Owner's Manual for Women*. Health Communications, 1997.

Doherty, William J., Ph.D. *Take Back Your Marriage: Sticking Together in a World That Pulls Us Apart*. Guilford, 2001.

Gabe, Grace, M.D., and Lipman-Blumen, Jean, Ph.D. *Step Wars: Overcoming the Perils and Making Peace Within Stepfamilies.* St. Martins Press, 2004.

Glass, Shirley P., Ph.D., with Staeheli, Jean Coppock. *Not "Just Friends": Rebuilding Trust and Recovering Your Sanity After Infidelity.* Free Press, 2003.

Gordon, Sol, Ph.D., and Shimberg, Elaine Fantle. *Another Chance for Love: Finding a Partner Later in Life.* Adams Media, 2004.

Gray, John, Ph.D. *Mars and Venus on a Date.* Harper Collins, 1997.

Gray, John, Ph.D. *Mars and Venus Starting Over.* Harper Collins, 1998.

Haman, Edward A. *How to Write Your Own Premarital Agreement.* Sourcebooks, 1998.

Harley, Dr. Williard F., Jr. and Chalmers, Dr. Jennifer Harley. *Surviving an Affair.* Revell, 1998.

Koman, Aleta, M.Ed. *How to Mend a Broken Heart: Letting Go and Moving On.* NTC/Contemporary Books, 1997.

Krasnow, Iris. *Surrendering to Marriage: Husbands, Wives & Other Imperfections.* Miramax, 2001.

Krasnow, Iris. *Surrendering to Yourself: You Are Your Own Soul Mate.* Miramax, 2003.

Leman, Kevin, Ph.D. *Living in a Step Family Without Getting Stepped On.* Thomas Nelson, 1994.

Lusterman, Don-David, Ph.D. *Infidelity: A Survival Guide.* New Harbinger, 1998.

Markman, Howard; Stanley, Scott; Blumberg, Susan L.; and Edell, Dean S. *Fighting for Your Marriage.* Jossey-Bass, 1996.

Meyerson, Mitch and Ashner, Laurie. *Six Keys to Creating the Life You Desire.* New Harbinger, 1999.

Naylor, Sharon. *1,001 Ways to Have a Dazzling Second Wedding.* New Page Books, 2001.

Pittman, Frank. *Private Lies: Infidelity and the Betrayal of Intimacy.* W.W. Norton & Co., 1990.

Porter, Dahlia. *365 Reflections on Being Single.* Adams Media, 1999.

Robbins, Riki, Ph.D. *Betrayed: How You Can Restore Sexual Trust and Rebuild Your Life.* Adams Media, 1998.

Safier, Rachel. *Mr. Right Now: When Dating Is Better Than Saying "I Do."* Jossey-Bass, 2004.

Smalley, Gary. *Making Love Last Forever.* Thomas Nelson, 1996.

Smart Marriages, *www.smartmarriages.com*

Stepfamily Association of America. 1-800-735-0329 or *www.saafamilies.org.*

Subotnik, Rona, M.F.C.C., and Harris, Gloria G., Ph.D. *Surviving Infidelity.* Adams Media, 1999.

Tessina, Tina, Ph.D. *The Unofficial Guide to Dating Again.* Macmillan, 1998.

Vaughan, Peggy. *The Monogamy Myth: A Personal Handbook for Recovering from Affairs.* Newmarket, 1989.

Index

About the Author

Loriann Hoff Oberlin, M.S., is the author of many nonfiction books including *Writing for Quick Cash, Working at Home While the Kids Are There, Too,* and *The Angry Child* and *Overcoming Passive Aggression,* both cowritten with Dr. Tim Murphy.

She has appeared on numerous television news segments offering her commentary as well as on the *CNN Morning News* and *Sally Jessy Raphael,* and she is a frequent guest on talk radio. Ms. Oberlin served as the online divorce pro for Oxygen.com and she contributes to leading publications. While writing the second edition of this book, she was a graduate student in clinical community counseling at Johns Hopkins University in Maryland, where she lives with her current husband and her two sons.

Ms. Oberlin is a member of the Stepfamily Association of America, the American Counseling Association, and the National Council on Family Relations, a group devoted to family life education.

Reach her through her Web site at *www.loriannoberlin.com.*